C000246551

COMMANDO

By the same author

The Royal Marines Total Fitness

COMMANDO

Survival of the Fittest

ROBIN EGGAR

JOHN MURRAY

© Robin Eggar 1994

First published in 1994
by John Murray (Publishers) Ltd.,
50 Albemarle Street, London W1X 4BD

The moral right of the author has been asserted

All rights reserved
Unauthorized duplication
contravenes applicable laws

A catalogue record for this book is available from the British Library

ISBN 0–7195–5305–9

Typeset in 12/13 pt Bembo by Wearset, Boldon, Tyne and Wear.
Printed and bound in Great Britain by The University Press, Cambridge

To Jacqui, Jordan and Rowan,
and to the memory of my father
John Eggar

Contents

Illustrations

(between pages 116 and 117)

27. Mark Wolsey posing during Crash Action
28. Russ Corn receiving the Sword of Honour during Pass Out
29. Pass Out

The author and publishers would like to thank Matthew Ford for permission to reproduce Plates 1, 4, 5, 6, 7, 9, 11, 12, 13, 14, 15, 16 and 18. The remaining photographs were taken by the author.

Acknowledgements

THIS BOOK COULD never have made the long yomp from champagne-fuelled conversation to hard cover reality without the cooperation and unflagging enthusiasm of Captain Mark Wolsey RM who volunteered his own services, those of his Training Team and of Young Officers (YO) batch Sept. '91, and kept pushing all of us when spirits flagged. My personal thanks for their support and for putting up with endless dim questions from a 'fat civvy' also go to all the Training Team SNCOs: Billy Baxter – especially for the last few miles over Ryder's Hill – the ever self-effacing Tom Coyle, Dai Phillips, Paul Redding, Graeme Foster, John Atkins, Toby Broomes and Lieutenant 'Evs' Everett. As for you YOs, some talked more, some less and some never stopped but without you there would be nothing. I owe you all a debt for allowing me to share your lives, your pain and some of those deepest, darkest secrets. Thank you for the dagger to: Brian Adcock, Phil Ashby, Paul Attwood, Dan Bailey, Bob Baxendale, Mark Collins, Russ Corn, Tim David, Pete Evans, Andy Goldsmith, Andy Harker, Stan Harris, Trevor Henry, Steve Hussey, Charlton Jackson, Pete Joy, Matt Lodge, Rob Lunn, Pete Manson, Andy McInerney, Jason McQueen, Jools Ostling, Andy Parlour, Gavin Parr, Mark Robinson, Andy Rowley, Philip Shetler-Jones, Matt Skuse, Matthew Stovin-Bradford, Mike Tanner, Rory Thomson, Neil Watkinson, Mark Webster, Martin Wood and Jeremy Woodall.

The Royal Marines were exceptionally generous with their time and facilities. At the Commando Training Centre at Lympstone the Commandant Colonel Mike Taffinder was encouraging throughout. At Officers' Training Wing Major Matt Sturman, Captains Andy Shaw, Gordon Messenger, Steve Newing, Mark Bailey and Damian McKinney, and Wing Sergeant Major Colin Grice answered my endless questions with tact and forbearance, while the charming staff of the Officers' Mess kept me fed and watered. At the Press Office in London Major Bill MacLennan, Captain Simon Haselock and Colour Sergeant Dieter Loraine proved invaluable and generally managed to circumvent the massed ranks of bureaucracy. (It should, nonetheless, be understood that the views expressed in the book are mine and not necessarily those of the Ministry of Defence.) Thanks also to 42 Commando for a memorable regimental dinner in April 1993, and to the Officers' Mess at 40 Commando. No thanks, however, to whomever at HQ Belize who cancelled a projected trip to see 45 Commando in action at the eleventh hour for no apparent reason – sadly my loss is reflected in the book's final chapter. There will be other names I have accidentally omitted or unwittingly forgotten for which I can only apologize.

Thanks are not exclusively due to those in uniform and must be extended to Fiona Wolsey for meals, beds and encouragement during the Thirty Miler, and to Nicola and Richard Ellis for getting married and so starting it all off. Without the efforts of my agent Julian Alexander there would be no book. My son Jordan never stops asking 'why?' but he did rush around Lympstone announcing 'Daddy done Thirty Miler, too!' When I started this project my daughter Rowan was not even a spark.

Finally none of this would have been possible without the love and support of Jacqui, who erroneously believed that in marrying me she would never have to set foot inside another military establishment.

Midnight, 4 September 1991

TOMORROW IT BEGINS. For real. In earnest.

It may be anticipation, it may be trepidation, bravado, fear or any of a mêlée of conflicting emotions but for one young man the approach of midnight brings no rest. The echoes of forced laughter, the unnatural gaiety, the stiff jollity of early evening, going through the motions of a formal ritual at best misunderstood, dissembling before those who are already members of the Commando Club – all those moments have been washed away into the darkness, faint echoes lost somewhere between the estuary and the Equator.

He walks out of the Officers' Mess, strolls away from the lure of another drink at the bar (there will be time and to spare for that), through the double doors, down between the cannons and their gleaming brass barrels. He walks, for he does not yet know how to march, slouching along in blue blazer, one hand in his trouser pockets, the other trawling through what was once a perfectly decent haircut. As his shoes crackle over the tarmac of the parade ground, his torso involuntarily snaps into a semblance of attention, sagging again as he skirts the wire fence that surrounds the ammunition dump.

Then he is down – down on to the grass and gravel of the bottom field. The bottom field waits as it always has done – waits patiently, for everyone, everything, comes to it eventually. The thirty-foot ropes hiss their welcome, writhing gently in the wind. The sea breeze ripples across the static tank, disturbing the surface eddies as if some feral prehistoric beast lurks there. Silhouettes – a creation of man but deliberately made uninhabitable – swirl across the field like an unfinished game of Tetris^{TM}. A field of small walls, tall walls, nets that catch feet not fish, ropes like snakes and ladders that travel across but never up, tunnels like black holes sucking what little light surrounds them into nothingness, tunnels that lead nowhere.

Some buildings, so it is said, absorb and retain the emotions of those people who once lived and suffered there, sending them back as ghosts. If the Commando Training Centre has ghosts they would be here. Especially on this night of all nights, this first night. The bottom field is a place of great pain and greater achievement, where today's ecstasy becomes tomorrow's agony, a place where once concrete certainties can trickle through fingers like so much powdered bone and where long cherished dreams can come true.

The ghosts of the bottom field may sense the presence of the novice. He does not see them, or feel them, for he has his own demons playing hopscotch from his groin to his gorge. This time he is ignorant and all the luckier for that.

The young man stands ten yards back from the perimeter fence staring out over the estuary, looking for the invisible water. Instead through the coils of razor wire he can see both the mud and the stars.

Greenhorns, not Green Berets

I don't know what effect these men will have on the enemy,
but by God they terrify me.

The Duke of Wellington

MOST OF THOSE who arrive at Lympstone's Commando Training Centre (CTC) to stay come via the back door, rattling along the Exeter–Exmouth commuter line. For the majority of the young men who began officer training at noon on 4 September 1991 their first sight of their new home was from the train.

The track seems little more than a casual afterthought squeezed on the last few yards of land left before the estuary of the river Exe. The tide is out, revealing an expanse of mud as black as the ninth circle of Hades. The mud is a far more effective warning about the necessity of boiling local shellfish for several days than the ineffectual notice boards that line the station. Even on clement days the wind always threatens to howl along the narrow platform, grandly christened Lympstone Commando, to blow the unwary over – bags, Bergens and all. Naturally the green-bereted Marine on guard remains firmly inside his little hut, nodding curt acknowledgement at flashed identity cards, stifling the suspicion of a sneer at the new arrivals. They may become real officers one day but right now they are 'Yo-yos'. One day the salute will have a meaning but that will not be till next July, when some and only some of them will wear their own green berets. Until then they are barely worth the raising of one eye from the gorgeous Star Bird baring her full-colour all.

The thirty-four Young Officers, plus a brace of Jamaican officer cadets, who comprise the YO batch Sept. '91 are due by noon. One is never even going to make it to Devon. A phone call arrives detailing the non-arrival of a certain Mr Bailey, and in the Officers' Training Wing (OTW) there is a flurry of activity as attempts are made to get hold of a stand-by officer, egged on by the Commandant who is upset, even personally offended, by the attitude of the missing man. There are, after all, fifteen or so potential Marine officers who have passed the Admiralty Interview Board but scored too low to make the final cut.

A steep narrow path leads these once and future civilians straight into the heart of their home for the next fifteen months: a trickling stream of young men semi-formally attired in blazer, shirt and tie, sometimes brothel creepers or for the really insecure a dark suit – perhaps the only one they own. For the first time they are truly alone. Despite all the preparation and buildup, despite being surrounded by others in the same boat, they stand around abandoned, among a crowd of equally isolated souls. There in that alien military environment, even those few who had spent university vacations with the Corps and thought they knew their way about Lympstone paid no more than a passing glance at the bottom field. They ignored the array of ropes and assault courses, shrugged off the giant static tank full of water, dank even by the muddy standards of the Exe. Soothsayer's luck, perhaps, for they will become familiar with its chill contents soon enough.

Others like Mark Robinson and Matthew Stovin-Bradford prefer to come by car. Stalwarts of the Rugby Club at Southampton University, who had managed to convince each other that it might be fun to become Royal Marine officers, they were running late for their arrival deadline. Burning along with the roof open on Matthew's car, they nearly missed the camp's front gate. It appears suddenly on the Exmouth road, leaping out on the right if you breast a hill driving much too fast. The dangerous road is spanned by a pedestrian bridge which all Marines are ordered to use at all times, even on timed runs.

If the truth was to be told (which it eventually was, but months later) neither was quite sure what he was doing there. Mark, at least, has a Services' background (his father is an army colonel) but dad's regiment had turned him down for being 'too cocky'. The pair had been in the pub playing dares one night halfway through their final year. After failing to impress a number of first-year girls by posing as astronauts they quickly discovered that Royal Marine officers had much more kudos. To complete the image, 'Chalkie'

(Stovin-Bradford) spent a long time parading around Southampton in a Marine sweatshirt.

'The culmination of our tall stories ended with us both arriving at CTC on 4 September 1991,' recalls 'Bob Rob'. 'I surprised myself by turning up feeling slightly perturbed about my impending doom.'

They wandered through the rest of that first day in a daze, sat without complaint while their brand new, guaranteed short but sexy haircuts were savaged by the camp barber, who charged them an extra two quid for the privilege, wondering what the hell they had got themselves into. Without exception all YOs are shipped off for a dose of tonsorial butchery, a not so subtle reminder that as of this minute their lives are no longer their own.

At that first lunchtime in the Mess three new second lieutenants, still in civvies for their uniforms will not be issued until the morrow, eat their lunch, chewing each forkful slowly as it turns to dust in their mouths. Steve Hussey, a shorn freckled lamb, surely too young, too innocent for this killer's job, and handsome young Woodall, with his single devil's eyebrow, talk to a brace of training officers, affording them a deference that hides the apprehension eating away at their stomachs. Their table manners are impeccable as if they expect the Commandant's all-seeing eye to be everywhere. 'Just wait till you see the Yo-yos' table manners go in training,' grins one training officer when they have bolted and run. 'By the end we might as well just pour it in a trough outside their rooms and let them dive straight in.'

Although he does not yet know it, the third YO, Neil Watkinson, educated in France and an economics graduate from Nottingham University, has already committed a cardinal sin. All the officers already know his name. Due to a genuine mix-up about starting dates, he is committed to being best man at a wedding on the first weekend of training – the only one when they are not allowed 'to go ashore'. Without knowing what he has done, Neil, who speaks with a somewhat fruity tone, his face furrowed and spotty, is both self-conscious and uncomfortable.

Across the polished Mess tables strange arcane words and phrases echo: 'I was threaders ...', '... went to the heads', 'anyway he was completely ball-bagged but he cracked on ...' With each unfamiliar expression a YO head jerks, ears flapping at the foreignness of it all. At least they can recognize 'yomp' because everyone knows that word since the Marines' epic march across the Falklands. Despite the khaki, despite the military badges of rank, one must never forget that the Marines are the Navy's soldiers and to emphasize this difference they continually use naval terminology mixed up with their own slang, leavened by a perpetual black humour that puts a darker twist on everything. Marine recruits are always 'nods', young officers always 'Yo-yos', Marines with a green beret become 'bootnecks' and any member of the Army is a 'Pongo'.

After lunch the batch all disappear into the hands of their drill instructor, Colour Sergeant Jordan, a ramrod-straight man of middle height and indeterminate age, with enormous tattoos decorating the length of each forearm and a career that included eight years in the Army, for which he has eventually been forgiven. He spends an hour or so explaining the rules and customs of 'cabin' living, though his primary responsibility is for batch drill, that side of forces' discipline hardest for civilians to comprehend. What it is supposed to do is mould soldiers into a single whole, to erase the danger of acting individually in combat where you have to be able to function as a unit.

When they march off initially they are reasonably together, a mite sloppy, some shuffling their steps and swinging their arms as if they remember how to do it only as an afterthought. Half a dozen give the impression that they have done this before – which, of course, they have. Another half dozen, including Chalkie – who is greatly relieved to be able to lose himself in the middle of a crowd of equally tonsorially challenged colleagues – appear to lack the ability to distinguish left from right, buttock from humerus.

'This isn't too bad,' says Colour Sergeant Jordan grudgingly, before adding with a bleak smile, 'But just wait until you see them marching for the first time. It takes weeks to get it right. I suppose it must be some psychological thing.'

At 1600 hours the batch are delivered to a lecture hall for a talk from their course officer, Captain Mark Wolsey. They are sitting slumped in three rows looking at each other out of the corner of their eyes. In he comes: tall, imposing, his forearms bronzed, his whole demeanour calculated to give one impression only – this, boys, is what you can become, but don't expect it to be easy. Jordan barks an order and with varying degrees of alacrity backs snap into an upright position. Wolsey is not here to deliver a pep talk. He introduces himself simply as 'the officer responsible to make sure you all have a fair chance of passing out'. An ominous portent of things to come.

He goes on to outline some basic rules about conduct in the Mess and in general. They are, he stresses, commissioned officers, not cadets, which requires them to conform to different standards in exchange for which they get to use the facilities of the Mess. (Royal Marine YOs all start off as 2nd Lieutenants.) Stand up when addressed by a superior officer. The Commandant has red tabs on his collar – an important rule to learn as their first sight of him will be in a lounge suit that evening. 'You are referred to as gentlemen and expected to behave like them. Loutish and slovenly behaviour will not be tolerated, too much and you're out.' He cautions against running up too high a Mess bill and advises prompt payment, something about which he has personal experience.

'You call all trained officers "sir" unless asked to do otherwise and that will only be in the Mess.' His delivery is firm, clipped, accent cut glass but not quite top drawer crystal. 'You refer to other batch members as Mr. You are to be in the right place at the right time, at least five minutes before your appointment. Leave is a privilege, not a right, but except for the first weekend when you may not go ashore there are no restrictions on weekend leave. Because of past troubles in Exmouth you are required to be clear of that town by 1930 hours. Otherwise if you wish to stay out all night that is fine, provided you are alert and on time the next morning.'

At this pronouncement a few half grins, swiftly hidden, pass between certain members of the batch. This bodes well, a licence to thrill, to fraternize with all the nurses and students of Exeter. Wolsey then introduces them to the SNCOs who will act as their Training Team for the next fifty-four weeks.

Colour Sergeant Jordan they have already met. The batch is divided into three sections, each reporting to a sergeant: Tom Coyle, Billy Baxter and 'Evs' Everett. Then there is the TQ (Training Quartermaster), Paul Redding, a bantamweight colour sergeant, and finally Toby Broomes, their PTI (Physical Training Instructor). To the batch right now the Training Team are still ciphers; their attention remains firmly fixed upon the person of Captain Wolsey. One day he may be affectionately referred to as the Boss but now he is the supreme authority figure to whom all must bow. Forget girlfriends, forget mothers, fathers and best friends; for the next year Wolsey is the most important person in their lives.

'I require 100 per cent effort and enthusiasm. You are under a microscope here, there is little that you can get away with and then not for very long,' he continues. 'There is no shame in leaving. While I will certainly not discourage the emergence of individual characters, the integrity of the batch shall not be compromised by the individual. I do not want to see any cliques or enclaves forming in the Mess. That is all.'

'Of course,' he admits later in the privacy of his own office, decorated with a polished Iraqi artillery shell and other defused souvenirs of Kurdistan, 'cliques do form, and some of the YOs will want to be alone, but it is important to put away personal likes and prejudices as fast as possible. From the beginning we will put people who already know each other into separate sections. The humour a batch displays amongst itself can be very black, even cruel, and to a large extent the batch acts as its own police force, decides who will and who will not make it through training. However one thing I cannot abide is gratuitous bullying. It does happen but if it comes to my attention the man responsible will find himself on warning.'

The warning system is the official weeding-out process with which the Corps can dispose of those whom it considers will not make the grade but who may be too pig-headed to acknowledge it. It is also used to get a YO to buck up his ideas. The first step is the Course Officer's (Wolsey) Warning – which lasts for a month. If no improvement is discerned this may be extended or the YO moved on to OC's Warning (Officer Commanding: Major Matt Sturman, the new head of Officers' Training Wing) which also lasts a month. The final step is the Commandant's Warning which lasts for three months. After that the YO can be 'withdrawn from training'.

(Even then some YOs refuse to accept the axe. Legend tells of one who was told by his Course Officer gently, 'Perhaps you should think about whether you really have what it takes to be a Marine officer.' Two weeks later the YO was still in uniform, still at Lympstone. 'I thought about it, sir,' he replied ingenuously after being quizzed about his continuing presence, 'and I decided I did have what it takes.')

'The warning system is designed to keep giving them the benefit of the doubt,' continues Wolsey, with the smile of a fox contemplating an unguarded hen-coop. 'I'll probably put a bunch of them on warning next week, reminding them that it can only get better from then on. The aim is to sort out the duffers a.s.a.p.

'Some people here have never failed at anything – school, university, sports – in their life. At some point I may have to close the door behind one and say "you will never make a Royal Marine officer as long as I am in the camp". Obviously if a chap is a brilliant field tactician but can't iron his kit properly some allowances will be made – but not many. A messy man, one who's always late, whose personal admin is just crap – if it remains that way he will eventually have to go. If someone is sloppy and slapdash with kit, the chances are he will be so with his men.

'That may sound hard but it might mean losing a magazine in the field – and in Northern Ireland that could end up booby-trapped and lead to the death of a Marine. When I was in Northern Ireland I would fine soldiers for lost kit. I charged a month's pay (up to £400) for it. Once a corporal lost a radio battery and couldn't find it. However the IRA did and they booby-trapped it; it kept appearing on walls all over the place, tantalizing us. Eventually we had to surround it from a distance, get in bomb disposal experts to defuse it. That's a lot of expense and manpower for one careless action.'

But what of more mundane matters, what of poor Mr Watkinson, caught between loyalty to a friend and his new master? 'I shall let him sweat a bit,' says Wolsey, 'but as it isn't his fault then I shall let him go … if he still wants to.' However Mr Watkinson, for all that he looks like a padre in search of a deserving religion, absorbs what must be done, learns quickly and stays in camp, risking the wrath of an old friend for an uncertain future. As if in reaction to this horrific experience of instant fame, he retreats for many weeks into a grey anonymity.

Every year the batch is enlivened by a couple of Commonwealth officer cadets. This is either part of the nation's generous foreign aid to its former colonies, or a way of balancing the defence deficit as these cadets pay handsomely for the privilege. The Directing Staff (DS) resent not their colour, but having to spend time on men who do not necessarily want to be standing in the freezing snow on Dartmoor or the Brecon Beacons – indeed, who may never have seen the white stuff before. The situation is complicated because for these officer cadets, while attendance is mandatory, it is basically an attend course: a bloody tough attend course, but there is none of the fear of failure which can both haunt and drive their British colleagues – just fear of frostbite.

Trevor Henry and Charlton Jackson, seconded with forty-eight hours' notice from the Jamaican Defence Force, arrive lugging heavy suitcases in late afternoon and already looking somewhat chilly. Jackson is resplendent in a pair of outrageous grey trousers that, while doubtless the height of formal sobriety in downtown Kingston, erupt out of the September sunshine like a running sore. Wolsey raises his eyes to heaven and murmurs, 'I won't say anything, just let the others in the batch exert some peer pressure.' An oblivious Jackson wears them to the welcome cocktail party and again in the morning before he is forced into uniform for the duration. Thereafter they are to be seen only during the most anonymous of runs ashore.

At 1745 half a dozen of the batch march towards their civvy suit parade. The two at the front who are obviously University Cadet Entry or Corps Commission lead the way in a semblance of marching order while the others drift along with their arms swinging casually. Different groups converge in different styles on the tarmac at the back of the Officers' Mess: a group of five wheel smartly around the corner, others slob along hands in pockets, falling in in a manner that will never be seen again and one the survivors would never believe now. Everyone is ten minutes early, Wolsey's warnings effectively absorbed.

At 1800 precisely Wolsey gives instructions on how to behave at the Commandant's cocktail party. 'There are sponsor officers – some of whom are civilians, volunteers who act as sounding boards, father confessors or just an essential piece of humanity to keep you in touch with the world outside Lympstone – who will make themselves known over the next few days, so you may talk to them without realizing it.'

Strung out in three ranks, all in suits, this is the first time the entire batch have been together. Peas in a pod they are not. Even in their freshly butchered hairstyles a few stand out by sheer size. Royal Marines tend to be of average height, stocky and wiry rather than built like lock forwards. Michael Tanner actually is a lock forward (playing for the Navy he broke three of England international Tim Rodber's ribs in an inter-Services game) and former England Under-21 skipper, with a head that appears to sprout direct from his shoulders. He in turn is dwarfed by Gavin Parr, who possesses an aggressive demeanour, huge Neanderthal features and the sort of haircut favoured by KGB hitmen in James Bond films. Gav is altogether not the sort of chap you would like to meet in a dark alley. In contrast the baby faces of Steve Hussey and little Matt Lodge appear as if they might be freaked out by a booing goose. Others look so young that Mummy might have packed their trunk before sending them off to Marine finishing school.

Inside the Mess the Commandant, Colonel Mike Taffinder, a compact man with a low centre of gravity and enormous bushy eyebrows looking much younger than his fifties, is a cheery relaxed host. His petite blonde wife, who has started to shake up tradition by changing the dads-only booze-up to a Parents Day involving mothers too, insists to all the YOs, 'Please call me Sarah.' They are so embarrassed they would rather choke than call the Commandant's wife by her Christian name. Yet Sarah, through all the jolly informal chatter, cannot hide her own concern at what Dan, her son from her first marriage, is about to go through.

Like all his new colleagues Dan Bailey, white blond hair and skin tanned dark brown by a year in the African sun, shrugs off the nerves that suffuse each and every one like an overdose of Brut – universal liars prattling about how confident they are. All come on like friendly hedgehogs, polite enough but hiding behind defensive spikes. All have at least one drink, perhaps a horse's neck (brandy and ginger) or a gin and tonic to furnish them with courage but as soon as they see one switching to orange juice they all follow suit. Nobody but nobody is going to blow his first night by getting drunk.

A studied contrast and striking compliment to the eventual outcome of Royal Marine training is how socially adept the trained officers are. Like chameleons they can blend into any social gathering and not just appear to be, but actually be, relaxed. Because they are supremely confident in their abilities they have no need to be arrogant, to brag.

The process of weeding out unsuitable candidates has already begun. At the party experienced training officers are eyeing up the new batch like horse butchers at a knackers' yard. To the untrained Mike Tanner looks a certainty.

Far from it. Tanner has a problem. Actually he has lots of problems. He is eighteen stone of rugger bugger and somewhere along the line Union captured his soul, seduced him with beer and comradeship. He has contrived to fail his first-year university exams not once but twice and at different universities, a monumentally difficult task which indicates a serious lack of judgement from a man once on a UCE (University Cadet Entry). Were it not for a naval officer – and keen rugby fan – who fought to keep him, he would already be out on Civvy Street and in debt to the Corps. As it is he arrives at Lympstone already under Commandant's Warning. Since this was deemed to be unfair it was changed to OC's Warning, giving him an extra month's grace to get his act together.

Mr Tanner himself has few doubts. 'I have spent all my life in the pursuit of excellence, this is the biggest challenge I have ever faced. Others may fail, but not me. Failure is not personal, it just means that person is not suited to life in the Corps.'

Physically while his prowess on the rugby field has managed to get him this far it may prove to be his ultimate downfall. He is built like a human tank, but many old hands at the party have already sized him up and found him wanting. Another naval officer admits that he tried to dissuade him from choosing the Marines during his (uncompleted) university degree course. 'He should be able to yomp for ever ... but his arms will not be able to bear his body weight, with pack and weapon, on the Tarzan aerial assault course. He is simply the wrong shape for a Marine, unlike say Mr Rowley over there.'

Andy Rowley has never failed any physical test. A triathlon expert without a spare ounce of fat on his body and a qualified teacher from Loughborough University, he moves as if he is already a lean, mean fighting machine ready to be cocked and fired. Already a couple of officers were sizing him up for the top slot, a serious Sword of Honour candidate.

Pete Joy is another whose record has him singled out as a potential high-flyer. Another UCE with a good history degree from Cambridge he carries himself with the physical confidence one might expect from a boxing blue; of medium height with dark hair, there is a chilling intensity about his stare, as if he were looking through and beyond you towards distant horizons only he can see.

Jeremy Woodall, 20 and a non-graduate, left Bedford School after A levels, a tall elegant boy who would not look out of place in the Guards. His father is a finance manager and he admits to not being 'very academically orientated, though I should be'. He failed his first attempt at the POC (Potential Officers' Course) and instead spent a year travelling around South Africa, Zimbabwe, had a month on a cargo ship to Hong Kong, three months in the colony and then a month in Japan. 'From a young age I've looked at joining the Armed Forces,' he says; 'if you're going to do something, do it to the best of your abilities. The physical side interests me, I'm not one of those people who can sit around all day doing nothing. I don't see myself as failing, though I'm reasonably open minded and I realize there is a lot of team work involved. At least I've got no girlfriend saying "come home, come home" and there is no family pressure.'

In contrast to young Woodall, Andrew Goldsmith is one of the older members of the batch, a week shy of his twenty-fourth birthday and a graduate of agricultural college – 'not Cirencester; they give us a bad name' – who tried his hand at tilling the land for four years but finally quit, primarily out of boredom. 'I was amazed I passed the Admiralty Interview Board,' he admits with the closest thing that passes for happiness on his lugubrious countenance. 'I'm not even that fit physically but I don't consider that to be the main problem.' Within half a day he has already acquired a reputation as something of an enigma, happy to stand by himself sizing up the opposition. Unlike the others he makes no attempt to hide his curiosity about his newly acquired colleagues; inside this haven of physical fitness, he is not ashamed to smoke a cigarette, defiantly drawing the smoke deep into his lungs, exhaling with a grunt of relief and then almost immediately lighting another one.

Goldsmith's intention, which right now he is playing very close to his fag packet, is to play the grey man. By nature a man who enjoys solitude, one who can find comfort standing alone in the middle of a crowded bar, he believes that if he can remain anonymous to other batch members he will be able to hide inside the crowd, and if he can avoid drawing attention to himself from the Training Team and the DS, he will sail through officer training. That is his theory anyway.

Unlike Mr Goldsmith, socially aware enough to be cynical, Gavin Parr is distinctly ill at ease in these surroundings. He carries his huge frame, all 6' 5" of it, as if it were a burden and he were Quasimodo at Prince Charming's Ball. Mr Parr is one of two Corps Commissions, Marines who have passed selection procedures for officer training. A King's Badgeman (a King's Badge is awarded to the top man in each recruit troop and only then if he is considered good enough) he is already entitled to wear the Commando green beret. Raised in Canada he first tried his luck with the Royal Navy – 'I left Dartmouth,' he volunteers, 'after a certain drinking incident with no regrets on either side' – before enlisting in the Royal Marines as a recruit. Although committed to becoming an officer there is something about him of a man who has been in training too long.

Gav is chatting to Jools Ostling and Rob Lunn, a short saturnine graduate with a first-class degree in international affairs, when they are interrupted by another YO who says in distinctly mid-Atlantic tones, 'Gentlemen, if I may interject ...' Andy Parlour appears out of place, his accent primarily American but delivered in stilted correct English of a kind hardly spoken any more, almost as if he were declaiming from the Declaration of Independence. Educated at Johns Hopkins University in Baltimore he is rumoured (incorrectly) to have achieved the highest score of all time on his AIB. Intellectually able, his major difficulty will probably be the physical demands. Or it may be that his foreign upbringing and different perspectives will alienate his batch mates. Inside any group during the process of coalescing together an obvious outsider can become a target, a focus around whom the rest can unify.

Gav and Jools disliked 'Mr Parlour' instantly. The two of them had already met on 'Mockerkin' – a course for testing leadership skills – and clicked. For Jools, at 21 a University College London graduate in economics and former National Bronze Medallist for rowing, this is the first time he has ever lived away from his south London home. He intends to enjoy it – which his alliance with Gav will probably help. They are obvious mates, natural allies – Gav, still with his 'nod' (recruit) haircut where individual hairs more than a quarter of an inch long would be put on a charge for disorderly conduct, Jools with an ingrained suspicion of anyone from public school. With each carrying a chip on his shoulder, together they are perfectly balanced, Gavin so huge as to be almost terrifying, Jools with a gift for mimicry and a razor tongue. The instant they nicknamed Parlour 'the Interjector' was not just a bitchy moment of wit but the nascence of the batch's sharp end. From then on Messrs Parr and Ostling made themselves the batch's mouthpiece, seemingly indispensable but actually vulnerable. Allowing yourself to become the loaded gun is fine as long as you stay clean yourself, but it doesn't take much for nastiness to back-fire, for a weapon to explode in the face of the one who fires it.

Strange how people see what they wish to see, how selective the memory is. The boys – for that is what they were then – mainly remember those first days as a time when they strutted their stuff like peacocks waiting for their feathers to grow. Yet talking to them is like talking to a bunch of parrots who all repeat the same lines, with just a few variations. Some, like Tim David and stolid dependable Pete Manson, are anxious to become absorbed into the furniture. While Martin Wood, fresh from talking up being a rufty-tufty Marine to his mates at Exeter University, is now confronted with the end of his fantasy and manfully coping with it by looking stricken.

The other Corps Commission YO has spent the past two years in a rifle troop. Andy Harker makes up for any lack of social skills by simply looking military, a feat effortlessly achieved by Andy McInerney who looks as if he was born to ride down Horseguards Parade. Others, like Brian Adcock and Matt Skuse, are so certain, so cockily confident that they deliberately seek out senior officers to impress their mates. Russ Corn is more considered in his approach; for the moment he, like Harker, can hide behind Yorkshire standoffishness while Philip Ashby, who has already earned a green beret on an SSLC (Short Service Limited Commission), approaches the cocktail party with the same amused 'I'll join in but you can't ever break me' look he will wear behind his eyes for ever. Eighty per cent of this batch are graduates – at the time a record for the Corps – while those with even less life experience behind them can be spotted easily and not just because they shave only twice a week. Only 19 or just turned 20, Rory Thomson, Philip Shetler-Jones and Tristan Harris are easily distin-guished by fresh faces and nervous expressions.

This is the batch's last night in civilian clothes. Tomorrow morn-ing at a time when most sensible people are thinking about break-fast they will have already been issued with their new uniforms and will be starting to acquire some brand new skills.

2

Of Officers and NCOs

Example is the school of mankind and they will learn at no
other.

Edmund Burke

LYMPSTONE WAS CO-OPTED as a Royal Marine base during the
Second World War and became the sole Commando Training
Centre Royal Marines – or in that initializing jargon so beloved of
the military, CTCRM – in the sixties. Compared to Sandhurst it is
tiny, more a military village than a small town, and can scarcely be
described as an architectural landmark, full of modern oblong eye-
sores that roll down towards the mud-flats. However it possesses all
the necessary facilities – a fully equipped hospital, a near full-sized
Olympic swimming pool, a church, banks and a sports shop, while
relics of the early days are still scattered about the camp. The
Commandant's office looks straight out at some ageing wooden
huts dating back to the war, a constant and deliberate reminder of
Corps history.

The Royal Marine Corps was created on 28 October 1664,
when the Duke of York and Albany's Maritime Regiment of Foot
was formed by the decree of King Charles II. Initially they were
known as the Lord High Admiral's Regiment, or the Admiral's
Regiment, the Royal prefix being granted in 1802. Over the next
three hundred years the Marines distinguished themselves at major
engagements both on land and sea; their first battle honour was
1704 when 1,800 British and Dutch Marines attacked and captured
Gibraltar; at Trafalgar it was Marine Sergeant Major Secker who
cradled Nelson as he lay dying on the deck of HMS *Victory*.

The Royal Marine badge shows a lion and crown above the
word 'GIBRALTAR' (the Corps' finest battle honour), itself crowning

half a globe (Africa, Europe and Asia – the US Marine Corps have the other half) surrounded by a laurel wreath. Underneath the globe is a fouled anchor and the Latin inscription 'PER MARE PER TERRAM' (BY SEA BY LAND). However relations between the Navy and the Marines have not always been smooth, the senior service viewing the Marines as a younger, brash and bouncy half-brother. The original and primary role of Marines on board naval ships was to prevent sailors mutinying against the harsh conditions under which they worked. On 13 July 1860 John Dallinger of HMS *Leven*, a private in the Royal Marines Light Infantry, became the last member of the Royal Navy to be hanged from the yard-arm. He had been found guilty of two attempted murders.

In the Great War the Corps served with distinction at the Gallipoli landings and the Zeebrugge raid. At the outbreak of the Second World War the Corps' strength stood at 16,000 men and ended up at 75,000 – 16,000 Marines were involved in the Normandy Landings of 1944. However it was the introduction of the Commando green beret in late 1942 which secured the future of the Corps. Originally seventy-nine army regiments were represented in the eight Commando brigades, of which five were exclusively composed of Marines.

In 1946, during the defence cuts that followed demobilization, the Corps displayed both foresight and flexibility. Realizing that they had to find a role to ensure their survival as an independent entity they took over responsibility for Commando training – which the Army has regretted ever since – and decided that all Marines would undergo it. (From then on every member of a Commando unit from the Navy doctors to the cooks and the drivers had to pass the Commando Course in order to be able to wear the green beret.) In an age of shrinking empire the Marines ceased to be just an amphibious infantry option and became an essential part of the country's defence force. Further intelligence in planning for the long-term future has seen them take on specialist training roles as diverse as Arctic and jungle warfare.

Royal Marine tours of duty in Northern Ireland have the tendency to be relatively trouble-free where despite inter-service rivalry – for the Marines are the Navy's soldiers – they are highly respected. 'In Northern Ireland,' says a former Army Intelligence officer, 'the Marines are close to the best. While the Paras have earned a not totally unfounded reputation for shooting and thinking of the questions afterwards, the Marines will explain to the local community exactly why they are there and what they are going to do.'

The long-term future of the Royal Marines – who had just been forced to disband 41 Commando in 1981 – was secured by the Falklands War. A tiny garrison, Naval Party 8901, has been stationed at Port Stanley since the nineteenth century, and during the initial Argentinian invasion sixty-nine Marines, although outnumbered by hundreds, fought back until they were ordered to surrender by the island's governor. In taking back the islands 3,520 Marines were crucial to one of the most ambitious – and risky – amphibious operations in history. The yomp across the Falklands from San Carlos to Port Stanley has become the stuff of legend. Aside from its strategic significance what it did was prove that Marine training not only worked but was an essential option for modern warfare. In the end there is no substitute for the man on the ground, provided he knows what he is doing – and provided he is led by officers who he knows are at least as tough and resourceful as he.

It is part of the Corps ethos that both officers and men should be trained at Lympstone. They go through the same experiences – though officers have to complete the Commando tests in faster times – the same pain. The Marines do not, have never done, and never will recruit boneheads from public schools possessing private incomes, the right accent and the ability to master a horse. They are tough, certainly, but their rigours are tempered with a considered, at times almost intellectual approach.

The selection process for Young Officers is rigorous and painstaking (as it should be since it costs £1,000 per week to put an officer through training) for the Corps are looking for a flexible man who can combine physical strength with quick-response thinking. Each YO has already completed a three-day Potential Officers' Course (POC) at Lympstone and then gone through the Admiralty Interview Board (AIB) at HMS *Sultan*, a naval shore base at Gosport in Hampshire. Being a smooth talker with the physical constitution of an ox is no guarantee of acceptance – perceived commitment counts for much more.

The POC tests for the physical and mental stamina required – three days in which thirty hopefuls are whittled down to ten or less. First they have to pass the USMC (United States Marine

Corps) fitness test – eighty-five sit-ups inside two minutes, sixty press-ups in as long as it takes, provided it does not take too long, forty squat jumps in one minute, eighteen pull-ups, a three hundred metre sprint in five sixty-metre legs in under forty-one seconds; all followed by an afternoon on the Bottom Field climbing ropes and being shown how to get around the Tarzan Course. The next day they get to play on both the Tarzan and Endurance Courses as well as giving a three-minute lecture to the rest of the course on a subject of their choosing. The final physical test is to jump in the pool from the three-metre board, wearing full battle kit, then swim sixty metres.

For every ten that pass a POC, only three or four may get through the AIB – a further two days before a panel of five (generally comprising a Royal Marine colonel, a personnel selection officer, a Royal Marine captain or major, a Royal Navy officer and a civilian headmaster). Candidates have to know about Naval and Marine history and organization and are tested for mental alertness by being asked to describe how they would cope with certain life or death scenarios. Both potential psychopaths and gung-ho patriots might like to be Royal Marine officers but the job of the AIB is to prevent such potential liabilities ever setting foot in Lympstone. Some people will always slip through the net – despite official denials to the contrary those with military connections might get a positive nod if they are on the borderline – but generally the AIB does its job with a ruthless efficiency that can leave a teenager exhausted and shuddering with newly discovered fears and insecurities.

In YO batch Sept. '91 thirteen have opted for a full career commission (a minimum sixteen years' service), six of whom are UCE (University Cadet Entry). A UCE is selected by the Corps at the age of 18 or so and signs on for a full career commission. Prior to going to university he will undergo the first four weeks of YO training and will then spend four to six weeks of his summer vacation attached to a unit. The three or four years spent at university will count towards promotion seniority. Graduates also earn more – £34.55 per day (£12,610.75 per annum) as against £30.14 (£11,001.10) for non-graduates. Full career officers can leave at any time, although UCEs must stay on for seven years after graduation.

Another UCE, Philip Ashby, was no stranger to the Royal

Marines: in the year before he went up to Cambridge he had taken an SSLC (a nine-month course in which he took and passed the Commando tests, as well as joining a Commando unit in Norway). An SSLC has no commitment to join the Corps; indeed Ashby was the exception, for the idea is to go on and become a captain of industry who can act as an ambassador for the Marines, spreading the word in Civvy Street about how wonderful the Corps is.

Ashby is the third member of the batch entitled to wear a green beret throughout training – the rest are stuck with the giveaway blue. The other two green berets are the Corps Commissions who initially joined the ranks and have already completed their thirty weeks of recruit training. Corps Commissions do sometimes find themselves at a disadvantage intellectually for all the others have academic qualifications that place them in the top five per cent of the country. However, intelligence alone is no indicator of how a YO will fare.

A YO batch is a peculiar, almost unique, organism, made up in this case of thirty-five individuals all with their own individual prejudices, phobias, preconceptions and beliefs, both ingrained and learnt from personal experience. Some already know each other through university or UCE. Robinson and Stovin-Bradford are already 'best friends', as are Rowley and Adcock. What they all have in common is a lack of self-doubt; to their minds just to be here is to be one of the élite. For them to become a disciplined unit, in which individual desires gradually become fused into a desire for a single goal, requires a strong outside force. A leader.

It is example that makes a man. Corporate dynamics have it that inside any tightly defined group structure individual members of the group will eventually take on many of the characteristics of the group's leader, whether he be charismatic or a ditherer – imitation becomes either a form of camouflage or the sincerest form of flattery.

Should some advertising whiz kid ever want to cast a Marine for a TV commercial Captain Mark Wolsey would probably get the part the moment he walked into central casting. He looks the way people imagine a Royal Marine officer should look. Six foot two, 31, he moves with the grace of a natural athlete; handsome, yes, but there is a chilly edge in his light brown eyes that forbids him from ever being too pretty. He wears his green beret as if it had been there for ever. The jaunty, insouciant air he conveys would be infuriating were it not clear that this arrogance is founded on a bedrock of confidence gained through experience. He talks well but with a middle-class accent bred not in a country seat but from the BBC. Although married he keeps up a raffish air by driving a BMW convertible and a Harley Davidson motor bike. A cool guy with cool toys, who relaxes by eating extra hot Vindaloo curries, the only danger he can never foresee is the one where his personality might roll into self-parody and caricature.

Wolsey's height and neo-aristocratic bearing lead his colleagues to joke about him being a Guards officer on secondment. He is not at all popular with his contemporaries, some of whom can wax obscenely eloquent on the subject's shortcomings. This may be professional jealousy as despite early peccadilloes Wolsey is marked out as a high-flyer. Or it may be personal: anyone who makes the hardest physical challenges in life seem as easy as buttering toast, and then reminds you how easy it is, is at the very least aggravating. On the other hand SNCOs and men who have worked for him have called him 'the best officer I've ever served under. Despite that cocky front he actually listens to and cares about his men.'

Officers very rarely take more than one batch through the fifteen-month training schedule. Because of the enormous influence a course officer has on YOs he is selected with particular care so the final nod is often given by the Royal Marines CG (Commandant General) personally. So Wolsey was obviously highly regarded. 'I didn't know Mark before he arrived,' says Colonel Mike Taffinder, 'and I will admit I was concerned by his reputation. However I spoke to a former CO of his who told me he had total confidence in Mark. He came into my office and the very first thing he said to me was "I've met this man who wants to do a book on the batch ..." He wasn't short of confidence, that's for sure.'

The batch quickly nicknamed him 'the Cardinal' but any pejorative tone vanished within weeks as awe turned first to respect then to love. For them 'the Boss' was the bee's knees, the ultimate Corps role model, and anyone criticizing him suddenly found themselves facing the potential wrath of thirty-five YOs.

In fact within the Corps Wolsey is physically the exception rather than the rule. If one can make such a generalization Marine officers are, like the populace at large, usually of medium height but they differ in that they possess an innate sense of self, a physical confidence that breeds the respect without which the basic ethos which governs the Marine esprit de corps would crumble.

Broadly speaking Marine officers break down into three types, but only two are likely to find their way to the top of the Corps ladder – sword wielders and pen pushers. There are romantics and pragmatists, and those in the middle, who can be discounted over the long haul. The twain are forever engaged in conflict, all the way up from YO training to CG. Actually the conflict is more apparent than real for the two are locked in a symbiosis, both needing the other to make the system work.

The pragmatists are the quieter types, coldly efficient, who run by the book because that is the way it is. They are adaptable but uncomfortable if their superior prefers to flout regulations in order to get things done. Their sense of humour may be non-existent, or concealed so as not to detract from the job, or so dry as to be witty only in hindsight. Their Marines respect them, do not question their decisions but are not allowed to love them perhaps because that would be too frightening.

The romantics have a maverick spirit that the Corps, to its credit, tries to channel but not to expunge. They have fire and flair, or hair-trigger tempers (as many a poor computer has found to its cost). They can be charismatic and terrifying because, simply put, they are always potentially dangerous, an incident waiting to happen. They still hang on to extravagant notions, whether they be lowly troop officers who go AWOL to sort out a girlfriend or senior officers who may still let their hearts rule their heads.

There is little doubt where Major Matt Sturman in charge of OTW (Officers' Training Wing) sits. He had been in the chair for less than a week when YO batch Sept. '91 arrived, so from the off was learning a new job. Unfailingly polite and operationally unflappable he has the air of the concerned housemaster at an old-fashioned boys' public school. He is a worrier who joined the Marines relatively late and because of this finds following the rules the more comfortable course. Physically Sturman is around 5' 9", of slight build, with thinning fair hair, a round face and a perpetually furrowed brow. Temperamentally he and Wolsey are poles apart, so from the outset clashes were inevitable.

On paper, everything in Wolsey's career looks fine and dandy. He was a UCE, chosen by the Corps at eighteen and paid through Nottingham University, where he studied – though that might be rather economical with the *actualité* – philosophy and enjoyed the pecuniary advantage of a salary while a student, before passing out of Lympstone in 1982 fourth in his batch. 'I was told I was up for the Sword, until I completely cocked up my final written exam,' he says with no trace of regret. 'Winning the Sword of Honour doesn't mean that much when you get out to a unit.'

He returned to Lympstone after two years serving as commander of Zulu Company in 45 Commando. Following a tour of duty in Northern Ireland he went to Northern Iraq immediately after the Gulf War. His middle years, however, are rather more shrouded in mystery and throughout the course YOs would spread rumours of his having gone AWOL and of charges that hung over his epaulets like the sword of Damocles – while there were murmurings amongst Corps contemporaries that Wolsey was too reckless, too loose a cannon, to be put in charge of tender young officers.

'I was a bit wild during my training – one time we had all our shore leave cancelled for six weeks,' grins Wolsey recalling his days as a YO. 'And while on a rugby tour we did try to blow up Sandhurst with thunder flashes. There was another incident in a pub that ended up all over the *News of the World* – fortunately they thought it was army officer cadets, otherwise we would have been in the shit.'

War stories bring out the ego in any military man and for Wolsey it still rankles that he finished his YO training just after the Falklands War ended. However going into Northern Iraq was some compensation. The Marines' task there was to help the UN enforce safe havens for the Kurds, to protect them from the Iraqi army in the aftermath of their abortive rebellion at the end of the Gulf War. When he talks about it, absent-mindedly fondling a defused grenade he borrowed from the Republican Guard, it is all matter-of-fact, the way soldiers often talk about situations that could have got them killed, as if denying the dangers bans any night terrors. Facing down a Republican Guard colonel in open ground with both sides aiming machine-guns at your head and ready to open up with everything they've got is one thing; sneaking into Iraqi barracks in the middle of the night to 'liberate' their weapons – everything from Kalashnikovs to anti-tank launchers – might be considered another even if it simply confirmed suspicions that the Republican Guard are no more élite troops than are Millwall supporters. Such clandestine operations gave the men a great deal of munitions – the kind that do not have to be accounted for to the Ministry of Defence – to let off in the desolate, deserted valleys outside of Sarsing.

Underneath such tales always lies a separate agenda, for such actions mask the frustration at what the Marines were *not* able to do in Kurdistan: that they could not really help the people they were supposed to help and were constrained by both UN regulations and higher authorities. It's tough to play a policeman who can only shoot back after severe provocation, difficult to negotiate with enemy soldiers who simply do not know that they have just lost a war, and if they have heard it simply do not believe it. Another plus for Marine discipline, another lesson Wolsey has learnt that must be passed over to his new charges.

Inside OTW are various officers with responsibility for different aspects of training. Some like Captain Bailey are the orderly unsmiling types, others like Gordon Messenger and Andy 'Shagger' Shaw have a zest for life that is communicated to the YOs even through the most mundane of subjects. There is even a Pongo Captain, whose major task appears to be organizing the Final Exercise.

However the most important people as far as the batch are concerned in these early days are the SNCOs in their Training Team. Although during Wolsey's first briefing they might have been overlooked, these are the ones who count – not just because they'll call a YO 'you stupid cunt ... sir', but because if you can't get on with your NCO in your first troop command you are dead (sometimes literally).

Marines like to boast that any of their corporals could out-perform a Pongo sergeant and with their Training Team the batch have struck especially lucky. The most immediately striking is Tom Coyle, an acerbic Glaswegian with a tongue that can flay the arrogance off a graduate with an alarming, inventive but always scatological turn of phrase. Six feet tall, wiry, with that ubiquitous Marine moustache favoured by SNCOs and a great many officers, captains and above, he is a PW1 (Platoon Weapons Instructor First Class), a crack shot with any number of weapons who served in Northern Ireland in various capacities about which he will say little. Ulsterman Billy Baxter appears almost a Coyle clone – a little taller, a little wirier, a fraction thinner on top. He's an ML2 (Mountain Leader Second Class) whose career was nearly terminated after a parachute jump in which another jumper floated beneath him whipping the air out of his chute. He fell like a rock to the ground, breaking his back in several places. Quieter than Coyle, he may not possess the range of the Scotsman's vocabulary but he can voice his opinions just as witheringly. Despite initial appearances to the contrary Billy is more considered and open, less wild than Coyle, who in the final analysis is comfortable but trapped within his well-ingrained prejudices.

The third section SNCO is 'Evs' Everett. Of heavy build, with a russet complexion and sandy hair he looks more like a farmer than a Londoner. He will leave at Christmas to become a Special Duties Officer, which means that his role will henceforth be in administration. His replacement is Sergeant Dai Phillips, another PW1, which causes much merriment as all Team jokes can now begin, 'There were four Marines on an exercise, an Englishman, an Irishman, a Scotsman and a Welshman ...'

Formerly a Royal Greenjacket, Colour Sergeant Paul Redding is Course Instructor and TQ, who has just transferred over to the Marines after passing the All Arms Commando Course. It is a strange appointment to put him in with YOs, as he has yet to serve in a Commando unit, and though to the other SNCOs he will always be a Pongo, right now it is worse – he is a Pongo without a clue of how real Marines do things. Redding is an odd mixture of erudition and working-class mores, telling tall stories of tarts in Thailand at one moment and talking of what he read in the *Observer* the next.

The final member of the Training Team is Sergeant Toby Broomes, a black man of medium height and impressive musculature. He is the batch PTI, responsible for building their strength up so that yomping across Dartmoor carrying 110-lb Bergens filled with all the essentials of field living becomes second nature rather than a long drawn out torture.

The first task of the Training Team is to make sure that the batch acquire some basic skills. Very quickly and in a manner that they cannot forget. Washing and ironing will do for a start.

Learning to March in Boots

No man is an Island entire of itself; every man is a piece of the
Continent, a part of the Main.

John Donne

THE FIRST WEEK in CTC is known as 'J' Week – or Joining Week
– supposedly a gentle introduction to the rigours of training ahead.
In the scheme of pre-dawn starts and post-midnight finishes it is,
but at 0740 on the morning after the cocktail party the batch are a
little unsteady in their bravado, a trifle shell-shocked by the
experience. It probably did not help that they were aroused from
their restless slumbers by YOs from the May '91 batch masquerading as Physical Training Instructors and were put through what was
to be the first of many 'beastings' at 3 a.m. A ritual as old as drinking till you puke, they knew it was coming, but it still meant no
sleep.

As students they never had to appear, let alone function, at this
sort of hour – 'My week at Uni started at ten on Monday morning
and finished at three on Tuesday afternoon. The rest of my days
were devoted to beer, golf and rugby,' mutters Chalkie. This is the
last time they will be lined up together in civilian clothes; henceforth they will be always be a group in uniform. From now on
things will never be the same again.

They are paraded by Colour Sergeant Jordan down to have their
'phot' (picture) taken for their ID cards, rail cards and for the batch
book, and a poster of all their mug shots is given to each YO and
soon adorns various offices in OTW. This poster is a symbol of survival for as soon as someone quits their photo is crossed through –
two broad red or black strokes that excise them from the present
like some outlawed desperado in the Wild West who has just met

an untimely end. The ritual of the cross reduces one to an instant non-person.

Some YOs, one in particular, took the ritual of blanking out faces to its extreme. Appointing himself judge and jury he blacked out some sixteen faces on his poster, deciding unilaterally that among others Goldsmith, Evans, Collins and McQueen would never make it. By doing so and boasting about it to those he thought were his mates, he also appointed himself batch executioner. As a prophet he was to prove as accurate as any Delphic oracle – spot on about half the time – but as with anyone so certain, so arrogant, there is always a glaring flaw. Time as a helix often brings the axe back down on the executioner.

Phot complete, it is time to go through the next ritual – Picking Up Kit. For the outsider this is an amusing exercise. Half a dozen poor souls who have committed one of the worst offences known to the military – they have failed to fill in forms detailing shoe, waist and collar sizes in advance – wait forlornly in the wings, while their twenty-nine colleagues stretch the length of the corridor gazing in bemusement at this giant cardboard box. Woe betide the inquisitive one who dares to open, or peek inside, his box before the stores quartermaster bellows out his instructions.

'Put bag travelling one behind on the wall,' shouts the QM, as the YOs pull out a most unfashionable beige hold-all. Shetler-Jones holds out this object at arm's length, viewing it as if it were suffering from a highly contagious form of leprosy. 'You have until Tuesday morning to change any kit. Now open the box. There you will find six winged collars – check it is all there because if you lose anything you will be charged from now on.'

So it goes on – Pussers-issue trainers, Pussers T-shirt (blue) … (Although to the outsider 'Pussers' always sounds rather derogatory it is not. It is one of the most frequently used naval slang words, referring to any item of Navy issue. 'Pussers Foo-foo', for example, is a foot and body talcum powder issued for use in the tropics) … shoes (black) shiny, khaki denim trousers, everything that might be deemed suitable for a Marine. Not however for a Shetler-Jones whose expression could grace a Bateman cartoon. Eventually, with a gesture that will become all too familiar as the months roll by, he shrugs his shoulders, unrolls his Just William grin and staggers back to his cabin in the Officers' Mess clutching the boxes, which appear to be specially designed to be slightly too big for anyone other than an orang-utan or Brian Adcock to carry comfortably.

There is much moaning among certain YOs upon hearing that they will not be issued with their own personal weapon for another five days. 'You'll just have to use your bayonet, then,' a sharp rejoinder comes echoing down the corridor. Alongside innumerable medical and dental checks – 'it's to see if we're still alive and capable of biting the enemy to death' – learning how to care for kit and to keep individual cabins so tidy that the dust salutes on entry are the lessons drummed home over the first two weeks.

The cabins are functional rather than luxurious, furnished with bare necessities and quickly decorated with pictures of soon to be ex-girlfriends. The partition walls are so thin that everyone becomes instantly familiar with their neighbours' choice of music. Tanner's love for the Royal Marine Band's Greatest Hits is not generally shared by his colleagues. Communal showering and washing and ironing in underwear means each man soon becomes accustomed to the sight of his colleagues' equipment. Any residual gentility and shyness is rapidly eradicated as everyone confesses in turn to 'having a swamp' (urinating) in their cabin sink.

Just to make the experience more enjoyable the washing machines – huge industrial Maytags, big and tough enough to scrub a small Marine sparkling – are placed out of bounds. All washing has to be done by hand. Then there is the ironing. For most of the batch up until this point ironing is something either done by Mummy or not done at all. Their first efforts would have been better had they fallen in the latter category.

To Gav Parr, fresh – if that is the right word – from thirty weeks of recruit training, the Officers' Mess seems like the royal suite at a luxury hotel, the hand washing a small price to pay. 'Joining as a recruit I felt I was stripped of every right I ever had as a human being and was immediately given the feeling that the next thirty weeks of training were unattainable. Being given my very own cabin with my own sink is a definite high, so is being treated like a human being rather than some form of retarded pond life.'

At this stage those with any previous military experience are much in demand. Parr and Harker, the Corps Commission boys, could charge for demonstrating their expertise. The UCEs, as well, already have enough basic knowledge to get by, having been through the first four weeks of training before they went up to university. Mike Tanner so looks the part, barking out his instructions in an authoritative tone, that on arrival some of the YOs believed he was their Course Officer.

Throughout those first few days the individual members of the batch are eyeing each other up, trying to work out who is who, discovering whether preconceptions are being realized or confounded. 'The first week was, to be honest, a little strange,' admitted Tim David, with his languid but sharp wit, after the first ten weeks. 'When I decided to join up last December I didn't know what a Royal Marine officer was like apart from the common media perceptions of dagger-clasping screaming commandos. Matt Skuse and Mike Tanner lived up to this but the rest of us were a bit more student-like and relaxed. Mike was so keen that it was only two days later I realized he wasn't already a fully trained member of the DS. We all had our suspicions of Andy Harker. I thought he was a corporal inserted as a mole to keep the DS one step ahead. Even now I'm not too convinced, he's too good at everything. Mr Shetler-Jones still hasn't grasped that the Guards is more of a social pose and that you get dirty in the Marines.'

Shet himself who after his AIB interview had been expecting to find a batch consisting of 'thirty-four editions of Matt Skuse and one Andy McInerney' found it particularly amusing to be 'called a cunt collectively for the first two weeks'.

Inside his head Mike Tanner is already a Marine officer, has been for a couple of years. Chalkie and 'Bob Rob' Robinson had met him over the summer at a rugby pub in Twickenham. 'A mutual friend introduced us when he heard we were going into the Marines,' chuckles Robinson; 'the next thing we see is this huge person crushing our hands and saying something like "2nd Lieutenant Michael Tanner Royal Marines, M Company, 40 Commando." We were terribly impressed with his command of the jargon and military bearing ... until we got here and found out he was just one of us.'

Despite all that wild-eyed aggression Mike underneath it all is a bit of a pussycat. All he has ever wanted to be is a Marine officer, so he wants to help everyone else to become one too. 'People misread me,' he says, 'I was genuinely trying to help. As a UCE you do those first four weeks before you go to Uni and when you come back you do them all over again. The first time I went around like a headless person, getting to bed at three and up again at five to clean the toilets with a toothbrush. Everything was chaos and I remember nothing about it; the second time it was all so much simpler and clear cut. It's nothing to do with how intelligent you are, anyone without experience finds themselves in a complete tizz. I was trying to help.'

For Rob Lunn a Marine bursary – '£1,200 a year and a drink with an officer once in a while thank you very much' – has not prepared him for being issued with what appears to be half of all the kit in Lympstone and being told it has to be ready for inspection in the morning. 'Being completely unused to admin and "globe and buster" folding I followed the only course of action open to me: I flapped.'

For Bob Rob the memory remains the stuff of nightmares: 'I floundered below a morass of kit, wondering whether I was about to sink or swim. Whatever university had done for me it certainly hadn't prepared me in advanced ironing techniques. My disorganization reached new heights when I managed to prepare only one bayonet for a kit inspection which failed to make up for the rest of the omitted stuff.'

Struggling with domestic responsibilities under the unforgiving gimlet eyes of the Training Team is particularly hard on a couple of the batch. Mark Webster, a Wigan lad with a degree in business information technology and a brother who is a lance-corporal in the REME (Royal Electrical and Mechanical Engineers), cracks after a mere forty-eight hours. He tells Wolsey he wants to leave, thinks about it for another day then changes his mind, but his mind is already set in dither mode. Uncomfortable like Jools Ostling with the very concept of an officer class, unlike him he has not found a comrade to drink with. Once a YO starts to question his presence at Lympstone he is forever on the precipice of quitting.

'I believed I would become a Commando the second I entered the main gate, and would immediately be thrown into a cohesive team for hard work and quick progress – I hadn't reckoned with the ironing board. Within four days our conversation centred around which detergent would get clothes really clean and how best to iron a shirt,' says Martin Wood, who for all his macho talk, looks perpetually on the verge of tears, struck dumb by the unrelenting abuse of the SNCOs. Every time he saw three stripes approaching him he got the shakes. Indeed during those first few nights he did cry himself to sleep, but was man enough to admit it to his mates later on. This was a big mistake. Marines, even trainee

Marines, can only countenance certain types of failure. Being perceived as a wimp is not part of that agenda.

Once the inspections start Chalkie, for all his cracks about changing his application in order to join the SIS (Special Ironing Service), really catches it. It is, he admits, largely his own fault for setting himself up as the batch clown. 'I've always been a gobby bastard,' he smirks, 'and I came to the Corps after a month in Portugal, where I had a great time but got seriously overweight. I know nothing about soldiering and I haven't worn a rucksack since I spent two days on Exmoor at fifteen when I got lifts going uphill from passing cars – the batch have called me Sherpa-Bedford since I told them that.

'Naturally the first thing I tried to do was bullshit Colour Sergeant Redding that I had worn a pair of socks I hadn't. "Have you changed your socks?" "Yes, Colour Sergeant." That wasn't very bright as it is the sort of thing you can check quite easily!'

It was to get better still for Chalkie. One inspection later Redding, having discovered that all his shirts are neatly folded in the right place, that even his tapes are standing to attention, suddenly asks: 'Where's your raincoat?' 'I haven't been issued with one yet, Colour Sergeant.' 'That's no excuse !' Bang ... everything goes flying across the cabin floor. These days he laughs about the unfairness of it all; back then it was everyone else who thought it was funny.

While most YOs quickly took the inspections and the verbal insults rained upon them by the Training Team with equanimity and good humour – an unlimited source for jokes and tall tales – Pete Joy found it tedious and intellectually insulting. 'Along with the majority of the batch I'd spent the previous three years or so responsible for using my own time productively and keeping my room as tidy as I saw fit,' he says. 'I soon found that I resented the vast length of time spent in admin and the intrusion of inspections. Perhaps I was disposed to be more critical than most but I found Initial Training boring and a waste of time – I hadn't spent three years at university to be a laundry slave.'

On Tuesday 10 September the batch did their first Basic Fitness Test, a benchmark that is used at least twice a year on Royal Marines. Consisting of pull-ups (as many as you can manage), burpees, sit-ups, dorsal raises and press-ups (as many as you can manage in a minute), it is followed after a reasonable breathing space by a 2.4 kilometre (1.5 mile) group run which must be completed within fifteen minutes. There is then a further 2.4 kilometre individual run which must be completed in under eleven and a half minutes. For a YO batch with an average age of twenty-two this test should not present difficulties.

Chalkie managed it. Just. Adcock, Rowley and Harker sailed through, of course. Mike Tanner failed, as did Mark Collins and surprisingly Andy Goldsmith. The excuse he gave was that he was trying to help Tanner along. The SNCOs who have heard every excuse ever invented were unimpressed, though in the weeks that follow, his physical capabilities are never again questioned. For Goldsmith failing a test that most pass and then swinging a line is not the best way to sink into batch anonymity. It was however an indication of the power of Tanner's personality that at a point when nobody in the batch truly knows him, when they – unlike the Training Team – have no reason to doubt his fitness, when all they can see is the incredible hulk, one of them should risk failure to push him on. Or, alternatively, it might be the first spark of a nascent batch spirit.

That afternoon Sergeant Broomes introduces the batch to IMF (Initial Military Fitness), a series of synchronized Swedish PT exercises designed to bring them to a standard where the Bottom Field and its associated tortures can be approached in relative safety. And there are the ropes to climb, thirty feet high and it hurts like hell every inch of the way to those who have not got either the upper body strength or unlike 'Shaggy' Ashby (an extreme rock climber) the technique. 'For a good laugh you should see Tanner trying to climb a rope,' Parr drops in one day, but then he's experienced and you can see other wannabe high-flyers like Russ Corn dying fifteen feet up in the air, a fly with one leg trapped in a web, frightened of falling, so frightened of hanging out as to be hanging on.

Training moves gently on through lectures ominously entitled 'It Could Happen to You' (concerning the dangers of friendly fire), 'March Discipline/Care of Feet', the riveting 'Corps Funds' and 'Why a RM Officer ?' (delivered by the chaplain); through painstaking hours spent learning to strip and assemble the SA80 Assault Rifle, map reading, radio and communication skills; through endless hours of IMF, swimming and the unit boxing finals where the mild-mannered tones of Neil Watkinson did not prevent him beating Rob Lunn into near concussion, and Matt Skuse's reputation as a 'cheesy biff' plummeted still further when after losing his bout he went up to the Duty Student and apologized 'for letting the batch down'.

So inexorably on to the field. CTC is blessed with having one of the world's bleakest and potentially most dangerous training areas waiting on its doorstep: a place where the weather can change from bright sunshine to blinding sleet, clag into zero visibility within seconds, a place that on a foul day – and there are several hundred foul days a year – makes the yomp across the Falklands seem like a dose of *deja vu*. That is Dartmoor.

Before Dartmoor always comes Woodbury Common. A mere four miles from Lympstone, Woodbury has its hidden dangers. It is home to Peter's Pool and the tunnels that comprise the first two miles of the Endurance Course – probably the hardest of all Commando tests – so Marines learn to know it well. It is home, too, to a unique medical condition known as Woodbury Rash which has found its way into the textbooks. The Rash infects the body with pus-filled sores leaving scars which like a bad marriage never really go away. The other main danger to training is civilians.

Civilians like to walk their dogs there, which for a perfectly cam-ouflaged Marine can be a salutary if insanitary experience. During their training recruits are sometimes given a live chicken upon which they must feast for some days; legend has it that a busload of pensioners enjoying their constitutional happened upon a bunch of nods chasing a chicken around trying to hack its head off with a bayonet. Other stories have a girls' school outing chancing upon an NCO machine-gunning his troop all standing and 'dying' to atten-tion – it may have been blanks but their acting was enough to unleash many an attack of the vapours. The rule with Woodbury Common is simple. If you are going to fuck up, do it at night.

The first YO exercise on Woodbury, aptly titled 'Tenderfoot', came in Week 4. 'Phys' (Physical Training) has still not got any bet-ter for Mike Tanner. As a runner he simply doesn't cut it, trailing in behind the others. 'My training is for short twenty-yard bursts of speed, I'm just not prepared for this, my stamina is not up to it,' he admits. 'But I'm determined to work on a special programme in the evenings when I've done all my admin. If I get it right I should have from seven every night. But I am looking forward to going into the field.'

Tenderfoot is important for the YOs because it is the first and only time where they receive basic practical fieldcraft instruction (in comparison recruits have four different exercises to practise their skills). From this moment they are expected to be able to put up a bivvy (a groundsheet and some rope) with a minimum of time, understand the fundamentals of camouflage, stalking and concealment, the necessity of wet/dry routines (always sleep in dry clothes and socks, change back into damp ones in the morning). At night they learn that their equipment has to be readily accessible so that they can move everything in the dark. With so much to learn in so little time the Team are ruthless in looking for weaknesses; holding the smallest mistake up to ridicule drives home the standards that have to be upheld.

The YOs are still amazed by the amount of kit they have to carry in their Bergens (though at this stage it is a mere 60 lbs compared to full military operations where they have to add in radio batteries, ammunition, five days of rations and anti-tank weapons to give an average pack weight of 90–110 lbs). Inside their jackets are binoculars, a map case, a clasp knife on a lanyard, and the various belt webbings combine to an ingenious whole. There is 'fighting order' which is a series of webbing pouches (pronounced 'pooches') attached to the belt, with a bayonet, water bottle and basic rations. Then there is the assault pack, two bigger pouches zipped on to the side of the Bergen that can then be removed and zipped together to make a small back pack which gives a Marine enough to survive in the field for a minimum of twenty-four hours.

The weather is kind on Tenderfoot so spirits are initially high; the unwary have drunk all their water by lunchtime, having omitted to find out whether they will be getting any more. Andy Harker sits under a tree, his water scarcely touched, as if expecting the world to cave in at any minute. Others are busy heating up boil-in-the-bag rations or munching on a snack. Generally they are very cool, if grousing a touch about lack of sleep, water and what some consider the meaningless nature of their activities. 'It ain't too hard so far,' says one speaking for all. There is even time to compose the first two parts of the section sex fantasy letter to *Penthouse*, interspersed with ribald comments about one member's failure to 'trap' (pull a girl) in Exeter – unlike Jools Ostling who has won the competition for the first batch member to get laid.

By 0900 the following morning it is a different story. Those unaccustomed to camping are short of sleep and temper. The morning inspection does not help matters. Corn and most surprisingly big Gav are pulled up for having a filthy weapon. Major Sturman considers this to be inexcusable behaviour in a Corps Commission and wants him banged on a warning right away. Both Bailey's and Shetler-Jones's personal admin is a total mess, though the Training Team are confused to find that Shet has a mega-dirty razor. 'I didn't think that Wendy had to shave yet,' comments Coyle. Trevor Henry and Neil Watkinson are pulled up for dirty Mess tins.

Then it is time for morning PT led by Wolsey, who gets a narcissistic pleasure in stripping down to the waist and showing off his manly torso, a distinct contrast to the equally bronzed but cherubic shape of 'Seven bellies' Stovin-Bradford. The run is sharp and mainly uphill and on the return to camp Collins collapses. He says: 'I was having difficulty breathing, my saliva was very white ['foaming like a dog,' adds a bystander]. I had got a bit of double vision on the run back but when we sat down everything started to get darker and darker until it went black. Then I passed out.' He is shipped back to the sick bay at Lympstone where he remains until the following morning.

Wolsey insists that 'there are no punishments without reason here'. However the penalty sometimes appears to outweigh the crime. Sergeant Baxter's section have left their camp site 'strewn with gash' (a few wrappers and a couple of soup packets). As a penalty for this act of wanton eco-vandalism the entire section have to run around a nearby knoll twice in full assault order, a quick lesson in the collective responsibility once so beloved of the Tory Cabinet.

In the afternoon they go on a quick three-mile stroll to familiarize themselves with the route for the Night Navex (Navigation Exercise) while in the luxury of their giant tent the Training Team have their weekly discussion about how the batch are getting on. Some they pass over quickly, others are discussed for five minutes, their characters and motives stripped right down to the bare bones, and adorned by Sergeant Coyle's florid similes and imaginative metaphors.

Pete Evans catches the sharp end – 'he's leaking admin like the Bermuda Triangle'. Webster has gone down with a mysterious hip ailment. To the Team physical weakness is a symptom of deeper problems. Baxter sums it up: 'I never knew a good man who got hypothermia or frost bite.' They are worried about Gavin Parr, who's trying to get pally with the sergeants but avoids eye contact with Mark Wolsey. His Mess tin was so shiny that Coyle is convinced he has a spare one stashed in his kit.

Everyone falls over when Redding describes how Shetler-Jones knocked on the tent door before inquiring, 'Excuse me, where's the loo?' Coyle employs his most withering summation – bare of four-letter words – by suggesting he should be forcibly transferred to the cavalry. To him to be called a Percy Pongo (so christened because all Marines believe that the Army never wash) is far more damning than 'motherfucker' or 'cunt', which are employed so casually and so often as to become terms of endearment. Coyle also wishes to discover why Watkinson chose the Royal Marines 'when there are perfectly good jobs teaching Open University'.

Others get more charitable treatment. UCE Pete Joy is excused a dirty weapon; a compulsive note-taker, he is considered bright, alert and should finish in the top half-dozen. So too should Paul Attwood, whose TA experience is showing through, and Matt Skuse. To the Team Ostling appears quiet and efficient though he remains in the background, while Parlour seems a bit overawed and eccentric but is 'a good potential CO'.

Everyone wants Tanner to succeed – the officers, the sergeants, his own batch. He has already stamped his personality on the batch, bawling out one guy for not doing his job, while on another occasion, on sentry duty, he was conversing with Coyle *sotto voce* when Robinson stomped up – ignoring all the rules on keeping quiet at night – so Tanner backhanded him in the face without even looking like Baloo unleashing a heavy paw. With a weapon in his hand he is like a bull in a china shop, firing on automatic from the hip, while the rest of the batch grin, 'That's Mike Tanner'.

Part of this desire to support may be the realization by some of the seemingly less fit that not only are they better than they first thought, but also that Tanner, who to his peers originally seemed like a primeval force, is very much weaker than they are. At the moment he is a slow motion tragedy, inexorably rolling towards failure, gathering momentum despite universal attempts to stop it.

The Night Navex is a cinch. There may be no moon but a cloudless sky erupting with stars means visibility is perfect. Most of the YOs are back in under an hour. Parlour and Joy fail to report in to the Team so are sent back out to pick up all the markers. Wolsey goes to bed grousing that it is too easy and muttering, 'Just wait until the morning.'

In the morning inspection Parr gets a real going-over from Billy Baxter. It was decided that Billy should inspect him – so it didn't look like a conspiracy – and go through his Bergen to look for that extra Mess tin. Instead they find a dirty razor and a foam bottle, both non-Pussers issue and therefore banned from Tenderfoot. Parr looks like a little boy caught red-handed in the orchard, a difficult performance for such a giant. The second man to be inspected, he quickly packs up all his kit and then stands in line glowering for half an hour as the rest are dealt with. Whereas most of those finished with are quick to help their peers, uncharacteristically it takes him a long time before he grudgingly helps a couple of the slower ones assemble their rifles.

With all gear stowed it is time for the morning PT. Wolsey orders them to strip down and sets off on a cross country run. It is hard work, up and down hills, at the top of which they do press-ups with the Boss in the centre, a spider inside his web. Twice up the hill and Tanner is flagging badly, with a couple of the stronger runners on each elbow willing him on until Tom Coyle takes over for a subtle chat – interesting to watch because of the ease with which one party converses while the rugby forward can only gasp. (The conversation touched on Tanner's fondness for the social side of rugby and the odd pint of beer. It obviously worked, as a week later at the batch wine-tasting while others were getting stuck into swallowing not spitting Tanner was nursing Diet Coke.)

On the route home Chalkie is starting to go white, saliva foaming at the teeth; eventually he just leans forward and throws up in the middle of the batch. Not a pace missed, all continue running back to the camp.

At 0930 'Evs' Everett gives a lecture on 'Selecting a Route' to a group of extremely shattered YOs. Some – like Thomson – have their notebooks out in front of them but pencils hang lifeless in the right hand below exhausted eyes, with the hair on the back of the head glistening with sweat. Much of the lecture is obvious – avoid skylines, open ground, use a big wood rather than a small one where you might be trapped, always have a route out as well as a route in. The modern soldier also has to be permanently aware of the dangers of attack from the air and that modern buildings afford only temporary cover from a heavy machine-gun. There is a five-minute break between lectures (conducted on a magnetic board with pre-set headings) in which a couple light cigarettes and Evs lobs half a dozen apples into the group. 'Incoming,' yells one as the apple bounces straight off a hapless head.

They then embark upon a camouflage exercise which in the bright autumn sunshine looks strangely ludicrous, thirty-four grown men in the undergrowth with their clasp knives, coming back looking like Fern Man or refugees from the White Heather Club. The object of the exercise is to break all lines of symmetry on the body – especially head and shoulders, the line at the bottom of the helmet and also the oblongs of the pack. Standing in line in their camouflage they all look slightly ridiculous but the exercise is not a game. The aim now is to walk, amble, crawl, whatever, until you are within one hundred metres of a nearby knoll, then fire a shot. The observers on the hill have to spot you and radio-in walkers to fix the position. They get another shot with a walker within ten metres, then another with him touching the helmet. It can be both surprisingly easy and terribly difficult to spot a camouflaged figure if it does not move.

Collins's collapse on Tuesday was a cue for the instructors to stop probing for weakness and set out remorselessly to expose one that has surfaced. The doctors want to keep him in for a couple of days, so Wolsey drives back to CTC and demands that he come straight out. The point, Wolsey explains, is that he wants Collins to start the four-mile yomp back into camp so that it could be said that he failed it, not that he never did it. 'Now is the time we have to show him the hard side. What is the point of him going on for another six months and then failing the Commando Course. It is a waste of money.'

Collins comes back out brandishing a sick note as if it were a Kevlar vest, claiming that he is only available for light duties. This goes down like a cup of cold sick with the Team. Shown the note Tom Coyle merely exclaims in his thickest Glaswegian accent, 'I've seen it, Mr Collins, now what do you expect me to fucking do about it?'

In the afternoon they practise CQB (Close Quarter Battle) for the first time, walking a path with two live and two still targets, checking their reactions. The rules are simple: spot them, fire two shots, hit cover, fire another couple, then move on. Thomson missed one target completely, walking past looking at the dead 'live' body. Tanner went around blasting on full automatic while Shetler-Jones tried hard not to wet himself. While awaiting his turn Parr caught forty winks – the sign of a pro – the others chatted on in desultory manner and Collins polished his excuses.

With the air of a malingerer he hung back until the very last on the CQB, like a *News of the World* reporter hoping to make his apologies and leave. 'I've had flu for five days,' he says. 'I was feeling terrible when we came out and the PT just finished me. It's not really fair that I haven't had time to recover but I do realize that there will be no opportunity to relearn these lessons.' His basic lack of physical fitness is explained away because 'I had a job working twelve hours a day for the past three months so there wasn't enough time to do proper physical training'; a strange attitude where a three-month summer job is more important than a career.

The Wednesday Night Navex was harder, as the batch had no prior knowledge of the ground. It went pretty well for the Team, if not for five YOs who got lost. Concealed behind an RV(Rendezvous) point Wolsey heard Shet announcing to his partner, 'I have no idea of where we're going, I'm relying entirely on you.' Colour Sergeant Redding was stuck at the final checkpoint with the limping Webster who regaled him with tales of misery – how he wasn't making any friends, how this wasn't for him, and so on. Eventually all bar the missing five gathered together and were given the undoubted treat of going through Peter's Pool in the last hour before midnight. It was a warmish night – for October – and they all slid in uncomplaining, up to their shoulders in a viscous liquid more closely related to mud than water.

'I was soaked through,' recalls Andrew Goldsmith, 'covered in mud, squelching back to a pitch-black bivvy site and knowing that as soon as we got off to sleep we were going to be rudely awakened for a crash move. I started to laugh because I realized that there was nothing else could happen to me right now to make it any worse. The Cardinal was jogging alongside and he said in that cut-glass accent of his. "Tell me, Mr Goldsmith, have you ever been happier?" I had to laugh because in a sense he was right. It certainly beats the hell out of farming.'

At 0100 the Team who have been sitting up chewing the fat and munching on egg banjos (fried egg sandwiches) called for a crash move. Like many a fiasco in three acts it starts encouragingly enough with the two sections closest to the path actually managing to find their way to the edge of the wood. Their state of *déshabillé* however is more extreme. 'So who's slept in their wet boots, then?' muses Coyle. 'At least nobody seems to have lost their rifle,' as they stagger past dragging ground sheets, Bergens slung over one shoulder. One YO has his entire worldly possessions in a plastic bag. 'I picked my Bergen up by the wrong end, sir,' he confesses, an admission which requires no rejoinder. Henry and Woodall have lost their helmets and only Harker, Parr and Tanner have their act together.

The scene degenerates further as the third section, poor unfortunates buried a hundred metres deep inside the wood, manage to get hopelessly lost in the blackness; a couple head deeper into the trees, forgetting in their blindness that the road is down hill. God knows exactly what they have all lost – everything from a rifle cleaning kit to odd socks, bungy cords and dozens of tent pegs.

Bob Baxendale in charge of one of the first two sections has managed to shove most of his kit into his Bergen. However he is not too keen on being told to do things he does not see the point of. Told to put someone in charge of the rear of the section, he storms back past three YOs snorting and swearing. 'A potential shit in the making,' hisses one of the Team.

Everett administers a bollocking, reminding the bemused YOs that in the field they have to be ready when their men fail, that their assault packs are supposed to be affixed to the side of their Bergens at night to cover such eventuality and that fighting off a surprise enemy attack cannot be done with a ground sheet in one hand and a pair of boots in the other. He sends them off to bivvy up in the dark with the hint that another five hours remain between now and dawn. Sleep comes easily to a batch showing signs of exhaustion.

The morning will be far worse for they have to yomp back to Lympstone. That first big yomp is hell for all but a few, and will always rank among their worst memories. Tim David had coped well until the final day when he lost a magazine and a pair of binoculars in the crash move. It was as if he had lost a member of his family: his morale snapped. 'The worst four days for me on the whole course were Tenderfoot,' he says later. 'I'd lost my magazine going through Peter's Pool. It seems so trivial now, I've lost countless things since, but I thought I was going to be in a lot of trouble. In the crash move I learnt that the pocket on top of a Bergen is to identify which way up it goes on your back. I left everything behind and came out with an empty pack. Finally I blew up on the yomp and was driven back to CTC in the Sherpa. I was miserable.'

He was not the only one. Collins caved in after a mile, whimpering, 'Please sir, I'm not feeling very well.' Of the Jamaicans Charlton Jackson confirmed Tom Coyle's prophecy – 'Tomorrow the Caribbeans will meet their closest friend for the rest of the course ... the safety vehicle' – but Trevor Henry confounded it by finishing even though he was dying on his feet. Steve Hussey, who until then was doing very well in an unobtrusive way, failed to make it, as did Jason McQueen, Andy McInerney (who had a major boot and blister problem which made walking almost impossible), Parlour and Thomson.

Robinson confounded expectations despite carrying a Bergen that was so badly packed and lopsided it looked like the Leaning Tower of Pisa and the Team thought he'd be lucky to make it to the end of the lane. Chalkie, Mike Tanner and Rob Lunn all came through but admitted if it had been another half mile they'd have rather lain down and died.

'I got close to quitting on that yomp from Tenderfoot,' recalls Goldsmith. 'I was ready to wrap then. If someone had asked I'd have said "yes, please" but there was no one standing next to me. I didn't think physically I could do it, my mind was strong but my legs wouldn't work. It was hell, or rather it seemed that at the time, already the memory is fading and it starts to seem a bit easier. I just remember the damp clothes, the wet boots and the heavy Bergen – yes, I know we had no ammunition, no rocket launchers, no radio batteries – but it still seemed to weigh a ton.

'The hardest thing is to keep your head upright staring straight ahead for as long as possible. Once the head drops you start to stare at the feet in front of you, desperately trying to keep up with the front group because if you're on your own you're finished. The next thing you start to do is look at your own feet, watching them go back and forth like a couple of puppets, and you start to think about the pain in your feet, the blisters grow bigger and bigger, you imagine you're wading along through a swamp of your own blood, you don't know whether the liquid running down the crack in your arse is blood or sweat. Then you start to hate and that keeps you going for a bit.

'You've come up a long hill, you're straggling a hundred metres behind the main group and then out pops this civvy photographer with a smiling face and those fucking silly red boots, snapping away, pointing that lens in your face and you feel like you're going to die and it'll all be on film and you want to hit him, smash the camera and his silly grin but you know if you stop you'll fall over and you'll never be able to get up again so you go on and it keeps hurting and you keep hating.

'I finished but I felt as if I'd failed and that hurts as much as the pain in your legs and the ache in your shoulders. I did learn to yomp that day on Tenderfoot so since then I just get pissed off and it gets me through.'

Shetler-Jones finished the yomp in pretty good shape, smiling his carefree smile as if this was just another gentle stroll in the woods. The grin never wavered when as punishment for the unique achievement of failing all three inspections on the exercise he was sent in full kit to immerse himself in the static tank. He was also placed on Course Officer's Warning. At least he did learn one thing – not to call his Bergen 'a knapsack' again.

Wolsey dished out warnings to more than a quarter of the batch. Bailey, Collins, David, Parlour, Parr ('he was so surprised,' said Wolsey, 'his jaw hit the floor'), Stovin-Bradford, Thomson, Watkinson and Wood while Mike Tanner was told he would have been on one if he wasn't already because his phys was a long way from scratch. The warnings distressed far more than the blisters, some of which were raw wounds the size of a fifty pence piece.

'When Wolsey told me after a few weeks he was putting Dan on warning my heart sank,' said Taffinder. 'When Dan had first decided to go for selection I had rung up CG and warned him that he might make it and was he happy that Dan should go through training at Lympstone when I was Commandant. He laughed and said, "No problem, and if you have to sack him you can always get your deputy to do the dirty deed." "No, I'll do it myself," I said firmly, "and then I'll tell Sarah."'

There are things that hurt more than learning to march in boots. At least nobody has wrapped. Not yet. But they will. And soon.

4

Fear of Failure

We are neurotically haunted today by the imminence and the ignominy of failure. We know at how frightening a cost one *succeeds*: to fail is something too awful to think about.
Louis Kronenberger, 'The Cart and the Horse'

ON SUNDAY 20 OCTOBER the batch moved down to the Kent coast to practise live firing on the ranges at Lydd and Hythe. St Martin's Plain Camp lies on the outskirts of Folkestone, just past the Euro Tunnel Exhibition Centre – all neat modern white-painted stressed steel and glass. In contrast the camp looks as if it were built in a hurry to repel the threat of the Napoleonic invasion and has not been renovated since – row upon row of wooden huts packed full of young, light-fingered cadets who proved totally capable of nicking Pete Manson's helmet when he left it unguarded for a moment. (His week plummeted from bad to disastrous when he lost his wallet containing his ID and credit cards walking back from the chip shop.) It is also the place where the Army comes to train for tours of duty in Northern Ireland. Sergeant Coyle has spent two years there so knows precisely where to find all the muddy puddles and streams – ideal for crawling through at the end of a tiresome day on the ranges.

Six weeks completed now and still the batch are *virgo intacta*. No one has left, walked or been pushed. A bookie would not offer any odds on Collins surviving until Christmas but Webster's long face makes him an equal favourite to take the long walk first. The difference between the two doomed men is that one has condemned himself. Although a few of the batch have warmed to Webster's lugubrious countenance and sardonic, self-disparaging wit, he simply is not happy, will not let himself relax, while Collins has been accused by the Training Team of being fawning and servile, ingratiating himself by asking questions. So at last the batch have a unified front, a live target for their verbal sniping; they do not give a toss for him and there is no undertone of sympathy or comradely concern in the remarks slung in his direction.

However, it is not just these two who are lucky to be still around. A Night Navex on Dartmoor the previous week had ruthlessly exposed weaknesses in some of those on warning ... and one who was not. Map reading is a skill that all Marines have to master but if an officer cannot get it right he has no business in the Corps.

The disasters started with Brian 'I've-never-failed-at-anything' Adcock, who began the exercise boasting of having a good sense of direction and promptly got lost within five minutes of setting out. Shet also got completely lost, but displaying the sanguine unphaseable temperament that has now endeared him to the Training Team, announced happily, 'I've been around in a few circles but it's jolly good fun' – a remark that left both Coyle and Baxter at a loss for words. Mike Tanner was very late, typically so determined to finish he failed to follow lost procedure (which requires that after a certain time limit expires you must head for the nearest main road and wait there until you are picked up by a safety vehicle), pressing on to the end while the DS were scouring roads looking for him. They were not best pleased.

As for Chalkie it was even worse. If a first prize for complete incompetence, breaking regulations and non-Marine behaviour were to be awarded he would have won it hands down. The batch have already put him on a sponsored diet and while the seven bellies are down to five and sinking fast the phys is still killing him. It has not, however, broken his spirit, nor his inability to keep his mouth shut. 'On the Night Navex first off I got hopelessly lost,' he recalls. 'I'd gone round and round in circles and eventually was so fed up, I switched on my torch and tramped through the wood shouting.'

'I just heard this voice crying out "hell-ooo" as if he were on a ramble in the park,' confirms Coyle. 'Hell-ooo' is now considered by the batch to be an essential part of Marine Night Navex equipment, second only to the compass.

The real drama occurs first thing Monday morning when Andy Parlour – the oldest member of the batch – resigns. He had expressed doubts to Wolsey earlier but the crunch came when his girlfriend discovered she was pregnant. She lived in Brussels and, according to Wolsey, had already had personal problems resulting in an abortion, but was not prepared to go through that again, so the gentleman was obliged to stand by her ... or was this a fortuitous excuse to get out with some honour? Wolsey gives him the week off, sends him off to Ostend on the ferry to talk it over with her. Then he will have to come back and enjoy a week at Lympstone going through all the paperwork. Once a YO goes away to mull over his future it is usually only a matter of time. For if commitment wavers this early it seldom recovers – though Mike Taffinder can recall one early waverer who went on to win the Sword.

The YOs delight in speculating about the dear departed, even if not party to the full reasons. Desperate to fit in and obviously of some private means, Parlour had resorted to some pretty strange methods to win friends and influence the batch. Andy Harks was reeling under the shock of a final poll tax demand for over £200 when Parlour asked if he could 'take care of that' for him. Harker just looked through him as if he didn't exist. 'He lived in the cabin next to mine,' says Ostling. 'He was always knocking on the door asking if he could help me with anything. It seemed like he was the one who needed the help.' Mike Tanner had been scrubbing his basin when Parlour bounced in, like Top Cat, asking if he could help. 'I still had to clean the outside of the windows which I hate as it involves hanging halfway out, holding on with one hand and polishing with the other. Andy Parlour grabs the duster and starts cleaning away furiously. Well, that left me nothing to do so I turned on the tape player, sat down in my chair and read a magazine, watching this Yank millionaire clean my windows. It was bizarre.'

Tanner is relieved that somebody has gone. The feeling may not be personal but it is essential that somebody leaves. 'All everybody has talked about in the first few weeks is who is wrapping and until somebody does wrap there's a lot of pressure,' he says. 'It's like a big game of Cluedo but once somebody does go and people stop talking about it, it eases a lot of pressure off everybody else so they can start settling down, start being honest with each other. Until now there is loads of front up, people hiding behind masks. Now perhaps we can get on with learning to be Royal Marine officers.'

For some it was a great load off their shoulders: no longer would they be the first one to quit. Webster suddenly seems more relaxed and starts attempting to integrate – if by being rather irritating.

'I couldn't quit while Bryan Adams was at Number One,' he announces, starting to whistle an off-key version of '(Everything I Do) I Do It For You'. Even after fifteen weeks at the top of the charts, the Canadian's version sounds much better than the one from Wigan. 'You've been saying that since you got here,' chips in Hussey. 'Why don't you just do it, get on with it, man.'

Range firing can be an unpleasant experience if the weather is shitty, with the winds, rain and hail sweeping off the English Channel straight into the firer's face. Otherwise it is at best extremely dull, at worst excruciatingly boring. Although part of YO training is a six-week course on how to be a range officer, company live firings are invariably run by the qualified SNCO instructors. The result is that the officers often have to sit around all day reading the papers and thinking up new ways to entertain their men during breaks in the firing. Out of this mindless tedium has come such wonderful creations as Helmet Man, Woolly Pully and favourite of all – Shingle Man.

In the lunch break (range regulations are very specific: Firing must cease by 1230 precisely and will recommence after the lunch break at approximately 1330 depending on whether 'the idle fat civvy has finished his lunch'), after the batch have wolfed down their 'haybucket' lunch of 'pork Wellington' (sausage roll by any other name) and thick soggy chips that saw better days in an earlier century, it is time to play. Helmet Man is where the poor subject has to wear and carry as many helmets as possible hanging off his clothing, leaving him festooned like a Ghostbusters Christmas Tree decoration; Woolly Pully is the same with sweaters … but Shingle Man is the one everyone wants to play, provided the sun is shining and the pebbles are dry.

First, however, there is a cabaret interlude where Webster and Goldsmith perform 'The Laughing Policeman' – 'it's the first time I've seen Webster smile in weeks,' notes Coyle – aided by Ashby's wonderful rib-cracking laughs while Wood juggles with three oranges. Three section volunteers have their clothes filled with pebbles … pockets, trousers, shirts and jacket pockets (if they take the jackets off it takes three men to lift them). A well-packed Shingle Man is carrying over 100 lbs in extra weight – more than a fully loaded Bergen – and is so uncoordinated that if he falls over like a turtle on its back he cannot get up again.

Naturally, as with all Marine games, there is a competitive edge to the proceedings, in that the losing section has to clean everybody else's kit. Shetler-Jones looks like a caricature from a French and Saunders show, a giant scarecrow with an enormous belly and a figure that appears bloated by a combination of beer and steroid abuse. The race across one hundred metres of shingle is hysterical and eventually after leading most of the way he falls over ten metres from the finishing line and can move no further.

Shet is fast becoming the batch mascot, the butt of their wit but not a malicious target. 'He is the only man we've ever met who carries his rifle as if it were a fashion accessory,' comments one mate. Even at his most excessive and useless he has Billy Baxter in stitches – 'his men will like him because he is odd, eccentric and nothing ever seems to get him down'.

'We invited his parents to the Parents Day next month,' adds Wolsey, 'and got a nice thank you letter telling me how much Philip was enjoying his training.' To which Coyle can only add that he cannot wait to discover what singular sub-species of *homo sapiens* could ever have sired such a specimen.

One sure-fire way the batch have discovered to get fifteen minutes of free entertainment is to ask Tom Coyle what he thinks of the SA80 Assault Rifle. As a weapons specialist he has many opinions on the rifle, none of which would please its British manufacturer. 'Everybody in the Army has to pass a basic proficiency test with the SA80 every year. The problem is that most of them are just clerks and drivers who fire the rifle but once a year, when they have to hang around five hours for three minutes' firing,' he says. 'It has a 4x4 scope so is much easier to fire up to 300 yards. Otherwise it's a shitty piece of equipment that easily falls apart. It can only be fired right-handed, unless you want the ejected rounds to take your eye out. Bits fall off it the whole time and it cannot cope with any extreme climatic conditions. Why is it that Britain has not manufactured a decent weapon this century? Just in case you're wondering, the Lee Enfield .303 was invented in 1888 and we were still using it after the Second World War.'

The Lee Enfield was so accurate it was still being used as a sniper rifle in 1980. The SA80 is unlikely to last two decades. Hailed by its British manufacturer as a highly accurate and fully automatic weapon, the answer to all the modern infantry's problems, it has exceeded only the expectations of those who doubted it in the first place: at present it is worse. Coyle's comments on the SA80 were borne out by a report in 1993 on the rifle's performance in the Gulf War, where sand clogged the works and certain parts of plastic moulding broke too easily. It has cost the taxpayer millions to iron out initial design faults and as far as the Marines are concerned it simply does not do the job they need it for. It is all very well lugging it about in training firing blanks but the YOs were never impressed with it in its LSW (light machine-gun) version with the longer barrel and bipod stand. They would rather carry an old-fashioned GPMG (general purpose machine-gun) any day and sod the extra weight.

Coyle's method of making live firing more exciting and demonstrating the fallibility of the SA80 was to borrow a few Heckler and Koch MP5s, allowing the boys to loose off a few rounds and learn about other weapons. The HK is very useful in Northern Ireland because of its size and firepower. He has not yet started on shooting with the Browning 9 mm automatic – 'God help them, or us, as most of them cannot hit a barn door and that goes for the officers who carry the pistol on duty at Lympstone'. Coyle, of course, can hit a man-sized target at a hundred metres.

Mark Wolsey's technique – as one might expect – is to let the YOs blaze off on automatic. It is one of his pet theories. 'Instructors hate firing on automatic, the accepted doctrine is that firing on auto is wasteful, inaccurate and generally a waste of time. Initially it is all of those things but automatic fire is one of the SA80's capabilities, so why not learn to use it. When training for operations, I divided my company into squads, had them stand on the thirty-metre mark and loose off full thirty-round magazines in one burst. The first time nobody got more than seven shots on target; by the eighth mag it was between twenty and twenty-five. That proved my point, so when patrolling operationally I would always have two or three of the patrol with their weapons on automatic. If the enemy pops out of a hedge in front of you with an SMG (sub-machine-gun) you don't have enough time to drop into the prone position, so squeezing off a mag on auto will make him jump for cover even if you're not on target.

'The other point is that loosing off on automatic is fun! Hopefully when the batch go on to their units they will keep introducing it to their men, who will not get so bored on range days. You must be happy and comfortable with your rifle – after all it is your best friend.'

Cocky, arrogant and confident Brian Adcock is so capable and fit he is cruising; he sees training as an attend course that he will pass easily, which gives him the leeway to play jester. At the end of the day's shooting he cheeks Redding who promptly gives him press-ups. He thinks the NCO's joking until the number starts going up in exponential thirties. After eighty press-ups even Brian is looking a little puffed.

Upon their return to camp the batch are run down a hill to crawl through a muddy stream. The only one excused is Pete Joy – which is ironic as he has acquired the reputation as the scruff bag of the batch. He had actually done what he was ordered, changed into civvies and cleaned up before going to the Mess for 'scran' (food). 'It was a complete accident,' he confessed later, 'I wasn't paying attention.'

If such punishment seems harsh it is deliberately so. Marines hate appearing anywhere in dirty kit, without clean faces and finger-nails, considering that to be something only Pongos do. It is also, as Wolsey explains, designed to encourage the development of a batch spirit. 'Teamwork is starting to come through. They have been punished for not doing things the same. Like a morning inspection when some were wearing their dress belts, and others had them laid out; it wouldn't have taken a moment for the Duty Student to issue an instruction for all to follow.

'Other essentials are to be on time, to erase the casual nature of civvies. I am never late for any appointment, always early,' he con-tinues – nor is he boasting: off duty Wolsey is infuriatingly punc-tual. 'Loss of kit equals loss of efficiency. I am also trying to encourage imagination and initiative – when given a task not only to carry it out but to think of interesting ways of doing it.'

Seven weeks in and the batch, like a slow motion Polaroid, is developing its own personality. Certain characters have emerged sharp and fully defined, others remain blurred silhouettes in the background, or fuzzy around the edges. However like Janus they have two faces, one for the Team, one when alone together. What the Team see is often only what the batch wishes them to see; the Team may dislike a YO for professional reasons but if the batch like him they strive to protect him. If the batch don't like you, as Collins has discovered, they will just leave you out there to hang slowly twisting in the wind of the DS's displeasure. To the Team Ostling is a grey man; to the batch he is their cutting edge, the mimic who answers the phone, convinces Rob Lunn's girlfriend she is talking to her man, who promptly announces he doesn't want to see her any more.

'Now it does seem very amusing, but at the time I wasn't very happy,' says Lunn. 'My girlfriend had had a lousy day at college and wanted cheering up. Jools listened to her for a bit then snapped, "Oh do stop whining and pull yourself together," and put the phone down. I had some serious explaining to do the next day but she did see the funny side. We stopped going out soon afterwards.'

As the personalities gel and find mates to whom they can unburden themselves the beginnings of a social split can be discerned. It will become known as 'The First XV' and 'The Wankers', with a few who can float between the groups at will and a few more who think they can. By Lydd and Hythe there are three basic divisions – the lads, who enjoy beer, rugby, more beer and girls in roughly that order; the 'graduates' used to a more solitary existence, and finally the oddballs.

The batch regard Pete Joy as a weirdo who has been known to run up and down the corridors howling at four in the morning. A Cambridge boxing blue, they joke that he had his memory scrambled in the boxing ring – 'he's punch drunk'. He sometimes seems to be on a different plane from the rest of the batch and during drill McQueen found himself facing Joy who had done an about-turn for no apparent reason. Five weeks in, he appeared to lose control, bayoneting a cardboard rifle target. But put him in an Exeter nightclub flirting with a pretty girl and he is instantly lively and witty company.

Throughout the course the Team keep a 'batting order', a chart to judge how the YOs are doing. At stake is the Sword of Honour, something which Wolsey believes to be overvalued and divisive, and as the Pass Out date comes ever closer a certain amount of manoeuvring and uncomradely behaviour will be seen among those who consider themselves viable candidates. When they assess the YOs the Team constantly grade them in wide bands as a pointer to how they are doing.

Mike Tanner is definitely one of the lads. Physically he is still doing badly but he is so popular with the batch and Team they say it will be a sad day *when,* not if, he goes and are expecting a good leaving party. Currently struggling in the bottom eight, his confidence remains unalloyed. Mike admits to having lost a stone, and believes he is keeping up after managing to start and finish in the first five on a four-mile run. 'The Navy selector called to say he was playing me at prop,' he complains. 'He didn't seem to think being in training was any excuse as he lives for the sport. By the time they've finished with me here I'll be a flanker!'

Much to the surprise, not to say horror, of the batch that other oddball Andy Parlour returned from his visit to the pregnant girlfriend in Brussels, having changed his tune. Despite earlier refusals to countenance such an act, she had opted for an abortion, and he had thought once more of resuming his commission. 'I've made up my mind now. I'm going full ahead for the Sword of Honour, sir,' he announced to a bemused Captain Wolsey.

As is so often the case, Dartmoor was to prove the catalyst for change. Even in summer it can be a treacherous place, for fogs and storms blow in direct from the Atlantic. The perfect visibility of one minute can become a stumbling whiteout moments later; temperatures plummet to freezing, abetted by icy rain that stings and burns the cheeks. Prehistoric storms for prehistoric terrain.

In late October, soon after returning from the ranges at Lydd and Hythe, the YOs made their first real acquaintance with Dartmoor, a time when the Lady of the Moors can be a real bitch. She blew hail and bitter sharp drops of rain horizontally into their faces, reducing the line of sight so sharply that the point man of the section was all but invisible to the last in line – it was not a day for stragglers. In those conditions nylon waterproofs merely postpone the inevitable; with their tendency to retain heat they prevent the body breathing, so the sweat forms and stays inside until eventually it soaks everything – denims, shirts, underwear – right through to the bone.

By 1530, with night bringing down its blackout curtain as the batch finally reached their bivvy point in Brisworthy Wood, Parlour and Collins simultaneously reached breaking point. Parlour squelched over to Wolsey and offered his resignation for the second time. It was accepted and on a waterproof sheet with a waterproof pen he wrote out: 'Wednesday 30 October 1991. 15.40 p.m. I hereby resign my commission in the Royal Marines, effective immediately. 2Lt A.N. Parlour RM.'

Mark Collins, meanwhile, had run out of articulating excuses and withdrawn totally into himself. The rest of his section were rigging their bivvies in the rain; he just sat at the foot of a tree buried inside his poncho, wishing his head could retract inside his hunched shoulders, the picture of misery made flesh. Eventually he mustered up the spirit, forcing his legs the necessary twenty yards to walk over to Wolsey. 'I'd like to speak to you tomorrow, sir. I don't feel I have the motivation to spur myself and thirty Marines on.'

Rumour is a most fecund mother but according to batch legend during his final interview with the Commandant, it became known that Parlour was the lucky recipient of a trust fund that ran into several millions, so while he had no need to work he had considered that the Marines would make a very good hobby – 'something to do with my life'. This is not a wise thing to say to any professional soldier and any remarks about third thoughts that Colonel Taffinder might have been harbouring were held behind tight, unamused lips. The batch had invented various other stories embroidering Andy Parlour's life, including one that his parents were both very Christian – Baptists, possibly – and were extremely unhappy with his girlfriend and that he wouldn't get any money until he married. Unsympathetic as the batch were to his presence in the group, it made scarcely a ripple in the pond when he left. A year later few of the survivors could remember anything about him except for his accent.

Matt Lodge, one of the quieter men, gave Collins his epitaph. 'If he had been quiet, a little more humble, then his initial lack of fitness would not have been a problem. Certain people might not have encouraged him, but they would not actively have campaigned to get rid of him. They made it quite clear he wasn't popular, and because he wasn't confident he came out with a lot of brash bravado which annoyed people.'

Mark Webster, unhappy for so long, was the third to go and ironically the one most missed by the batch. He could never make his mind up and even when he returned from another week at home (dispatched by Wolsey to think about it) while part of him wanted to stay, another part was still undecided.

'At that point,' says Wolsey, 'I made his mind up for him. I explained that this wasn't something where you could sit on the fence, the training is so intense that it demands total commitment. It isn't an opinion poll, a Don't Know vote is really the same as No. He had first expressed doubts after forty-eight hours in camp and all of us on the Training Team felt that if he hadn't made his mind up he was going to continue in the same vein for ever. It costs a lot of money to train an officer and it's a waste to keep on when you know they are going to fail, that's why sometimes we can appear unduly harsh on a man.'

'I suppose we always knew that Mark Webster wasn't going to make it, so the week down at Lydd and Hythe we all decided we'd actually try to get to know him,' says Chalkie, who in contrast to the departed had got his act together. 'We did and he was a nice guy whom everybody liked. Maybe if we, and he, had made an effort earlier he wouldn't have actually gone but I doubt it. To a certain extent and for a certain length of time the batch can support an individual, but eventually he has to make the decision as to whether or not he really wants to stay. Mark's problem was that he had wrapped internally and could never get over his suspicion that the Marines aren't some élitist middle-class organization, the Masons in green berets.'

For Martin Wood, seeing his 'two best friends Webster and Collins quit' was his lowest point on the course since he had stopped blubbing in the privacy of his cabin. To Tom Coyle, it was 'good riddance to a triumvirate of scrotes'. Unlike the British way with sporting heroes, gallant failure is not lauded by the Royal Marines; it is simply not acceptable. To kill yourself finishing is acceptable, to live but fail is not.

Three down, thirty to go. The batch spirit had been strengthened by the casting out of those who did not fit. 'It would be naïve to say that we were now an élite cohesive fighting machine, all as happy as Larry, but the mood has certainly changed,' wrote Bob Rob, before he knew what Eye Opener was to do to him. 'This change has been stimulated by the experience of shared hardships, of shared ales and mainly by the departure of a few long faces who didn't really want to be here.'

Most of YO training seems to involve physical hardship but the Corps are also keen to make sure their officers turn out as gentlemen. Unlike the Guards, life in a Royal Marine Mess is relatively informal, but two or three times a year they hold a Regimental Dinner – a monumental piss-up to be sure but a formal monumental piss-up, where all the rituals and traditions of which the Marines are justifiably proud are honoured and celebrated. On Friday 1 November the batch enjoyed a practice Regimental Dinner, in the

Officers' Mess at Lympstone, before which Shetler-Jones delivered a very stylish grace. Dressed in black tie – Mess kit costs several hundred pounds and nobody was forking out that until they had a green lid to wear in the day – they enjoyed a full dinner designed to teach Mess etiquette and the correct behaviour. With all the table silver laid out it was not a case of the Mess Manager saying 'this is the knife for the paté, this is your soup spoon', but the YOs were encouraged to ask questions, so they could get it right in the future. The Mess Manager also explained the relevance of the silver candlesticks in the middle of the table – they were a present from King George V and should always be lit towards the end of a formal dinner.

The Loyal Toast at a Marine dinner is drunk seated – a Naval tradition dating back to the days of wooden ships with low ceilings in the wardroom, but a privilege only granted to the Corps in the 1960s. The port decanter is always passed to the left but the bottom is not supposed to leave the table. During dinner officers are not allowed to leave the table for anything – which has resulted in several YOs who have partaken of too much liquid refreshment being forced to relieve themselves in an empty wine bottle. This rule is only relaxed during Ladies Nights, for the fairer sex are allowed to leave. Smoking, too, is forbidden until permission is given by the senior officer presiding.

For most of the YOs the dinner proved an enjoyable experience. They watched, learned, asked questions and drank far too much. Chalkie Stovin-Bradford, a former chorister, proved that underneath the extra bellies there still lurked the voice of an angel – as his rendition of 'Te Luce Ante Terminum' proved. However Jools Ostling found the tradition and ritual both irritating and unsettling, confirming his view that the place was full of 'middle-class wankers'.

Just another three days on Dartmoor and that is the first ten weeks completed. Then it's a mere five-week cruise to Christmas leave and the chance to get some sleep while stuffing yourself with turkey.

The Training Team call those three days on Dartmoor 'Exercise Eye Opener'. Most other descriptions would involve the use of many four-letter words. Eye Opener, three days of roughing it on Dartmoor in November, is the YOs' last chance to get their fieldcraft together. After this, as exercises concentrate far more on tactical training, there is no time to screw up on personal admin. It was hard, it was very wet, reinforced by having to strip naked, shove all their clothes and Bergen inside a bivvy bag and push the lot across a freezing pond. Woe betide anyone whose bag leaked for there would be no opportunity to get dry clothes on and the man would go down with exposure.

For some it still seems easy enough but at the same time as Tom Coyle and Billy Baxter are sitting by a roaring fire in a Princetown pub and speculating on potential Sword of Honour candidates, helped by copious pints of lager and bitter, three miles down the road, protected from the gales by a wall all of eighteen inches high, one of their favourites was having serious doubts.

'Can I handle the workload?' thought Andy Rowley. 'Why am I crawling through this puddle while the Training Team look down on me in delight? Why am I folding a waterproof jacket to the size of a magazine at three a.m.? Where's my mum? Why does one only remember the bad times? They can't all have been bad – waitress-served meals, I like the uniform colour and they haven't cut all my hair off – yet !

'It is not the money and it is not the women that led me to join the Royal Marines. I can't remember what answer I gave at the AIB but it was certainly not on the tip of my tongue at 6.30 last night when I was cold and wet and fairly much in bits. Tenderfoot came and went with a smaller bump than I had anticipated and before long we were firing live rounds. My girlfriend hates the idea of guns – I must admit I still flinch when I pull the trigger. Not an old sweat and hardened killer yet. Will I ever be? Could I kill somebody? What I really want to know is when you are in bits and you are absolutely threaders because you are hanging out and you are absolutely icers why does somebody decide it's time to stand by and off we go for another beasting? I want my bed.'

Pete Joy, too, was finding life in the field no more exciting than he had ironing and washing for Britain. The intention of YO training is to turn out Royal Marine officers who can command a troop of men, but at this stage there are only a strictly limited number of training command appointments and for a man like Joy who perpetually craves intellectual stimulus there is a limit to how long he can wait. In his case perhaps it was too long.

'In the field only one of us could be Troop Commander per day, three more Section Commanders,' he says. 'It was Week 14 before I was a section leader in the field, Week 29 before I got to try commanding the batch. The rest of the time life in the field involved nothing more stimulating than nasty weather, heavy loads, long yomps and bored cold nights on sentry against a non-existent enemy. I often imagined my friends from college doing useful, mentally stimulating work and then sleeping in their own bed at night, while I spent 95 per cent of my time in the field and at CTC doing tasks any strong fool could do and felt disappointed. Of course people like Phil Ashby and Matt Lodge felt the same to an extent but to them the end (to command a troop) justified the means and they were more patient. Unfortunately I coped with my boredom by "switching off" into thoughts of elsewhere and got myself a reputation for low alertness that helped me fall foul of the DS on several occasions.'

Chalkie already knew what it meant to fall foul of the DS and on Eye Opener he had mixed fortunes, as he recalls. 'Mr Crane, one of the SSLCs who joined us on the exercise, lifted spirits enormously, when on attempting to cross a stream, he tripped on his run up and submerged completely head first into the water. For some reason our rather graphic description of the wet and dry routine did little to raise his own morale … Unfortunately I awoke the next morning not feeling very well. I ate sausages and beans but had a feeling this would not be the last time I saw them. Felt a little better at having passed the inspection and celebrated by having my sausages and beans make their reappearance and then their encore. I had mixed feelings about being pulled off the yomp and sent back to Lympstone in the Sherpa.'

His mate Bob Rob was also pulled off the final day's yomp despite his protestations that he could easily manage it. With three miles already covered before dawn the rising sun revealed that the undead colour of his skin would have frightened off a vampire. Bubbles of Persil saliva were frothing from his lips and his eyes were rolling in his head, unable to focus on anything other than a middle distance he could never have reached. The previous day he had put down his rifle and gone off for a pee without it. Sergeant Baxter went nuts and ordered him to crawl through a puddle until he was soaked through. He remained wet all day. By the evening he was in an appalling condition, unable to get warm despite being forced to drink endless cups of hot tea. Some of the batch mumbled that the punishment was out of proportion to the misdemeanour. Bob had little to say on the subject but since that day he has been wedded to his SA80.

The final yomp was another calculated test of character. The YOs marched a mile to their four-tonner lorries, loaded up and were then ferried two miles, dumped off and told that they had four hours to reach a rendezvous, otherwise they would have to yomp still further. The ground looked deceptively easy except that it cut across Fox Tor Mires, the original blueprint for the man-swallowing marshes in *The Hound of the Baskervilles*.

Aside from one of the SSLCs who disappeared up to his neck, screamed in panic 'I'm dying' and had to be levered out by his section, the marshes were crossed safely. At the height of the climb around the cross at Childe's Tomb Trevor Henry, who by now was feeling the cold, suddenly yelled out.

'What the fuck is this white stuff, man?' he said pointing at the white flakes whipping across the moor, sugar-spun moths dancing to their inevitable death upon his black cheeks.

'It's snow, Trev.'

'No shit, man. I never seen snow before.'

He made it to the four-tonners in time – they all did – but, doubtless suffering from this sudden freezing culture shock, Henry shuddered uncontrollably on the way back to CTC. 'A few cuddles and Mars Bars soon sorted him out,' recalled Martin Wood. 'The final message we learnt there was that even if the individual goes down the team survives.'

Wood still had much to learn. He was missing the point, for in extreme conditions if an individual goes down, frequently he will take the team down with him.

5

The Prince Edward Factor

There is no loneliness greater than the loneliness of a failure.
The failure is a stranger in his own house.

Eric Hoffer, *The Passionate State of Mind*

'SOMEWHERE OUT ON Dartmoor, being steadily erased by the rain and lying on an only passingly solid mixture of marsh grasses and water, is a cowpat with my boot mark on it ... it only takes seconds to soak a combat jacket and hours to dry it out again. Similarly it takes only fifteen minutes to make a hot drink but the benefit is enormous. The lesson for today is "brew up or go down". It's all too easy to yomp, head down, eyes half closed, looking at the boots of the man in front – pretty soon you start to lag behind. Chocolate in a jacket pocket is twenty times better than chocolate inside a Bergen.

'Favourite jokes were from the Dartmoor safety video. "If the first step comes up to the ankle and the second up to the knee, the third should be backwards." All very well but when the water covers your ankle for most of the time you start to have doubts about the efficacy of the rule. Smiling is definitely worthwhile, it stops the face freezing up and should be attempted at regular intervals.'

The Andrew Goldsmith describing his adventures on Eye Opener is not the same man as the defiant chain-smoker at the Commandant's introductory cocktail party. Hiding inside the batch was always going to be difficult for such a confirmed individualist. (Others like Pete Manson and Tim David were to be much more successful.) He remains sardonic, so stubbornly nicotine-addicted that others have, in surreptitious ones and twos, come to join his smokers' club. His comrades (Ostling and Parr) have nicknamed him 'Deep Throat' (because of his deep voice) or 'Bubbles' because he can never get that 'God I'm so miserable' look off his face. The difference now is that he is part of the team, universally respected, even liked, but allowed to hang out with the friends of his choice.

He hides it well but Goldsmith is chest-expandingly proud of being a Royal Marine officer. At social functions he has a habit of swinging the lantern, exaggerating already tall tales. Inside CTC he has picked up Marines for not saluting him, which does not go down well with others in the batch. He does not care for he does not want to be a member of the First XV.

'There are cliques but I choose friends of the moment who suit my mood. This batch is so varied that if you want to be infantile there are people to go out with, get completely slaughtered and make an ass of yourself, who go into town, pretend to be a touring rugby team and take all their clothes off, with not a small amount of prompting from me,' he says. 'I was an original founder of the "Get Naked Club" which has made spontaneous appearances in nightclubs throughout Devon. Pete Evans and Rob Lunn are great for a quiet drink but Rob, the happy troll, can also swing and be a mad little bundle of fur. I get on well too with Stan Harris who has just cracked his twenty-first birthday and regards me as an old man.'

'At the beginning it was conform or die,' he recalls. 'I had some problems settling in. One of the great spokesmen of batch feeling was Jools, a death-watch beetle to people, ticking away in their bed-head calling "time". If he decided he didn't like you it was because the batch didn't, so early on he and I had a tense relationship. He issued nicknames to the batch, he caught on to the fact that I was content to be a loner if I had to be, the grey man at the back. I started with a survivalist attitude, which probably wasn't great for social relations.

'Ultimately you cannot masquerade in training, it will find you out. Either that or you will become something else and fifteen months is a long time to pretend to be something you are not. People have changed already, whether because of training or because they have relaxed. It seemed harsh at the time but the system thins people out. If the system fails to do it, the batch will.

'I think people who join the forces have never lost the joy of running around the woods going "bang bang" and I bet most of them got pissed off with having to count to a hundred if they were dead. I liken the batch to a pack of wolves, hunting animals. As soon as somebody goes down, physically, mentally, the batch ups and turns and savages that person so that they either get up and survive or fall and fail.'

The wolf pack is an analogy the batch themselves return to time and again, perhaps as an excuse, perhaps simply as a means of explanation. However, a YO batch is not just any old wolf pack; they are being trained to be superwolves, for each one has to be capable of leading his own pack. The competition to be best is tough, one difference being that when a young lieutenant gives his troop orders they do not question them, but if there are any holes in a YO's orders, his colleagues will not just point them out but may jump into them boot first.

At the same time, as Goldsmith has already acknowledged, you simply cannot expect to pass the course by yourself. At some point everyone, however prepared, however physically fit, however motivated, will be brought to a point where they will want to give up. It may be the Atlantic gales whipping through Dartmoor, or the insidious Welsh damp at Sennybridge that creeps into the very marrow of your bones, chilling you so you think you will never be warm again. Even the fittest can fall to a niggling injury, a groin or hamstring strain that never has a chance fully to recover, so the pain keeps grinding on and on, tightening with each weary step as if a torturer were applying a thumbscrew turn. It might be sitting in an Exmouth pub, whining interminably, three-quarters drunk and deep into self-pity, after the Dear John letter you have just received from your girlfriend, which enables you to join the fastest growing club in the batch – the dumped.

That is the time you need your oppos; someone who will brew you up a 'hot wet' (hot drink), while you shiver in your sleeping bag wondering whether dying might not be an easier option. Or maybe they are just there at your shoulder on another interminable yomp, whispering encouragement, pushing you on, checking their step to yours but never reminding you of the fact that you are slowing them all down. Maybe they just listen to how much you loved Fluffikins and refrain from being gratuitously cruel until breakfast the next morning, by which time they have told everybody else.

Inside the batch it has to be one for all, all for one. Otherwise you end up like Prince Edward. It isn't easy being both Royal and a Royal Marine.

Matt Lodge knew all about Prince Edward's unhappy attempt to become a Marine officer. He had been there. Matt is never going to be tall but back in September '86 he was only eighteen, fresh from school, gung-ho and naïve with it. He had been at Lympstone for all of ten days when he went home to pick up his motor bike, crashed in the fog and smashed up his left knee.

He carried on with training until Christmas leave but could not do any IMF or intense physical exercise. In the New Year the knee was diagnosed as having ruptured ligaments that were not going to recover for a minimum of twelve to eighteen months. Matt applied for and was awarded a UCE so went to Birmingham for four years to read French and Russian. 'It was quite exciting and a bit depressing. I hadn't been able to prove to myself I could do it. It haunted me to a certain extent but without doubt I was too young the first time. It was a blessing in disguise. Going to college was hugely valuable in enabling me to grow up. I have become a keen exponent of the idea that people should not go straight from school, anything rather than come in fresh.'

Privately the Marines admit that the Edward incident was a public relations fiasco. As Prince Philip is the Captain General of the Corps, whether Edward passed or failed both sides were on to a hiding to nothing. Speculation at the time had it that the Marines thought having a real-life Royal in the Royals could help insure against the inevitable defence cuts, although to do so might mean lowering the tough standards upon which they prided themselves. The sad thing for the Prince (for whom, it must be said, few Marines ever express sympathy – but then they are not the most sympathetic of people) is he never really had a chance. If they had to do it again the Corps would now insist on covering all the security aspects themselves.

It is not as if CTC were not already guarded, so the introduction of private detectives simply reinforced the natural barrier between prince and paupers. Matt Lodge, who was similarly placed apart from the batch by his injury, remembers how impossible it was for Edward to integrate with his batch mates. And even Marines are not immune to the snobbery of hob-nobbing with Royalty. How do you address a prince who drops his weapon in a puddle – 'you stupid bastard, sorry your Royal Highness, no disrespect intended to your mother'?

Similarly what is a YO going to think when he wants to go into town, get rip-roaring drunk and try to trap a bird when instead he is detailed to go out and have a Perrier (not drinking is almost a capital crime) with HRH. OK, so he's never been able to hang out with the guys, be normal, but isn't this his chance? Of course he has also got those bloody Special Branch officers hanging round him like vultures. It looks as if they are his real mates, not us in the batch ...

'Sept. '86 was an unusual batch,' says Matt judiciously. 'I still to this day don't know whether it was because I was injured – which is a nightmare because you immediately become separate, instantly cease to be part of that shared experience, and the bonding of the batch should never be underestimated – or because Edward was in it. By contrast with that batch I was immediately struck by how well we all get on, which has largely been due to the Team and the Boss.

'There was a problem with Edward. The Course Officer was very different from Wolsey, he was particularly worried about the impression the batch gave. He bollocked one YO for making him look bad in front of the OC – I was gobsmacked, where did his priorities lie? The SNCOs didn't know where to put themselves with regard to Prince Edward. It was a very poorly advised decision for him to join the Royal, but in purely personal terms there was no reason he couldn't have done it.

'Every exercise we went on there was a Range Rover with two Special Branch officers half a mile behind us, it restricted the whole thing. We couldn't go on a run ashore with the lads in the same way. We'd pop down to the wine bar in Topsham, but Edward wasn't a drinker. He had enough social problems in terms of mingling because people were not quite sure, he didn't muck in. It would be unfair to blame him totally. Physically he could hack it but, as I am testament to, it is not the physical thing that is crucial, it's up here in the head. It is in the mind, being part of the batch, getting on with the batch, the feeling of not wanting to let your mates down, feeling a pride because you don't want to let yourself down in front of them, it matters a lot more what they think than what the OC might say.

'The guys in the Sept. '86 batch probably wouldn't have that much good to say for him at all because prior to his going he had proved to be a bit of a prima donna on field exercises, hadn't been felt to pull his weight, the classic example of someone who wasn't that sure of himself in a command appointment, so he imposed himself by shouting and being authoritarian. That simply doesn't work, the batch reaction is "on your bike".'

In fact the batch's reaction was rather more extreme. When it is a YO's turn to give an O group (Orders Group) it is generally done in a low-key manner. Instead the Prince had treated them like a drill sergeant bellowing at a bunch of raw recruits. This did not go down well with the batch, who later in the day exacted their own little revenge by ragging him. They rammed mud in his ears, in his mouth, right up his nose, poured so much inside his shirt he could have been Mud Pie Man, instead of his nickname 'The Apple Juice Kid'. Later everyone laughed it off as high spirits but it was a coded warning to Edward to get in line and treat his equals with the respect they gave each other. The message was received and understood, but instead of getting tough the Prince got going.

'I respect him for saying this is not for me,' says Matt Lodge. 'All credit to Edward for dropping out, that takes as much courage as staying in.'

Perhaps more. Despite the natural flurry of tabloid press speculation Edward's resignation from the Royal Marines after Christmas leave was the best thing for all parties, honour being satisfied all round. Sometimes it is much braver to say 'No, this is not for me.'

6

Social Hi-jinks and Ruined Love Lives

I got a kindhearted mama, do anything in this world for me,
But these evil-hearted women man, they will not let me be,
I love my baby, my baby don't love me.
Robert Johnson, 'Kindhearted Woman Blues'

EARLY ON IN training the batch attended a tactics lecture from Andy Shaw. It was one of his classics. The lights dimmed and the audience was bombarded with a series of violent images of war, shots from the movie *Platoon*, of blood, of death and destruction – a salutary if Hollywood reminder of the ultimate reality they had volunteered for. Shaw opened his lecture with the immortal words: 'Gentlemen, this is the hardest thing you will ever do. Your wives and girlfriends will leave you, and at the end of training you will not be the same man.'

Everyone laughed, they knew the rumours but they were going to be different, their girlfriends were not going to leave them unless they decreed it. When they began training, all but a handful of the YOs were enjoying stable, monogamous and frequently live-in relationships, usually germinated and encouraged in the hothouse environment of university. All of them understood intellectually that fifteen months at Lympstone would put new and intense strains on these relationships, but none of them knew just how difficult it was to be. It did not take long to learn.

The others had arrived with a very different set of priorities, their intention being to carve a swathe through the womenfolk from Exeter down to St Ives and from Exmouth up to Edinburgh. That too, alas, was to prove not quite as easy as anticipated.

For Andy Goldsmith coming to CTC was not just the realization of a long held ambition to join the services but also a huge breath of freedom. 'All my time at agricultural college I was thinking about joining up but the only thing that slowed it up was a long-standing girlfriend who nearly finished the whole idea – which may account for my cynicism about relationships,' he says. 'We split in my last year at college when I had to make the decision which fertilizer company to join and where I was going to get my mortgage. I suddenly thought, "Sod this, I'm too young to die", and realized I regarded settling down as death.'

Goldsmith's attitude was mirrored in many of his comrades in arms, even those in steady relationships. In choosing a career in an all-male profession the YOs were compartmentalizing their professional and their love lives. Having chosen the lure of travel, danger and excitement as their first love they were placing any girlfriends in a subsidiary role. Nor are they – at the beck and call of superior officers and of training schedules designed by a misogynist of *Jihad* proportions – the masters of their own destiny. Love is a sensitive flower, it can collapse easily under a ton of shit. To survive and flourish, as the old clichés have it, relationships have to be a two-way street, full of give and take. Of necessity, for it is not entirely their fault, a relationship with a YO is a three-lane highway going his direction, with a cycle path going the opposite way. You give, they take. If you want to call them up on the phone because you've had a bad day, chances are they'll be out playing Boy Scouts on Dartmoor or you have to drag them out of the bar with the catcalls of their mates tolling in their ears.

It is a case of: 'Would you come down to Lympstone? I'm free for the weekend ... well, sort of ... we may be woken rather early on Sunday morning for an exercise briefing. You won't mind, will you, I really want to see you ... How early?... It could be as early as 0430 ... well, if that does happen I expect we'd have until 1000 to get ready ... what will you do then? Well, lots of the guys will have their girlfriends here as well, you get on with Lisa and Katie, don't you?'

Added to that a YO's girlfriend has to cope with that most impenetrable side of the masculine psyche. Sitting in the Double Locks, enjoying a full English breakfast washed down by a couple of pints of Old Peculiar, Mike Tanner is the perfect example of male bonding; all his adult life has been spent in pursuit of two goals, a green beret and an oval ball. His personal idiosyncrasy, he jokes (except he is not really joking), is that 'I don't really like any-

one who isn't a Marine or doesn't play rugby.' Fortunately for
Mike's love life his girlfriend Helen also plays rugby.

After a while in training, the sad truth is that most YOs feel like
Mike. He is more comfortable with his mates than he is with his
girl, and those mates – well, some of them are not only single, but
predatory with it. Take any group of young men from an all-male
environment – a sports team, a boarding school – and you have
immediately created fertile soil in which a Male Chauvinist Pig
may graze. If you then confine this group in an environment where
the only women they come into day-to-day contact with are waitresses, secretaries, Wrens in uniform and very occasionally senior
officers' wives who must always be treated with respect, you have
built them a sty. Further subject them to intense physical and mental demands and you have designed an MCP with an enormous
amount of energy to burn off once he leaves an open prison where
there is little outlet other than drinking beer.

The close, intimate bonding that develops between YOs during
training (and indeed between recruits) can to the outsider appear to
have homosexual undercurrents. The Royal Marines have a schizo-
phrenic attitude towards a subject that is guaranteed to drive military
men puce with embarrassment and rage. They are simultaneously
outrageously homophobic about the very concept of a gay Marine
and adamant that it simply does not and cannot happen. They are
frightened, perhaps, because the very concept of sexual intimacy
defiles and sullies the purity of their relationship with comrades in
arms.

'Two blokes huddling together in a bivvy bag in the depths of a
Dartmoor winter is perfectly acceptable to the Corps. It is for
survival not for sex,' says Colonel Mike Taffinder, who speaks
diplomatically for almost every Marine. 'Homosexuality, on the
other hand, undermines discipline and that's why there's no place
for it in the Corps. When the shit hits the fan a man is far less
likely to issue a life-threatening order to his lover than to one of his
comrades.

'And anyhow, the Marines themselves won't have anything to do
with gays. Rightly or wrongly homosexuals are regarded as very
non-macho, wet handshakes and all that. Those who are that way
inclined will quickly realize that the only route to survival is to
leave. In my experience they are as rare as hen's teeth in the Royal
Marines. The only way anyone could survive as a homosexual in

this outfit would be for him to always look outside the services for his lovers.

'There are few real no nos in the Corps. Being a poofter and stealing from your oppo are two of them.'

Jools Ostling put it a whole lot simpler and nastier. 'If we found out that one of the batch was gay we'd kill him. And I mean that literally.' Calling someone a poof in the Marines is not just a gibe at sexual preference but calls into question every physical and mental characteristic that makes him a man. Statistics would have us believe there must be some gay Marines, but they must be very discreet and very brave. It is also not very wise to point out that many SNCOs and officers all have moustaches of the kind favoured in the gay community.

However, notwithstanding those prehistoric views, the Corps is fairly open-minded in its treatment of what people have done before they joined up. 'We know that at least 60 per cent of the YOs who join us have dabbled in illegal drugs,' says Taffinder, 'but as long as a man is clean when he's with us that's fine. We cannot pass judgement on what went before. Every man, every boy has certainly been subjected to if not an actual homosexual relationship, then something pretty close. All sorts of people come to us from all sorts of backgrounds and probably many have committed criminal offences, but that was before they joined the Corps. Provided they do not continue with those habits – that's the point.

'We can be supportive. One recruit found himself being blackmailed by an older man who was threatening to expose a sexual relationship they'd had before he joined the Services. He was terrified that if it were revealed he would be out of the Corps, or his fellow trainees would make life really hard for him. Instead we sought an assurance from him that the affair was in the past, we reported the blackmailer to the local police, the recruit passed out of training successfully and is now serving in a Commando unit.'

Before any serious attempts at 'trapping' were undertaken the first task confronting the batch was to bond together. The mating ritual of young men requires that it be done in front of other males and in the ongoing initiation an abject but honourable failure rates almost as high as an actual pulling. Building this rapport among relative strangers first requires the quaffing of countless pints and the swapping of life histories, suitably embellished in the telling. The progress of England towards the Rugby World Cup Final established an immediate common interest between the plethora of rugby players, as did their mutual affinity for ale, a natural corollary of the sport – perhaps it has to do with washing all that mud out of your mouth.

(There was some remarkable rugby talent in the batch. In addition to Tanner, Bob Rob, Chalkie, who had captained his County Under-21 side, and Bob Baxendale who had chosen a career in the Corps over taking up professional Rugby League forms, Jeremy Woodall has since played Sevens for the Corps. The upshot was that the batch XV went on to beat Dartmouth Naval College in their annual fixture, a fine achievement for a team taken from a class of thirty-five young men as against one culled from two hundred.)

Having established groups of like-minded souls the next question was where to go hunting. The batch had two initial choices. Both Pete Manson and Martin Wood had been at Exeter University and still had friends there which provided an entrée into student social circles that most of the YOs could easily slip into should they choose. However, neither Pete nor Martin were naturally gregarious; both kept that side of their lives separate from the batch, using it as a personal escape valve rather than something to share. Wood was soon after to become a batch target – a situation he did not help by withdrawing socially. He often appeared to view YO training as part of his post-graduate studies in politics. From the outset he spent most nights off hanging out with his old chums, before staying over at his girlfriend's house and arriving back at CTC before breakfast.

Pete Manson is by inclination a quiet chap, happy to bask in anonymity and let things pass him by. He had a hole-in-the-heart operation when he was a young child and has a huge scar running down the front of his chest. This only inconveniences him in that medically he cannot fly fast jets though he would like to be a helicopter pilot. Very reserved and old-fashioned in his outlook – a batch mate once described him as 'the YO most likely to still be a virgin at the end of training' – Pete would tend to hang around Lympstone at weekends and go ashore with his civvy friends in Exeter.

Which left Gav Parr, fresh from his thirty weeks of recruit training, who knew the seamier side of the local night-life, all the hang-outs and clubs favoured by the nods. Harry's in Exmouth is a local

legend, renowned as a place to go to meet Marines. Although the
town was officially banned to the batch in the early weeks, they
soon found this welcoming hostelry. The music and ambience are
definitely secondary to the main purposes of first social, then sexual, intercourse. Generations of spilt beer have given the floors
their own special sheen, so it is advisable to keep shuffling your feet
in a semblance of following the beat – this prevents them from
becoming anchored to the floor by a superglue derived from hops.

Gav and Jools quickly became habitués of another nod hang-out
in Exeter where anything goes and frequently does. 'With a girlfriend up in Edinburgh, I began by resigning myself to fifteen
months of alcoholic gymnastics with intermittent flights up north,'
commented Bob Rob, after being taken on Gav's guide to the
fleshpots. 'My problem seemed compounded during the Ostling
and Parr guide to local clubs when we were confronted by nothing
but "inbred Janners". The aforementioned pair have since gone on
to defend their alarming traps with these bribes of "horrendapigs",
refused by all those who wish to remain healthy in mind and body.'

The dangerous duo quickly established themselves as game for
anything and anybody. Ostling won the award as first YO to score
long before Tenderfoot and promptly established a league table.
'Me and Gavin got the biggest scores,' he says with a wicked grin
like a kid who has just been caught with his hand in the sweetie jar.
'We had a chart, did a survey. Charlton had a high score as well
once he got into the routine.' As with any group of young men on
the rampage penis size became a subject of endless discussion and
speculation. Unlike most groups where they all lie about it and it is
impossible to verify anyway, everyone was soon aware that Gav was
not just a tall man.

For the insatiable few, early medical lectures on the dangers of
AIDS and the use of prophylactics were frequently ignored. 'Safe
sex – we didn't believe in it,' reports one anonymous YO, who like
so many young men and women believes it will never happen to
him. 'I did three women and came inside them without wearing a
condom but I did have an AIDS test later as some of them were
pretty dodgy. I did catch something once. I got penicillin for it, I
was starting to come out in a rash.'

Like that rash, the desire to let off steam within the grasp of a
locally available girl soon began to spread and seep through to
many of those in relationships. Fidelity became a law to which they

paid lip-service rather than obeying it to the French letter. After all they were now spending most of their time in closer proximity to their comrades than their lady friends. 'There is nothing that can be brought closer together than men sleeping together in green bags in various soggy locations, recounting past sexual failures or deviances,' commented Chalkie, before going on to admit that Mike Tanner was quickly and universally recognized as a 'great trap in a bivvy bag when cold out in the field'. Shared hardship can prove a greater bonding than sex and so it was to prove.

The batch were slower to recognize and loath to admit how rapidly these changes were communicated to the outside world. Within the first ten weeks the YOs found it hard to face the outside world without a mate at their side, for they alone really knew what the other was going through. When girlfriends came to stay (there is a fairly relaxed attitude towards officers having a guest to stay overnight in the Mess, though permission has to be sought) they quickly found that outside of bed there was little time spent whispering sweet nothings *à deux*. In restaurants or pubs it would always be groups of YOs, each with their girlfriend, so the conversation would naturally turn to matters Marine conducted at high speed in shorthand and Corps slang (which takes a bit of getting used to). Chalkie's description of disappearing head first into a bog is only quite funny if you were not there. On the third time of telling it ceases to be even faintly amusing. Nor did it help the girls that they did not know each other, and were thrown together with a bunch of female strangers, expected to get on because their boyfriends did.

'My girlfriend Janie hated coming to Lympstone,' says Rory Thomson. 'Because there'd be four of us talking about some boring exercise and four girlfriends who didn't know each other and were expected to be happy about it. Not surprisingly they dropped like flies. I'd been going out with Janie since I was fourteen but our relationship was gone to shit by December. We struggled on but finally split up last June.'

From Week 1 the May '91 batch had been gleefully prophesying that most relationships were doomed. Sure enough the first 'Dear John' letters were appearing within the first ten weeks, the contents often interchangeable, the cries as old as time but no less understandable for that. 'We never talk any more.' 'You are so far away when we meet, either too exhausted or too drunk.' 'I don't know you any more, you're not the man I loved at college.' Old clichés from young hearts, hurt because they simply could not understand what their lovers were going through, knowing only that it excluded them and always would do.

Matt Lodge was determined to maintain his long-term relationship with Amanda through the early pressures, and when she got a job and moved to Exeter after Christmas Wolsey, a romantic at heart, prophesied an engagement once Matt earned his green lid.

'What caused so many break-ups? The regular and quite extended absences. People did actually change,' admits Matt, with the considered approach he takes to everything. 'We may not think we have changed much outwardly – though even there more than we realize – but our general attitudes and expectations certainly have. I think it can be quite difficult for an outsider to understand what we are doing, what we are going through. You can see our presentation at the end of year, see what we have done, but that doesn't give a feel for the pressures, the psychological pressure – for me there is a constant physical worry about passing BFT, then the Commando Course.

'What it is almost impossible to explain to anybody, but especially to girlfriends, is what the course demands of you. It is very difficult to give everything to training and still have much left to give to anything else. At one point at least in these fifteen months we will all be called upon to give most of what we've got and at that point you are probably stuck in a bog somewhere on Dartmoor and not able to get back into your cabin and write a long letter saying all the right things.

'Amanda is well aware of how the system works but no matter how much time I spend with her she is not part of the batch and never could be. '

Even on those weekends when the YO could escape from Lympstone the chances are that he would be physically shattered. The importance of sex rapidly changes from being a demonstration of affection into a bodily need, just another physical function. One girlfriend memorably summed up YO lovemaking techniques as 'a couple of kisses, a quick clamber on top, a loud grunt followed instantly by a snore as he falls asleep'. A far cry from weeks at college where there was plenty of time for foreplay, rest and even talking to each other.

Captain Shaw was far from encouraging for the lovelorn's long-term prospects, announcing, 'It doesn't actually matter if you finish training with your girl because the attrition rate among young troop commanders is almost as high. The best thing is to clear the decks, and wait until training is finished because then at least the girl knows what she's getting and has no rosy memories of lying around student bedrooms with someone with shoulder-length hair.'

Chalkie, for all his beer guzzling and laddish tendencies, was ferociously determined to keep his relationship not only alive but kicking. A major test of his loyalties came when he had to decide between attending the annual Army-Navy rugby game at Twickenham and the inevitable piss-up that followed it, or celebrating Katie's birthday with a West End show followed by dinner. He wisely chose the latter course, despite much barracking and accusations of being pussy-whipped.

'I see Fluffikins − as she's known by the batch − as often as I can,' he says, for once serious. 'It means for a whole weekend you don't have to see any member of the batch and you can bury yourself in her cleavage, you can become a civvy and do completely normal things like cooking. Katie has left university, has a good career of her own and cannot be told what she is doing with her weekends. To expect her to come out at my whim to wherever I am is hoping too much.'

As more relationships foundered − Andy Harker came back from Christmas leave having parted with his long-term girl − so the jokes and the sniping from the unattached got sharper, sometimes even vicious. 'One guy's girlfriend was reputed to be seeing someone else,' says Andy Mac, 'and they were teased mercilessly about this mystical other figure, Gazza, a Scouser scally (not to be confused with Paul Attwood who was also known as Gazza) she had picked up as a fresher. Since my girlfriend decided to join the Territorial Army, I get abused constantly about how she is sleeping with loads of soldiers. You just have to take it as a joke, which when you are feeling a bit low can be difficult.'

On occasions a joke which can seem like a jolly jape inside CTC is neither funny nor innocuous but simply malicious. 'Near the end of the first term,' recalls Pete Joy, 'some lout (everyone denied it, as the culprit would have got a real punching) told my girlfriend, when she phoned for me, that I'd gone AWOL two days ago and hadn't been seen since. This led to her ringing my dad in tears, who rang the guardroom and they sent the Duty Officer to find me (in my cabin all along). Very funny — but it just made me think of the batch as a bunch of wankers. This was one of the effects of CTC; many guys who were continually run from pillar to post and treated like kids took consolation in behaving like yobs and passing on some of the grief Lympstone visited upon them.'

Those like Steve Hussey and Joy, who disappeared every possible weekend and so chose to forsake the regular Saturday night piss-ups and trapping sessions, would catch a lot of flak (imbued perhaps with not a little envy) from their mates the next week. They were prepared to endure the ribbing because they needed the support to get through training. 'Getting away from Lympstone individually is important for the collective spirit of the batch,' adds Bob Rob cynically, after his girlfriend up in Edinburgh sent him his 'Dear Mark' letter long before the end of the first term. 'If nothing else, it gives Mr Adcock a chance to tell us stories of the ones that got away and Mr Skuse to show us the continental angles of the ones who didn't.'

'One of the least encouraging aspects of training — or perhaps it's because arduous training develops self-centredness rather than charm —' noted McInerney, 'is the way that an officer in the Royal Marines is regarded by the outside world and in particular by their eligible daughters.'

Unhappy with the 'horrendapigs' on offer in the local clubs the batch soon sought potential dates elsewhere — anywhere else. Goldsmith plugged himself into the Exeter medical hierarchy by dating a nurse — a smart move as nurses, too, work shifts, unsocial hours and enjoy partying hard. An Adcock and Robinson recce of the London scene, designed to preempt a possible batch strike on the heart of the nation, found a more fruitful hunting ground but also showed Mr Adcock's ability not to be able to recognize a transvestite. Ashby and Shetler-Jones somehow attached themselves on to the London deb scene, regularly driving two hundred miles up to town, to attend some smart society midweek ball before driving back to Lympstone for inspection at 0700. On one occasion Shet asked a colleague to pack his Bergen for the field exercise they were due to start on the following morning. He did so, but also added lead weights at the bottom of the Bergen. As these were his BFT weights, which cost money, he could not throw them away and ended up carrying an extra 22 lbs all exercise.

On the batch runs ashore it was apparent that they were unified at work but not at play. In the clubs Gazza's group would go off to trap girls whereas the rugby element would drink beer and not trap and then look at the others having a good time and say 'fucking hell that's what we want to be doing'. Pete Evans, despite lacking conventional good looks, was a regular on the club trawls and proved very successful at chatting up shell-shocked damsels. His technique was pretty sophisticated as well as designed to restore the good reputation of the Royal; as he was a tee-totaller and always sober he would wait until one of his drunken mates had offended some poor girl and then sidle up and, in studied contrast, be polite and charming.

Dan Bailey on the other hand became notorious for deliberately trying to muscle in on girls being chatted up by his friends. 'Dan was terrible, he tried to get his leg over this girl Gav was friends with,' recalls Ostling, 'she was only sixteen. If you were chatting up a girl in a night club he'd just come up, grab her top and try to wrench it off. Me and Gav were known for being pretty crude but he was more shocking.

'We called Dan the "social hand grenade", as he didn't seem to be able to judge a social situation. One time we went round to the house of these girls in Exmouth. They invited us to dinner, they were all dressed up, had made a real effort, cooked nice food and Gav and I were being well behaved for once. One girl was a bit fat so we called her Buddha but suddenly Dan picked up this squeezy thing and squirted her all over with cream. Gav and I were embarrassed and shocked – which didn't happen often.'

Other members preferred to concentrate on a bit of variety. One (who will remain anonymous to save his life) had two girlfriends who would be invited down to Lympstone on alternate weekends. Somehow he got away with this complex juggling act without either finding out about the other woman – but then he always did.

Two other YOs were not so lucky. They succeeded in trapping the same girl and both went to bed with her. Unfortunately both foreplay and consummation were captured for posterity by an assiduous colleague, who had bugged the room with a cassette recorder. This tape was kept and played back for all to enjoy later in the week. Naturally they never saw the girl again ... but somebody still has the tape.

7

More Pain: No Gain

An hour of pain is as long as a day of pleasure.

English proverb

LYMPSTONE HAS MANY traditions, most of which are printable, and it can never be said that CTC does not make full use of all its natural assets. The Exe estuary is one such asset. When the tide recedes it leaves an enormous expanse of mud so thick, black and cold as to make Charon believe the Styx had escaped the Underworld. One of the sacred and regular rituals of Royal Marine training is the Mud Run.

Usually mud runs take place as punishment for some crime. It might be as specific as the entire batch forgetting to salute a senior officer — one of Wolsey's natural failings which the YOs instinctively adopted — or as vague as the committing of a thought crime ('I know some of you do not want to salute senior officers') or demonstrating a particular attitude ('You are too arrogant' — another inherited behavioural pattern, one might think). Either way it's into PT rig, over the railway track and into the mud. The first steps are terrible, cold, damp, squishy, then it ceases to matter. Everyone else is in the same condition — soon only sky-blue flashes of T-shirt glimpsed amidst the brown, promptly exacerbated by the addition of press-ups and sit-ups in the mud. The only way to get clean is by being doused by a high-pressure fire hose. Perversely, even in mid-winter the YOs profess to enjoy mud runs.

Rory Thomson was enjoying his first mud run just before Eye Opener when something went between knee and groin. It was a bad time for such an injury, an unlucky stroke for a youngster already on warning. Rory got on fine with his mates, was consid-

ered to be one of the First XV but could not impress the Training
Team the same way. Eye Opener was a disaster.

An excellent runner but put a pack and boots on Rory and he
was immediately in trouble. Yomping across Dartmoor under a
fully laden Bergen in weather conditions that would drown a duck
made the injury worse. A small niggle quickly progressed into a
muscle injury. His map reading was diabolical, his admin shot to
pieces and by late afternoon on the second day, when he was asked
to inspire his section in a Practical Leadership Task (hoisting an
injured man thirty feet up to a bridge), so was his motivation. He
admitted later: 'On a personal level the PLT was where the lessons
were learnt – how was I to motivate a group of people who were as
cold, wet and tired as I was? Needless to say the task didn't go very
well, due mainly to my lack of experience.' He finished the exercise
but only as an automaton, obeying orders without question, not
giving them.

The Team were particularly scathing and recommended he be
placed on OC's Warning. 'He's so used to bollockings and failure
that he doesn't give a shit,' said Billy Baxter. 'He drops the ball every
time he's given it.' It is not easy for Rory, whose father Jonathan
Thomson is a Royal Marine Colonel who had just finished commanding 45 Commando in Kurdistan, where Wolsey had been one
of his company commanders. 'Rory used to play soldiers on
Woodbury Common as a little boy,' said his mother at Parents Day,
'now he's doing it as an adult.' There was never any question of
strings being pulled, for Jonathan Thomson is not that sort of man,
but in many ways it was a strike against Rory, as if it was expected
that blood would out, that he should know how to be a soldier
without being taught, that introduction to Woodbury Rash before
puberty meant he should know how to pack a Bergen the right way.

Instead the injury got worse and as it got worse he felt increasingly isolated and depressed. 'Initially it was almost impossible to do
any kind of phys,' he recalls. 'I remember being on sentry, lying in a
hole in Woodbury Common in the pissing rain – thinking this is
the worst place I could be. It was a mortar trench, just body deep
and it fills with water and mud after about thirty minutes, we
couldn't wear waterproofs as they made too much noise.
Fortunately we were going on leave three days later which kept me
going. I rested my leg over Christmas and after that I could do
phys, but it hurt a lot and ached for at least three hours afterwards.'

If Rory was losing it through injury – and he was not to be the only one – Pete 'Jabber' Joy had lost it somewhere on Dartmoor. Along with his rifle. Highly regarded enough to be a UCE, intelligent enough to get an upper second at Cambridge University, Joy impressed the Team for the first few weeks, but as he was a certified loner his colleagues were less convinced. At times he appeared to be only semi-switched on, going through the motions as if physical memory were enough; there were days when he was completely apathetic, focusing on a different plane of reality. Russ Corn, a friend at Cambridge where they both read the same subject, could not understand the change from a highly motivated competitor. (Spotting a loser, Russ quickly palled up with Harker, whose attitude to stragglers he shared, and became one of the prime movers in batch politics, one of the leaders of the First XV.) People joked about the boxing but there may also have been other, more personal reasons for Pete's mother had died a year earlier. Whatever the explanation, his reaction to the mindless tasks of cleaning, admin and long wet yomps had been to withdraw into himself and he was increasingly incapable of rousing himself from such self-imposed lethargy.

Grief counselling is not a Royal Marine skill, but even Wolsey was surprised on Guy Fawkes Night in Brisworthy Wood – now known to the batch as 'Wrappers Wood' – when Joy wandered up to him and announced in the same flat emotionless tone as if he had just seen another tor on the horizon, 'Sir, I think I've lost my rifle.'

'What do you mean you think you've lost your weapon, Mr Joy. Have you got it ? If not, where did you leave it ?'

'I think about a hundred metres up that last hill, sir.'

Naturally enough the SA80 is nowhere to be seen up the last hill. That is simply not amusing – well, maybe it will be tomorrow over a pint in the Mess but not right now and only if you can recover the damn thing. Thank God it's a clear night, so clear in fact you can see the fireworks exploding, the bonfires burning bright, all the way down to Plymouth. Bang goes the scheduled 2200 hours end to the Night Navex. So it was about-turn for the batch, the singing of whose new marching song, 'Pete Joy's Rifle', composed for the occasion by Parr and Ostling (to the tune of The Jam's 'Eton Rifles') grew somewhat less spontaneous and more forced the further they backtracked. It took four hours to find the rifle which was six and a half kilometres away. He had been yomping without it for over ninety minutes. The Navex finally ended at 4 a.m.

That is enough to place Pete on warning; he is also fined £150 and given a dressing down that makes the windows in OTW shake. In addition he is given an extra punishment. In Wolsey's office is a polished shell casing from a 155 mm Iraqi artillery howitzer. Any YO who has committed a heinous crime is given the shell, which he has to carry with him all over camp – even into the static tank if required, where it has to be held above head height – and keep sparkling clean until some other offender relieves him of it. While Pete's reaction is to appear surprised, as if he has done nothing to merit such punishment, inside he is devastated by his mistake. Wolsey is concerned because a man in possession of an automatic weapon but not of all his faculties is extremely dangerous and unless he improves – as most of the batch have done when put on his warning – it will take five months to throw him out. As a UCE he will never resign because that means paying back some £12,000 to the Corps.

For Pete the incident is humiliating, but what really hurts is this constant reminder he is lugging around camp. It does not help when he learns that the selfsame thing happened to a YO from the Sept. '90 batch, the difference being that he got away with it as a following section picked his rifle up and returned it to him. Just to rub salt into his wounds, that YO went on to win the Sword of Honour! You do need a bit of luck occasionally and Joy's had run out. The question is whether the incident will wake him up or drive him further away. Unfortunately he is not able to admit the stark truth of what happened, not able to say out loud 'I fucked up' and improve from there. Everyone screws up at some point in training, the essential thing is not to let it get you down, or hide behind a bunch of excuses.

'The batch were initially understanding and sympathetic – they knew it could have happened to any of them, what with inexperience, fatigue and preoccupation. I took the £150 fine and dressing down without complaint,' he says. 'However Wolsey's little joke of having me carry his wretched shell case for three weeks, wherever I went, as a punishment did me more damage than ever he realized. My morale and self-confidence were already shaken enough by my lapse without any further humiliation, and that three-week sentence forever fixed my place in batch culture as a dozy biff, something I had never been regarded as before. For a man with a degree (allegedly in psychology) [it was actually philosophy] I would have thought Wolsey would have known better than to rub my nose in it as he did.'

To the batch Pete Joy's Rifle was a trigger incident to set their self-policing into action once more. Joy had placed himself on the edge, proved untrustworthy. From now on he would be watched and if he was found wanting again, the pack would first disown him and then would actively seek to destroy him. Andy Harker, with the experience of Commando training already behind him, was becoming increasingly abrasive to potential failures and prone to hectoring people about minor details in the field that were their own or the DS's business.

'Harker got into the habit of getting on my back,' says Joy, 'delivering a diatribe on how to sit down with a Bergen on or how to yomp in the field, for all the world like the Wing Sergeant Major; the difference being that I could tell him to fuck off and go to hell. Perhaps such bossiness covered insecurity on his rise to commissioned rank but I expect it will serve him well in the Corps.'

'Self-policing wasn't ever a conscious decision,' explains Matt Lodge. 'Just as it is a supportive group to those who are struggling, there is no room in the batch for anybody who doesn't pull their weight. A couple of individuals tried their damnedest to make people wrap but that was a malicious decision and so it didn't work.'

Group theory holds that inside any bunch of people thrown together certain characters will quickly emerge – the leaders, the chiefs, the Indians, the jokers and those doomed to be the butt of that wit. Jason McQueen has come into the latter category. Of deceptively slight build, possessing an innocent face and the tiniest trace of a lisp in his speech, it was not that Jason could not cut it. He was very disciplined, tidy, efficient but lacked perhaps that indefinable edge, the charisma required to be a Royal Marine officer. A natural worrier, he was always getting worked up about little things. Rob Lunn remembers walking down the corridor at 1 a.m. having finally finished all his personal admin to find Jason worrying about how to clean the back of his radiator. His major misfortune was alphabetical, having a cabin next to Jools Ostling.

A natural mimic, in his self-appointed role as batch spokesman

Jools never knew when to stop. One of his favourite tricks was to answer the phone pretending to be other members of the batch. 'I answered the phone a couple of times,' he grins at the memory, 'once to Rob Lunn's girlfriend and once to Jason's mum – I didn't say anything rude to her. However Jason reacted badly to having the piss taken out of him.

'If you go into the Marines you have to be prepared to muck in, everyone had the piss ripped out of them. In a group like that everyone has to have their niche, there have to be people to have the piss taken out of them. The drinkers, me and Gav, were the piss-takers, the spear, the sharp end, we said what everyone else was feeling. In a group natural leaders tend to emerge and in the batch I was one of the dominant characters.'

A reasonable apologia; not quite 'I was only obeying orders', more 'I was only carrying out what everyone else was thinking, so we all must share the blame'. The problem was that while Jools is a forceful character, physically among the strongest (the legacy of years of rowing), he was into wielding power without accepting responsibility for it. Inherently uncomfortable with being an officer his alliance with Gav Parr, like a military *folie à deux*, was managing to bring out the worst in both of them.

'This is my first time away from home. I found it brilliant, that's why I went pretty haywire,' says Jools, unaware of the contradictions in what he says. 'I don't like being a leader, I can stand in front of a class, teach people ten years older how to row, that is due to my upbringing. My father is a mechanic who has his own garage, my mother is a nurse. I went to my dad's old school, Wimbledon College. Some of the masters, including the deputy head, I knew by their first names because of rowing so I was never phased by authority.

'I was disappointed when I got to Lympstone as most of the batch were from public schools. I thought it would be more down to earth; instead it was full of people like Major Sturman and Captain Bailey, they were a bit cheesy, narrow-minded. I knew the Army made you polish boots but I thought we got a stupid amount of washing and polishing and ironing. Obviously it is part of training, but you could train us better if they were modern about it. I have a brain and I have had to think to get a degree but largely as an officer you are just passing down others' orders.'

When the batch went on a run ashore Jools and Gav – still

defiantly sporting his nod haircut, just as he would flash his 'Made in Britain' tattoo – would go into Exeter and hang out at a nightclub cum pick-up joint favoured by recruits, not at the places favoured by their batch mates intent on meeting Exeter University students and nurses. 'I just don't think it's right having a divide between officers and men,' he insists. 'They have got to respect you, just calling you "sir" doesn't meant shit. I never picked anyone up for not saluting us, unlike the Corps-pissed guys like Tanner, Steve Hussey and Plug [Pete Evans].'

Yet Jools could never reconcile his deeply held, deeply felt egalitarian principles with the pride he felt in being a Royal Marine. 'There was this smugness you had when you went out, strode around thinking you were the best, you could fight anyone, fuck anyone, could do anything you wanted.'

The problem was that, now the batch was bedding down and most people had found a level where they were comfortable, Jools's position began to appear suspect. 'He upset a lot of people, he was basically pretty spiteful, you could wind him up hugely, he could dish it out but couldn't take it,' says Matt Lodge who was never a fan – but then he was later to suffer from Jools's over-developed sense of batch loyalty. 'It was all based on insecurity, he was probably the most insecure bloke I've come across. To cover his own shortcomings he would divert attention on to others.'

Worse, by picking on Jason, who while he may not have been that popular was never a designated batch target, for nobody doubted his commitment – except Jason himself – Jools passed, perhaps unwittingly, from official pricker of vanities into unofficial bully, chief persecutor. Even the First XV began to worry. 'Jools pissed his mates off, he was on the sharp end,' recalls Tim David, who after a shaky, nervous start developed a sharp, confident, no-bullshit air of his own. 'He was very worried and his defence mechanism was to be a vicious bastard. He gave me a lot of grief around Christmas, then I realized he had a problem and after that he went a lot quieter.'

Jason, meanwhile, had come to his own decision. He approached Wolsey in early December, requesting a transfer to the Naval College at Dartmouth. To everyone concerned it made perfect sense, was the ideal choice. Jason was more suited to the more rigid, technocratic hierarchy of the Navy. Once the decision was made he relaxed and during the last few weeks he spent at CTC, working on admin duties, until the time came to go to Dartmouth, he got on really well with the batch – even with Ostling.

'Before I went up to university at Cardiff I only ever wanted to join the Corps, they even gave me a bursary,' explains Jason. 'When I was there I joined the OTC and had time to think and I wasn't convinced it was what I wanted to do. I like physical challenges but I didn't like living in the field at all. Because I wasn't completely happy I had all these doubts nagging at me from the beginning. I didn't like it when Ostling started giving people like Parlour and Wood a hard time. He was a domineering character who was impossible to get on with. I got my grief from him early on too. Maybe it was a contributory factor but it wasn't the main reason for my decision to join the Navy. I really didn't enjoy it in the field and when I was discussing it with the Commandant he asked, "So you'd rather be in a warm grey box?" I said "yes" and I meant it.'

One of Captain Wolsey's little ploys to keep the batch on their mental toes was to make them write essays. These topics would be given to the batch just as they had finished all their personal admin, cleaning up after days in the field; or they would be paraded at midnight outside OTW and told to deliver them before going to sleep that night. The essay topics varied from straightforward accounts of 'The Training Value of Exercise Eye Opener' to more abstract concepts like 'Killing in a time of war is no different to killing in peacetime' and 'Do you accept the fact that you may have to sacrifice your life in the service as a RM officer and what might induce you to do this?'

The intention is both deliberate and obvious, to prove that you can still think clearly when exhausted, that you can force your brain to make logical plans and progressions under the most extreme pressures. At times in YO training it is too easy to slip into a constant round of physical pressure upon physical pressure, forgetting that the brain too must be stimulated to produce the all-round soldier. The essays also allow the Training Team interesting insights into what is going on inside the batch, for when people are tired they let things slip, reveal how the batch feel about certain of their number. Conversely it is a useful safety-valve, allowing the YOs to sound off about something that is really pissing them off.

Dan Bailey hates the essays with a deep loathing, for he is not the most dexterous of writers as well as being out of practice after a year in the African bush where there is not so much call for literary skills. It can take him over an hour to produce what history graduates like Corn and Joy can dash off in twenty minutes. Naturally it is easier for the graduates – with the exception of Matt Skuse who, in complaining that biochemistry and essay writing are mutually incompatible subjects, is hiding the fact that he suffers from a mild form of dyslexia.

Essays on the abstract topics, as one might expect, are virtually uniform in their conclusions. No YO is going to say that he is not prepared to either kill or sacrifice his life in the line of duty. Horace's 'Dulce et decorum est pro patria mori' ('It is a sweet and seemly thing to die for one's country') is the generally considered yardstick, not Eric Hoffer's 'To our real naked selves there is not a thing on earth or in heaven worth dying for'. Moral imperatives do not often loom large in Royal Marine training but Andy Rowley was once again questioning what he was doing at CTC.

Rowley was so fit that he could have passed the Commando Tests in his first week at Lympstone. Smart, intelligent and personable with just the right trace of arrogance, he would keep reminding Wolsey about who was the fastest runner but not brag about it like Brian Adcock. He was in the top four from the first week and an immediate candidate for Sword of Honour. He loved the phys – the problem was, he hated the soldiering.

Every member of the batch had had their dreams of jacking it in, all had bellowed them out into the freezing fog of Dartmoor. Rowley had raised his troop's spirits on Long Knight – the last exercise before Christmas leave – when with all of them huddled together and soaked to the skin he had said very quietly, 'I wonder what other job I could be doing now?' Then he went on and listed them all. 'Lawyer ... doctor ... traffic warden ... accountant ...' On and on for half an hour without drawing breath, while his mates laughed and laughed, adding increasingly inappropriate and obscene suggestions as the list grew and grew.

Except it was not so funny for Rowley. There was more to it than that. The night before Long Knight had begun, his girlfriend, fed up with the way their relationship was suffering, had given him the brush-off on the phone. 'Well, sod her,' he thought, 'I can live without the grief, I've got my mates to look after me.' Sitting in the pissing rain for three days gives a man a chance to think, to take stock. Through the bravado, through the jokes, Rowley decided his whole attitude to Katie had changed. The first thing he did when the exercise finished was sprint to the phone, call her up and make his apologies.

He went off on his two-week Christmas leave with serious doubts, only to find himself still too distant from Katie, miles away from his family, worried about whether he, like some of the others, was losing the ability to plan his own life. And there was Northern Ireland, too, always brooding in the background, that almost inevitable posting for a Royal Marine troop commander, yet he had only ever wanted to be in the Corps for the sports, the travel, the comradeship. The reality of actually being a soldier, doing what he was being trained to do, started to sink in and he did not like what he saw. He started to make excuses, claimed that he had not been told enough, that he had only ever wanted to be a sports officer. His girlfriend did not like what he was becoming so added her opinions to the pot. So did his mother … a steady drip drip drip, both stalactites and stalagmites forming in the cavern of uncertainty within his head.

What it all boiled down to was that he did not want to go to Northern Ireland. This was not a question of physical courage, or the lack of it, but the prospect of serving in a place where moral values are so twisted, so distorted, that only the very lucky, or very bigoted, can see things as cut and dried, as black and tans versus green tricolours. The reality is a place where all the issues are a blurry mass of greys and more greys.

On his return to Lympstone Rowley announced his decision to withdraw from training. Wolsey, Matt Sturman and the Commandant all tried their hardest to keep him – probably too hard because they did not want to lose a potential Sword of Honour man. Wolsey offered his own rationalization of his first tour of Ulster. 'What the fuck, we're all going to die sometime, so die young!' became enshrined in batch folklore but did nothing for Rowley.

His friends tried to keep him – God, they tried – begging him to stay, to change his mind. Brian Adcock was his closest friend, they had shared a house together for a year at Loughborough and it was probably Brian who had persuaded him to join the Marines in the first place. One by one they cajoled him, buying countless pints in pubs and bars all over Devon. To no avail.

'I'm not like Prince Edward, giving up because I couldn't hack it mentally,' he says. 'I loved that side of things. I don't have to prove anything to myself and I didn't want to have to put my whole life into the hands of the Royal Marines for the next five years. I don't need to do that. I was turning into a different man after the first fifteen weeks and I didn't like him much. So I left and I have never regretted it for a moment.'

8

Cutting Out the Cancer

We are not always very kind. The batch knows by instinct if it
has a cancer and deliberately sets out to cut or freeze it out, by
deliberately picking on the weakness and exposing it.

Phil Ashby

HUMANITY IS CHAOS incarnate, but even so it has established patterns of behaviour for itself that emerge time after time. Ancient Chinese military theory has always held that the true purpose of war is peace. To be a soldier is to live in contradiction.

Soldiers are always here, have always been here, will always be here, as inevitable to society as death and taxes; agents of chaos, tools of totalitarianism, harbingers of destruction, defenders of freedom, name them as you will. Soldiers have to feel anchored to something, whether it be a rule book, a rifle, an ideal, an institution. This is why they thrive in time of war, for when the outside world has fallen into a state where laws are abnegated, the basic rules of society eschewed, they alone know whom they must obey, what they must do. The job of the soldier is to destroy all the established, accepted structures of his enemy's life and then give him back new certainties.

Soldiers do not believe in Chaos Theory – so what if there are mathematical patterns inside the most random of things! But what is war but chaos? Nature is nothing if not ironic in utilizing those who cannot believe in the chaotic way of things to carry out and confirm the very thing they deny.

Before he is ready to embrace his chosen profession a soldier must first, like St Peter before the cock crowed thrice, deny his master. He must turn away from the world. And he must be prepared to be absolutely ruthless.

Martin Wood should have learnt that by now; instead he set himself up to be the target. Captain Andy 'Shagger' Shaw, a tough former merchant seaman, Corps Commission officer and Falklands veteran, was in charge of teaching the batch tactics – battle drills and troop attacks. The week before Long Knight, Wood was asked to give an O group in front of Colonel Taffinder and five members of the DS. He made a complete hash of it, from his apologetic presentation to factual and tactical inaccuracies that would have got his troop wiped out. Shaw asked the batch, 'Well, men, what do you think?'

'We knew they were crap orders,' says Mike Tanner, 'but out of loyalty we didn't want to show him up. No one said anything.'

'Come on, men,' Shaw erupted, glaring at Wood. 'It is time to cut out this bloody cancer.' The hands came up – first one, then another, a forest of khaki arms, until virtually everyone had a comment to make. 'He got the ground brief wrong', 'He got the mission wrong', 'He gave the wrong coordinates'. If there had been thought bubbles coming out of each blue beret they would have been far more personal. 'He's a biff', 'He's a wanker', 'He's a waste of space', 'He should stay in Exeter with his girlfriend.' The batch wolves now had a new target to snap at, one officially sanctioned as a danger to life.

After the miseries of Long Knight, where Wood compounded his sins by losing his binoculars, came Christmas leave. The YOs took off faster than a bunch of drowning rats on a rotting life raft given a last-minute reprieve by a luxury cruise liner. Every year in YO training Christmas leave proves to be a psychological crunch point. For some being welcomed back to the family hearth where they do not have to iron, wash or practise physical jerks for two weeks, where they are cosseted and loved by family and girlfriends (the latter doing the latter is demonstratively more important), is a reminder of what they are missing, that there are more high points to life than sharing a bivvy bag with Tanner. Life is more comfortable, more practical and downright enjoyable back on Civilian Strasse. Thinking like that, a YO will not last long back at CTC.

To others it is only an opportunity to catch up on fifteen weeks of lost sleep, to scarf down piles of good scran, sink a few dozen pints, brag to their mates and thus avoid questioning themselves about why they feel so alienated from friends and family. You used to have to sit around listening to great-uncle Henry's interminable war stories out of politeness, now he is the only one who is interested in what you have to tell. Tales of stripping naked to cross the pond at Foggin Tor back on Eye Opener do not impress old mates who work in offices, they would rather tell you how they shagged the secretary at the office party, or how they remain gainfully unemployed and never get out of bed until midday. The mundanities of everyday life seem like walking through someone else's dream, so fickle, so unstructured they do not make sense. Home is now perceived as Lympstone, heaven a place where all activities have their fixed time and place.

Mike Tanner greets his batch mates with typical New Year bonhomie – 'Great to be back on board, isn't it, lads … lads?' – the second 'lads' disappearing pitifully into thin air as the aforementioned rush off to the Mess bar, hissing imprecations and obscenities previously kept in check when under Mummy's roof. Poor Mike, all he is doing is articulating what most of them feel, back from the real world into their peculiar home. But there is a time to be gung-ho, just as there is a way to be welcomed back by Captain Mark Wolsey. Wolsey was sporting a black eye and severely fractured cheekbone after being jumped from behind by a drunken neighbour wielding a metal bar in the small hours of New Year's Day. For months afterwards the batch believed he had done it playing rugby, though the more fanciful insisted it was after a pub fracas with six Paras. The neighbour eventually went to jail for six months.

Wolsey's welcome back to Lympstone comprised a dawn parade on Exmouth beach followed by a PT session and a long swim in the sea. 'This is not a beasting,' he said. 'You will know when you have had a real beasting because Mr Adcock will stop smiling.'

Brian stopped smiling within the week but that was after Rowley announced he was quitting. Brian had been sulking for a while since his request to go to Moscow on the Combined Services Water Polo Team was turned down and his confidence had taken a knock after giving a couple of sets of bad orders and falling flat on his bony backside on Long Knight, but he has a natural ability to bounce back. He is not one for soul-searching but Rowley's leaving has made him think again. 'I had long chats with Matt Lodge about the whole thing, we were both UCEs and he was unsure too. It's all right when someone you consider to be a wanker goes, but when Rowley decided it wasn't for him it hit me very hard. He decided for several reasons, he didn't enjoy the sol-diering aspect which took over after Week 10; the tactical side and patrolling didn't interest him. Katie his girlfriend didn't like it, his mother didn't like the idea he was in the Marines, he had those negative things hammered into him over Christmas. Eventually we decided he had made the right decision, ultimately he wasn't a sol-dier. But we were.'

Rowley's departure shook the batch to the core, changed some of the rules. They were still thinking about it when they deployed on Eagle Eye, a welcome return to the field after a succession of lectures followed by an exam on military law. This is an OP (Observation Post) exercise where the batch, who are now assumed to be proficient at fieldcraft and capable of surviving in the wild, are divided into four-man teams, controlled by an HQ section. Each OP has to make a covert insertion under cover of darkness and observe a particular position for two days without detection before attacking.

May batch had told them about two endless days on Woodbury Common watching an old concrete bunker doubling as an outside toilet for every passing local, so morale was not high. Then they heard that they were going into a plainclothes operation in unmarked cars, not defending Lympstone against the dreaded black-hooded warriors from Redland. Despite a sudden cold snap that took the temperature to below freezing it turned out to be the best exercise the batch had yet undertaken.

'Mr Stovin-Bradford was immediately on the phone to all his mates,' wrote Bob Rob in his essay on Eagle Eye, 'saying that he was now going under cover in plain clothes, he was going out now and may be some time, and that all the information was on a strictly need-to-know basis. On arrival at Yeovilton, Mr Harker got all excited, saying that this was the sort of air hangar that the SBS used as assembly points, while others disagreed but said that the movie *The Wild Geese* was filmed from this location.'

Waiting for the best part of a day in a hangar, the batch reacted in much the way one might expect of servicemen on deployment. They 'slept, walked around aimlessly, smoked and chatted, shoved Chalkie around, wrote letters to each other's skirt then slept some more'. Others played scratch cricket and football while Joy appeared to be lost reading *War and Peace* (actually it was *To Kill a Mockingbird*, which turned out to be an equally bad omen). They then practised leaping in and out of the transit vans as quickly and silently as possible. 'The practice departures from the transits were fun,' wrote Tim David, 'especially when one drove off with guess who – Pete Joy – still inside. He claimed not to have realized the van had stopped.'

The covert insertion worked like a charm, the 9 mms were put away and Mr Stovin-Bradford sadly reverted from being Special Agent Double O S–B to plain GPMG gunner Bradford. The batch were operating as a full troop under the command of Matt Lodge, with Andy 'Mac' McInerney acting as troop sergeant. His task was to lead the troop into position at night, during which he was to learn that forestry blocks on maps are not always where they should be. 'I would like to skip over the footborne insertion phase,' he wrote. 'At each piece of plantation I was confident of my location and necessary bearing. On exit from the plantation I was apparently deposited in a random new site, amazed that none of the batch had punched my lights out. It was the first time I felt I was actually sol-diering properly.'

Stumbling through the undergrowth, crashing into trees, Chalkie found his beloved but cumbersome GPMG to be as 'much use as breasts on a fish', while Goldsmith summed it up in his typical sar-donic manner: 'When we moved it was covertly and though the scenic forest stroll sounded like the entire population of Greater Manchester simultaneously eating large packets of ready-salted crisps, the mood of silent night insertion was not lost.'

The object of the mission was to infiltrate into Bosnia from Albania under cover of darkness, then observe a camp of Croatian irregulars (Wolsey was determined to spice up the batch's interest in current affairs: at that time the Serbs were not yet chief bastards in Bosnia) and report all their comings and goings for forty-eight hours prior to a dawn attack.

By dawn things at HQ are going pretty well. Deep inside a dense wood a mile from the camp Lodge is juggling his command – six OPs and an HQ – with remarkable facility for a novice. Sergeant Coyle is impressed, an achievement which few young officers can manage: 'He had nothing to lose but we would not have held it against him if he'd fucked it up, doing so well is a bonus.' The HQ section had it easy. All but invisible to any passing Croat, rotating a couple of sentries to watch the open spaces for unexpected visitors, they have plenty of room to move around, to answer calls of nature away from the group, even smoke and brew up. Andy Mac spends hours applying his cam cream, as if he were a supermodel preparing to strut along the Paris catwalk. At the end of it he still looks a mess. Matt Lodge is having a ball; others may be tired after a couple of hours' sleep but being in charge is pumping him full of adrenalin. Leadership does that.

'If you have a command appointment you become invincible, you can walk through walls, carry your Bergen for ever,' says McInerney, still smarting after his problems map reading the night before. 'Moving in last night we ended up crashing through firebreaks but I didn't feel my Bergen at all. I don't know whether it appears like some sort of aura to other people but within yourself you feel special. The person navigating – no matter how much he is carrying – will always walk away from the others.'

A mile away inside the target, the tattered towels fluttering on a makeshift clothes-line outside a concrete bunker which dates from an earlier, if not bloodier war, are the only signs of life. Coils of rusty barbed wire and rubble cover all the entrances to the camp. A short unshaven man emerges smoking a cigarette: the brown Red Army greatcoat that reaches to the ground and the Kalashnikov slung over his shoulder mark him as a Croatian irregular – or would if these were really the foothills on the Albanian border and not an eagle's glide from Bovington Camp in Dorset.

If the HQ group have 'proffed' (Marine slang for having it easy) life in the OPs is rather harder. Their equipment is minimal, two sleeping bags between four, one man always on the radio, another observing while the other two crash out, all in a space that averages less than seven feet by three. To avoid detection they are forbidden to use their cookers so have to exist on hard tack, eating cold food from their ration packs, drinking from their water bottles. Warm bacon burgers are barely digestible; cold, they are disgusting. Nor are they a passive food, and because the YOs cannot leave their position calls of nature are answered inside the OPs. Pissing in bottles is simple enough but defecating on cling film is an acquired art. 'Crapping on cling film, particularly if it is blowing in the wind, takes practice,' informs Matt Skuse. 'To miss the film is not good and would and did result in much wiping of grass and manhandling of crap. At the end of the exercise we drew lots to see who carried the cling film in their Bergen.'

Three hundred metres from the camp Skuse, Parr, Henry and

David had a pretty comfortable OP though Gav complained that he had to stop Skuse turning it into a country cottage. 'One of the most amazing events was the way Trevor Henry was able to sleep continuously for three days, apart from the time he spent eating. Insomnia is obviously not a problem in Jamaica,' wrote David. 'Trevor did not respond well to the cold or to the cramped environment and we adapted to that. Parr snored and we adapted to that too. We learnt that four people can live together in a bush for a long time before a murder occurs. One day more might have pushed it a bit far though.' The highlight of their OP came when they spotted two intruders whom they considered highly dangerous. Mr Skuse's request to engage 'One woman-white and one dog-small' was turned down, much to his annoyance.

Within a hundred metres from the camp, covering three of the exits, are two separate OPs one of which you could walk straight past and not see, hear or smell a thing. Atop a small hillock in a hide entered two nights previously and lovingly camouflaged further in the few post-dawn minutes before life stirs below are Robinson and Adcock (who because of his triathlon physique, all muscle and no fat, feels the cold bitterly – his hands have gone completely white as if the blood in them had been drained off) tucked up in the sleeping bags they share between them. Shetler-Jones, clutching his rifle and pair of binoculars, is on watch while Goldsmith is manning the radio.

Goldsmith still wears that 'God I'm so miserable' look magnified because this OP is so close to the 'enemy': he is dying for a smoke and that is completely forbidden. He still has days when he switches off physically and mentally because it all seems so bloody silly. It is just prior to 1000 hours and a bridal veil of hoar frost still rings the hide. Unable to stir all day they have another below zero night ahead before the planned attack at dawn.

Others had it harder. Soon after dawn on the first day Stan Harris discovered his OP was protected by a single piece of heather directly in front of them and a patrol approaching from any other angle could have spotted them miles away. Even Harker, tired from the long yomp in, had not checked out all the angles, proving he was human after all. While Thomson, Ostling, Corn and Baxendale quickly realized that a blind and deaf Croat could spot them.

For Rory the whole exercise was just another episode in his on-going nightmare. In the new OP he and Jools, both starving and chilled from the ears to the big toes, decided to brew up. 'We lit a hex cooker and nearly started a forest fire. This was obviously a major mistake.' The smoke was spotted ('I think they've set fire to their bush,' remarked a Croatian irregular in faultless Liverpudlian), the OP compromised and they were forced to move again. They ended up exposed, with two observing over a small hillock and the other two sleeping in the bracken. Rory was at the very edge; living with constant pain while under pressure to buck up his performance has etched deep gorges on his drawn cheeks as they run away from the Bassett rings beneath his eyes. 'He looks like he's done twenty-seven years in Changi Camp,' commented one of the Training Team. By this stage the Team know he is not going to make it, so does Rory.

Pete Evans is furious when his OP gets tapped by the Training Team: they were walking past when they smelt cigar smoke. 'Who brought cigars on this exercise?' demands Coyle, trying very hard not to laugh. 'I did, Sergeant,' piped up Watkinson, who then received a bollocking coupled with threats of immersion in the static tank once they get back to CTC. A little unfair as it might have been Neil's cigar but it was actually Ashby smoking it! A typical example of Neil's rigid and exact approach, typical too of Ashby's chameleon ability to create situations and somehow escape their consequences.

The Team call Neil 'the Vicar' but he has already earned everybody's grudging respect. Even frozen through he just keeps going. On the yomp back from Long Knight he voluntarily kept at the back to encourage the stragglers – others were told to, Neil did it off his own bat.

The dawn attack was duly carried out with some panache. Although the batch have not been taught the correct military way to clear bunkers and houses Tanner improvises by charging in screaming while firing on full automatic, which would certainly have scared the hell out of a Croat irregular. Shetler-Jones, still not the most military of men, noted caustically: 'If we ever have the misfortune to go to war against anything other than semi-trained monkeys a great deal more thought and trepidation will have to go into our actions or a lot of our side will get killed.'

The main cause of these 'blue on blues' (casualties caused by friendly fire) was undoubtedly GPMG gunner 'Rambo' Bradford, who by employing a generous definition to the words 'covering fire' managed to fire off countless blank rounds most of which would have gone straight through Rob Lunn. Wolsey had jacked up a Navy Sea King helicopter to take the batch back to Lympstone, which gave Chalkie a chance to redeem himself. During the airborne withdrawal he stood at the open door firing the GPMG from the hip while the others scrambled aboard. The pilot took off at such high speed that anybody not holding on was flung up to the ceiling.

'Upon boarding the helicopter and firing out of the doors while taking off,' wrote Chalkie, 'I fulfilled all my childhood Action Man dreams. The flight back was of immense training value, it's quite an experience to achieve weightlessness, something which for me I never thought possible.'

Back at Lympstone it was time to issue another fistful of warnings. Two days later Joy was accelerated on to OC's Warning but came out expressing immense surprise as he had been expecting to be congratulated on coming top in the military law exam – 'That was the most challenging thing I've done since coming here,' he told a stupefied colleague in the bar. 'I got 98 per cent, but it never got mentioned at my warning review.' Nor was Joy impressed when Dan Bailey dropped in to chat one evening – 'He had the cheek to try and talk me into resigning. Although he denied it I had the feeling he'd been sent by others in the batch.'

Rory Thomson was told he was going on to Commandant's Warning. 'That was always the point at which I had said I would leave,' says Rory. 'Captain Wolsey had told me that being off phys affects your mind too and that is what happened to me. I thought about it for a while and then announced I wanted to leave. I was given a few days off to think about it which is always reckoned to be the point of no return – you have some home comforts and don't want to go back. Mike Tanner and Brian Adcock tried hard to persuade me to stay.

'I did have the opportunity to be back batched to the next YO intake in May which I sometimes wonder if I should have done, but I was so physically and mentally exhausted I couldn't face going through the first ten weeks again. I was so run down it didn't seem attractive. The funny thing is that no one ever knew what the injury was but it still hurt for a year after I left.

'My final memory is walking back from sick bay and the batch were marching past in good order off to a lecture. Someone, I think it was Matt Lodge, shouted out, "Good luck, Rory" – not the usual "you wanker". I felt sad then because I knew it was really over.'

Where the idiosyncrasies of someone like Goldsmith have become accepted by his colleagues and acceptable to the DS, Gav Parr is still struggling. Already two steps up the warning ladder he faces being put on Commandant's Warning – three months to buck up or he's out. Nowadays he even admits that it might have been better to go spend some time in a rifle company, shake the training cobwebs off and see what an officer has to do.

Gav's problem is simple but he's too stubborn to see it. It could be that he's unlucky and his course officer has it in for him: he and Wolsey do have personalities which if they were chemicals would explode. But Gav's problem is that he's still a nod at heart, stuck in recruit training mode where the object was always to see how much you could get away with. So the Officers' Mess is great, a comfortable cabin and lashings of grub served by other people, but making small talk with officers at a private wine-tasting session, that's not his thing at all, he'd rather be on the phone to one of his girls or upstairs idly thumbing through a favourite porn mag (he is the 'batch librarian'). Gav wants to win by bucking the system, which is a big mistake because the system is bigger even than him and what he does not understand is that, according to Wolsey, the system doesn't want to break him, only to prove that to be truly an individual in the Corps you must also be able to conform.

Two days after Eagle Eye Gav went up before Major Sturman because Wolsey wanted him on Commandant's Warning. Gav, like Rory – like most of them – had always said that if it went that far he'd quit, so he argues every point, leaning his huge body over the desk, bludgeoning, whining but sticking up for his rights. It is a bravura performance which wins him another month's reprieve but may be counterproductive. The next day Sturman is livid at letting himself be browbeaten by a YO and is determined that if he gives sufficient cause Gav will suffer for it in the future. Wolsey was not impressed but for more intangible reasons. To him that wasn't the performance of a true officer; a gentleman would have taken it as gracefully as possible and promptly pulled his socks up. What it means, of course, is that he has to give Gav another command appointment and reckon on him screwing it up. Next time he won't get away with it, for the rope is coiled and waiting for him to tie his own noose. His mates in the batch – and he has plenty for after a couple of early hiccoughs he has always been a team player – know what the problem is but he still isn't listening, he's still hanging out at clubs with Jools and his nod mates, pulling the birds, making up nicknames, focusing the batch energies at Wood, Joy and Evans and forgetting to watch his own back.

Pete Evans is a strange guy. Now the oldest surviving batch member, with a degree in physics from Durham University, he worked at Hunting Engineering for eighteen months before deciding he wanted a full career commission in the Royal Marines. Pete has a bunch of problems but one big one. The Training Team have not been impressed and consider him to be misplaced. He is great in the classroom but can be a wet blanket on exercise, offering little in support. He can give orders well and did so on Long Knight but is equally capable of being bitchy to his section if things don't go to plan. 'He's a fifth column sent from CND to cause trouble,' grumbles Coyle attempting to find an excuse to put him on further warning.

Pete's big problem is that he doesn't drink alcohol. This makes his batch mates uncomfortable for while they get pissed up, there is Pete sitting there sipping his orange juice not laughing quite so loudly as they are at those bad jokes. 'It doesn't help not drinking,' comments Goldsmith, who had found a kindred enigma in Pete. 'Being drunk enables someone to act like a child and because Pete doesn't the batch regard him as very boring, the sobering man.' Unlike the equally teetotal Andy Harker who possesses all the requisite military skills and has been constantly in the top three, Pete has struggled in the bottom five. And let's face it, Pete is not exactly an oil painting. Ostling with his customary strike at the jugular promptly christened him Plug, after the hideous cartoon schoolboy in the Bash Street Kids; others prefer the more refined ring of 'the Dashing Lieutenant'.

'I thought Pete Evans was a wally to begin with,' admits Brian Adcock. 'He was an easy target for taking the piss out of, wasn't very fit or particularly attractive in all respects. He hates Jools Ostling but he has a skin as thick as a rhino and so has never reacted or bowed to the shit he took, never had any problems with his own competence.'

Despite all these personal pressures Pete Evans is loving it. 'I feel very fortunate to be on this course. I can think of no other organization which would spend fifteen months training its junior managers,' he wrote before adding a caveat. 'I am surprised at the number of people who avoid work if they can. I have found the narrow attitudes of some people astonishing. Being in a closed system it would be all too easy to see nothing outside of the Corps and that would be a sad state for an officer to be in. It will take a considerable effort not to fall into this trap and a lot of the batch don't see this or don't really care.'

That is Pete's major saving grace. He knows who he is, what he wants and what he has to do to get it. He will not change to conform to batch mores so having a thick hide is essential. Pete is not going to fail, though right now the only person who believes that is Pete. The only obstacle to his green lid comes from certain members of the batch who want him to wrap. They think he may be pre-cancerous.

Mike Tanner has never wanted anyone to wrap, though he admits that he would rather not serve operationally with Messrs Wood and Joy. The Commandant's Warning that was Tanner's birthright on arrival at Lympstone has long been rescinded. Everybody loves Mike – the batch, the DS (save Tom Coyle who still has some lingering doubts: 'He's getting there but it's still touch and go whether he can actually pass the Commando Course') – so everybody wants him to succeed. It's been hard, he's failed physical tests, died halfway up a rope innumerable times, even collapsed on yomps, but he will not give up. He wants it so much he has dropped two and a half stone on a largely beer-free diet. Mike is a character; the Rambo who in an ambush, with the troop commander and sergeant hit, slings a wounded Ostling over one shoulder, fires his rifle on automatic with the other and leads the patrol to safety; the sensitive, considerate one who during a night patrol suddenly produces his birthday cake from the recesses of his Bergen.

Mike Tanner's only threat now comes from himself. He's raised the odds from 30:70 to 50:50 but that may still not be good enough. Just like any big family even the good ones, even the loved can get cancer.

9

Welcome to the Bottom Field

Wales is nice. Wales is sunny. The only way to visit Wales is
with as much ammunition as you can carry. Wales is the sort of
place where sheep go to die amongst friends and short, hairy
cave-dwellers take their own cues to the pub for company.

Andrew Goldsmith, 'The Opal Star Lament'

THE DAY BEFORE Eagle Eye, PTI Sergeant Toby Broomes introduced the batch to the delights of BFT (Battle Fitness Training),
soon to become a thrice-weekly ritual. (While the batch were
going through training, to prevent confusion with the Basic Fitness
Test, the name for Battle Fitness Training was changed to Battle
Physical Training – BPT – but they always referred to it as 'BFT'.)
In essence IMF (Initial Military Fitness) was a series of physical
jerks whose intention was to prepare the YOs for the more arduous
and specific military tasks ahead. Watching them go through the
motions in unison IMF can take on a pleasing choreographed,
almost balletic look until they come to the ropes where upper body
strength is paramount and an Ashby can shin up like a monkey
while a Tanner is in agony trying to pull his huge bulk twenty feet
off the floor.

On the Bottom Field PT rig is dispensed with, trainers left
behind in the cabin, exercises are all carried out in 'fighting order'
– khaki denims, boots, webbing pouches with 22 lbs of lead distributed evenly between them, plus the rifle. This is PT with one
function only and that is military. The ropes, like Jack's beanstalk,
stretch up into the sky and appear to be much higher with only the
clouds for a roof. There are many others stretching horizontal to
the ground, the longest over the static tank. The rest of the assault
course comprises monkey bars, climbing nets, scant wooden

bridges, walls and tunnels. The secret to success is just to go for it, forget thinking about the hows, whys and wherefores. If you worry about a particular bit, inevitably when you reach it your brain will freeze, the body will check in response and disaster will follow.

The original military application for all this rope work is designed to complement the Marines' amphibious capability. It is all very well storming ashore on a beach only to be confronted by a barrier of steep cliffs. Obviously not many commanders are going to send their men ashore if the cliffs are heavily defended as that would be tantamount to suicide and the Marines have never believed in taking casualties if they can be avoided. To them slow and steady takes objectives, not full frontal assaults. (In the Falklands War the Royal Marines lost a total of two officers and twenty-five men killed and sixty-seven wounded. By contrast the Paras lost twenty-three dead and forty-seven wounded in one engagement, the taking of Mount Longdon.) A beach landing into a bay surrounded by high cliffs would first be preceded by either an SBS (Special Boat Service) landing or an advance party from the Mountain and Arctic Warfare Cadre who would quickly scale the cliffs, secure the position from counterattack, and lay ropes and rope ladders down so that the rest of the company can get to the top where they will not be so vulnerable. Bergens will be hoisted up later.

Concerned that they were losing too many men in training with ankle and knee injuries caused by jumping off walls on to concrete or earth hard packed by countless boots CTC has now had the landing spots covered in gravel which research has shown will be more forgiving. Some old-timers grumble that all this new-fangled technology means the men are going to be softer; others argue that in these budget-conscious times it costs too much to treat injured men simply to prove a macho point.

For Mike Tanner the trickiest part of running the assault course in the required time is squeezing through the tunnel with a right-hand bend. He had lost all that weight before Christmas but is now starting to put on extra muscle again. Matt Lodge has always been concerned about whether he is strong enough to tackle the hardest physical challenges. Now with BFT he is face to face with his potential nemesis. The most difficult skills for him to master are the half and full regains off a horizontal rope. In a full regain you snake-crawl halfway across and then hang off the rope supported only by your arms; in the half regain you hang underneath the rope with legs still wrapped around it like a sloth. There is a particular technique for getting back up which most people manage, especially as the alternative prospect is immersion in the static tank. The pressure on your arms is enormous and until you get used to the extra encumbrance of pouches and rifle they are a real distraction, as well as adding in Matt's case an extra 15 per cent to his body weight.

If the first term was an introduction to soldiering skills, a taster of what is required and of the hardships that must be endured, the Easter term is a long hard grind. It may only be fourteen weeks but they can appear to stretch to infinity. There are still the dreaded drill periods and now new sword drill periods which initially resemble the antics of circus clowns trying to ape the knife thrower. The classroom lectures are increasingly directed at specific military tactics; the current affairs talks concerned with the geopolitical situations in areas like the Middle East and Northern Ireland. There is even a day when the YOs practise riot control techniques against a mob of very eager and potentially homicidal Marines.

It is assumed that by now the YOs can navigate their way to their objective; the job now is how to deal with it once they get there. This is the term in which they learn how to be soldiers. The theory of troop attacks, anti-tank defence, trench warfare and amphibious assaults is all confirmed by field exercises. It does not take long to realize that out in the field anything that can go wrong does and that Mr Joy should not be allowed to hold anything with an offensive capability more dangerous than a potato peeler.

In February the batch moved to Sennybridge in Wales for a back-to-back twelve-day exercise – Quick Draw 2 followed by Opal Star. The batch were not looking forward to their time in Sennybridge Camp and displayed a somewhat uniformed attitude towards the local inhabitants, instantly mollified once they discovered that a local pub had unexpectedly flexible opening hours.

On arrival Gav, the Duty Student, lined the YOs up and issued the immortal command: 'OK, there are two huts allocated to us. So it's the good guys in one, wankers in the other.' Everyone knew their place without being told, though Brian Adcock mused: 'Where was I to go? Where did the wankers have to go anyway?' before heading smartly for the lads' grot, while Steve Hussey after unloading the truck with a Bergen slung over his shoulder walked up to Gav and asked matter-of-factly, 'Which one did you say the wankers were in, Gav?'

Any division in the batch, however good-humoured, was instantly bridged when they spotted the common enemy. Until now the YOs had had only passing contact with members of the Army. 'Our bad initial impression of Wales was only forgotten when we rolled into camp and met a strange dirty group of people – Pongos,' recalls Tim David. 'It was my first encounter with this strange arm of our forces. The standard uniform of shell-suit trousers and dirty T-shirts set them apart from any nods I'd seen before, their amateur attitude to whatever they seemed to be doing reinforced my views that Sergeant Coyle was right with his "scabby Pongo bastard" description.'

The batch's limitless capacity to consume beer in a local pub – quickly rechristened the 'Crimson Carnivore' by Tom Coyle – taught them a vital lesson: Welsh pubs only shut when the last customer walks out. This phenomenon gave rise to the formation of the Half Past One Club (open to members of the Training Team as well as YOs), a discussion group in which frank and open views on members of the batch past and present were aired. After one incident on the live firing ranges the conversation became not so much heated as apoplectic.

Quick Draw was a live-firing exercise, but firing while on the move not at static targets, though Wolsey, for one, considers the regulations remove any real training value from the experience. 'Firing live rounds yards from people's heads when they are on the floor in section attacks or standing behind them eighty metres away and firing over their heads is not allowed unless the weapon is fixed on concrete stanchions in the ground and firing at a fixed point,' he explains. 'You are not allowed to wave it around, or disregard the safety regulations to make it more interesting.

'The experience of hearing the rounds go just over your head is important; it's unique, like a whip cracking, it breaks the sound barrier. It means that if you hear it for real in Northern Ireland you know what it is and how to react. The only thing you can realistically hope to do in training is get people to react to the unexpected and unpredictable, so you have to get them to think in a lateral fashion, not in a blinkered unimaginative way. Training varies enormously from year to year depending on the characters and personalities involved, meaning that each year you are turning out a different officer within certain guidelines and limitations.'

Accordingly the occasional liberty was taken with range regulations which showed the batch that reliance on the properties of blank ammunition during training can prove difficult to cure and proved especially sobering for the more hung over members of the Half Past One Club. 'The proximity of live rounds close to one's precious swede,' says Chalkie, 'called for special tactics from the outset and in addition the packing of an extra pair of trousers.' While Dan Bailey – who despite being described by the Team as 'the world's worst radio operator' had recovered from a poor start and was taken off warning before Christmas – comments: 'The exercise taught us that friendly fire can kill (or make people on the 9 mm range duck very fast) as effectively as enemy fire.'

'Much of the exercise resembled a five-a-side soccer selection ritual at school,' adds Robinson, 'where people jockeyed for position to be in each others' teams and tried to avoid the attentions of the fat guy with two left feet, who in this case manifested himself in the form of "dead-eye Joy" and other members of the self-styled sniper troop.'

These are oblique references to the incident that can only be described as Pete Joy's finest hour – though it might so easily have ended up as a real-life version of the climax to Sam Peckinpah's classic Western, *The Wild Bunch*. On the firing ranges one section were busy plinking away with their Browning 9 mms while on the range next door Joy's section were involved in a simulated attack firing live rounds. He was holding an LSW and firing it on automatic while running forward. Seeming oblivious to shouts from the Training Team he stormed into the 9 mm range, firing as he ran. Fortunately no one was hurt but several were, in their own words, 'scared shitless'.

Joy himself described the events as follows: 'We'd already stormed several target areas, veering first one way, then another, running like bastards wet and muddy. The sergeants were coordinating our movement by means of yells and gestures but with ear-defenders on and after firing several hundred rounds from my infamously awkward LSW human speech was almost impossible to decipher. Half deaf in one ear and with an ear-defender jammed in the other I took the DS's shouting (as it later transpired "Stop, stop") for yet another yell to move forward and stormed a falling plate [target] in a pit, firing my LSW at it from what turned out to be an inadvisable angle. My error was the result of communication problems in a high pressure situation – I simply couldn't hear what the DS were shouting and misinterpreted them. The batch was so impressed with my textbook demonstration of the dreaded blue on blue that it was highlighted in "Thought for the Day" and the chaps returned the favour by sniping at me for the rest of the exercise.'

As an excuse that sounds reasonable enough, but not when taken with other incidents like losing his rifle, bayoneting the rifle target in Week 5 and appearing to be in dreamland much of the time. Any lingering doubts his batch mates had about Joy ended in that fusillade. Most of them let the matter rest there, only making the odd snide remark. 'We only really came close to death once, when Pete Joy did his Mad Max psycho on a live section attack and nearly wiped out the group on the 9 mm pistol range,' noted Steve Hussey. 'The sight of men taking cover on the 9 mm range as Mr Joy let loose across the valleys offered confirmation to many of the previously unconverted as regards the danger of the less switched on man with an LSW on auto, no less than to Mr Lodge who was glad for once of his insubstantial height,' commented Russ Corn dryly.

However, the most damning indictment, which summed up the extent of batch feeling, came in Jools Ostling's essay on the exercise. Ostling, who by now was under a cloud himself, since he had fallen down in his command appointments on both Long Knight and Eagle Eye, let rip his frustrations most eloquently.

'The thing that stood out more than anything to me is how dangerously stupid Mr Joy is and how stupid the Corps is for paying him any more for a single day. Since he ran in front of friendly fire at Sennybridge he's been paid another £450 in wages when it must be clear by now that he's got absolutely no chance of ever finishing the course. He can't even look after himself so how could he ever be allowed to command thirty soldiers? He didn't exactly redeem himself on Opal Star – he hung out on the yomp in, made a bee-line for every hole, trench or bog whilst everybody in front of him stepped carefully round or over them, and on top of that, he also managed to lose his respirator. The guy is totally shot away, and he can't even see it. He's under the impression he's really good – the typical nutter who thinks he's OK, it's the rest of the world who are mad. The penny has to drop sooner or later – he's a liability.'

Quick Draw was summed up succinctly by Gav Parr: 'The weather was shit, the food even worse so it made for the perfect week of live firing. We did have the use of our Goretex which made up for the weather. However, we couldn't eat them, so we still had to put up with the food. When the live firing stopped the novelty of being in Wales quickly wore off and nobody wanted to meet Matt Skuse's relatives anyway.' After four days dodging bullets, but living in the relative comfort of the camp's wooden huts guzzling the finest local ale, it was time to hit the field again for Opal Star – a six-day exercise in which the YOs were to meet some other new and passing strange fauna.

'Now and again, strange vacant-eyed creatures hove into view, bleating nervously and picking their way open-mouthed in no particular direction. This I was assured was Percy,' says Goldsmith. 'The only real difference between Percy and the sheep was that the sheep had better ambush drills – presumably due to their higher intellect. Another strange creature met on this exercise was the Cloggy. Rustling and chattering through the night, this plastic bag wielding and amiable animal issues chocolate and hot coffee to anyone who'll stand still long enough. No one could say they weren't friendly but how effective as soldiers?'

Opal Star was a joint operation with Dutch Marine YOs on their final exercise. Much has changed in the world since 1704 when Dutch and British Marines combined to take Gibraltar. Then they were considered equals but now the difference in training techniques, skills and ability sets them far apart. Russ Corn, who by Week 20 was becoming certain that the Sword of Honour was his but for the drawing, announced: 'As the Dutch are considered able soldiers I quake to think what some of the other European forces have to offer.' It started with a helicopter insertion that unaccountably stopped twenty-four kilometres from the destination and necessitated a yomp in; after half way the Cloggies were so shattered that their Bergens were taken by four-tonner and they limped the rest of the way home in their fighting order.

The Cloggies might not have been able to yomp but Shetler-Jones still could not give a halfway decent set of orders. 'I was fortunate enough to witness this historic military event,' says Pete Evans, 'and the crucifixion which followed under the guise of Captain Wolsey's debrief.' Particularly memorable was this exchange: 'Yes, Mr Shetler-Jones, the patrol commander should carry a Bergen as well. No, you can't fit ten ration packs in your respirator pouch.' Despite this inauspicious start Shet thoroughly enjoyed 'his first decent command appointment with a bit of freedom to operate'.

Dan Bailey had a less successful time: 'As I was section commander the section trusted me unfailingly to find the way and not get lost. As I was section commander I trusted Sergeant Baxter unfailingly to find the way and not get lost. We arrived at 1030 having got lost.'

The batch were, for the first time, allowed to wear their 'Gary'. To a soldier in the field the scientists who invented Goretex are considered humanitarian geniuses on a par with Mother Theresa and Albert Einstein. A fabric that keeps you dry but also breathes, allowing the sweat to escape without letting any moisture back in, can make all the difference between being totally miserable and reasonably cheery. The only danger with Goretex is that if you get soaked inside the water cannot escape either.

Not everyone got to enjoy Gary's benefits on the yomp, which was immediately livened up when one section was crossing a small river. Neil Watkinson went to throw his Bergen over to the other side, missed and watched it fall straight into the fast-running stream and be carried over a waterfall. Eventually his section picked themselves off the floor and after commiserating with him, thinking how unlucky he was to already have wet kit, found the heavens opening and 'we all got pissed on, before we could get the Goretex out'.

'All the trepidation of spending five whole days in the field with the added bonus of a weekend thrown in was channelled into an irrational hatred of all things Welsh, at least for those tolerant, understanding charismatic Yorkshiremen in the batch,' recalls 'Shaggy' Ashby, unable to resist a quick dig at Messrs Corn and Harker, before digressing on to other matters. 'Before Quick Draw, I had failed to appreciate the diuretic effects of Pussers' tea, our urinary tracts are now as clean as the Virgin Mary's reproductive system while our bladders are like Garth's.

'The only time it didn't rain when I've been to Wales was in May, when it snowed. Anyway I was yomping along sweating my tits off, cursing the designer of that extra comfy load-carrying device on my back and my major worry was still that I was getting wet. After three hours in the haven of my Goretex I finally summoned the courage to peel it off. Cue rain. Kit on. Kit off. Kit on. Ad infinitum. Luckily the Commonwealth contingent [Henry and Jackson] was struggling, necessitating ten-minute stops every five minutes. Luckily I was carrying the radio so I could hear what was going on. Unluckily we seemed to be stuck in the largest re-entrant in Wales meaning comms were non-existent. Who needs sweat bands when you have the headset of a 351 channelling the sweat into your eyes and ears ? Oh well, at least I won't have to carry the bastard after tonight. Imagine my surprise when the change in orbat [order of combat] came through: Radio operator Ashby!'

In the varying terrain of the Welsh hills the importance of 'comms' was quickly driven home. After watching Adcock struggle with deciphering the same message for four hours Ashby kindly announced that from then on he was always going to put his most 'switched-on' Marine in charge of the radio. The message was hammered through a day later when Gav, still under a cloud and now on Commandant's Warning, was sent to do an OP on their intended target – a small dam.

For nearly twenty-four hours, soaked through to the skin despite their Gary, four YOs, concealed about two hundred metres from the dam, observed the comings and goings of the enemy. The problem was that they were lying in a ditch out of radio comms with their base. Back at the harbour position Andy Harker, now acting as troop commander, pontificated, 'Don't undertake any patrol without comms, it's pointless.' When Coyle finally found them, after an hour of searching which might have said something for the YOs' increasing ability to meld into the undergrowth but did nothing for his temper, his critical assessment can be roughly bowdlerized as: 'You fucking ignorant bunch of useless scrotes, if they can't hear you back at HQ you might as well be dead ...' Although Pete Evans, who had been suffering in the OP alongside Gav, was quick to support him, insisting that they had done the best possible in seriously adverse conditions, the big man bit his lip and carried the can, admitting: 'The orders I gave were not detailed enough and consequently the OP failed and I failed the command appointment – something I can ill afford to do.'

Some years in February Sennybridge can be under a foot of snow. This year everything was wet, the damp got everywhere, despite Goretex. If there was a gap between neck and collar, between lace and boot tongue it crept in, water droplet after droplet searching for weaknesses, chinks, holes – anything into which it could creep, fester and spread its soggy plague. Every time you breathed the damp hung in the air, hovering overhead like an aqueous falcon waiting for a rabbit to drop on and drown. Not so much cold as chill, but a chill that works its way into the marrow of your backbone, making camp there, ousting the previous inhabitant so that you believe that even if you get dry, you will never be warm again.

The YOs and the Cloggies had their 'troop harbours' in the same dank dark wood, surrounded by the same straight soggy pines, blocking out what watery sun there was. The method of setting out camp was different. 'I went to the company commander's orders group to find a neat symmetrical camping site and several very large stony-faced Dutchmen varnishing their weapons,' says Robinson. 'The orders were a general chat about the weather and a hazy chat about the procedure for the night attack but slightly scant in detail. For example, many of us had forgotten to bring our chequered picnic rugs and we did not know the words to their camp fire song.' He was however greatly impressed by the Cloggies' ability to eat even more and do it even faster than the batch, a feat until that time generally deemed to be impossible.

Charlton 'Jacko' Jackson and Trevor Henry found the mud and the nagging cold increasingly tough to cope with. By this stage on the course their initial positions had reversed. Neither had volunteered for YO training, they had been given forty-eight hours' notice of going to Lympstone and it appears as if they were pinged alphabetically, those JDF officer cadets with surnames ending A–G being sent to the less demanding environment of Sandhurst. For anyone brought up in a sub-tropical climate, England sweltering in a midsummer heatwave is still a one-sweater day, but Sennybridge in March, nestling in the rain shadow of the Brecon Beacons, is evil. The extra allowance they had been given to cover winter clothing stretched only to a set of thermal underwear, but long johns and Goretex alone cannot focus a wandering mind.

Trevor, the JDF equivalent of a Corps Commission, had enlisted as a private but on applying for promotion to corporal was offered the opportunity of a commission. He started the course well but as the grey winter days dragged on was increasingly running on empty; indifferent and deeply pissed off he contributed nothing, lagged behind on the yomps, slept through his turns on sentry and spent every other available moment inside the comfort of his sleeping bag.

Jacko, three years older, was better educated and had come through grammar school. He had been completely horrified to begin with, wrapping on the Tenderfoot yomp and wondering what the hell was going on. Although he and Trevor stuck together socially, Jacko was enjoying the charms of a great many young English girls and fitted more easily into the social groupings of the batch. Though he too was crippled by the cold he had dug deep and found a previously unknown reservoir of determination and spirit that impressed his batch mates. Although the Team were still underwhelmed Jacko was already talking about the possibility of earning his green lid on merit – something he believes never to have been achieved by a Jamaican before.

To their credit the YOs are colour blind and did not often resent their presence, understanding that unlike them the Jamaicans had no choice about being there. 'Trevor's different so we just have to endure it,' groans Harker. 'Like on this exercise and he's in his bag hunched up against the cold so we just say, "Don't worry, Trev, we'll make you a hot wet and cook your rations." Sarcasm never seems to penetrate, perhaps he doesn't understand Marine humour. He always seems to be dead serious with his line when he goes on sentry duty – "wake me up when you come to relieve me in a couple of hours".'

'It was tough for them, they did well to stick it out as much as they did,' noted Ostling. 'Everyone realized they would never have to see conditions like that again, they weren't going to do Arctic training in Jamaica! Russ had a go at Trevor for being useless once early on, but we considered that to be out of order. But occasionally Trev overstepped the mark, I was standing there when Gav thumped him.'

Because of the cold, sentry duty was carried out in two-man groups: each stood guard for an hour, staggered at half-hour intervals. Ostling takes up the story: 'Me and Harks were on sentry and Trevor dragged his sleeping bag up. They were ten yards away, Gav had already been on half an hour and said: "Don't get in your sleeping bag, you'll just fall asleep. I've been on with you before and you slept through the whole thing." Trevor was just saying "Fuck off", standing up for himself, which was quite brave considering it was Gav. Then we heard this boom and scrambling about. "Get out of your sleeping bag." "Fuck off." "If you say that again I'll thump you." "Fuck off." Boom. The next thing we heard was "I'll get you for this, next time I'll stab you like a true Jamaican." Trevor always was a bit of a waster, but he was better after that.'

A night patrol did not go too well for Pete Joy, who had earlier in the day had some problems with a mortar. 'Try as I might I could not make the 51 mm mortar barrel fit the wrong way round, nor could Sergeant Baxter when he tried. How we laughed when we realized our mistake. That night my respirator also went AWOL from under the top of my Bergen but Messrs Hussey, Lodge and Attwood gladly volunteered their services to help me look for it. I couldn't help thinking it was a pity I'd packed it at all.'

Hussey as section commander was less than thrilled: 'After a night operation my section were in need of rest and all had just got their heads down when I was informed by the troop commander that my section was tasked with doing a patrol to find Pete Joy's respirator. I did not perform my task well as all the section were "threaders" [fed up] about the whole idea and ready to let him pay the price for a new one. We found it and were able to return back to the harbour to find out we were on sentry – life's a bitch!'

At least a night ambush went well. At 2300 hours they had installed themselves just inside a small copse less than fifty metres above a well-used track and after installing various trip wires settled down, preparing to wait for several hours (encouraged no doubt by the stories Billy Baxter had entertained them with earlier in the day of the time 'I waited three days in an ambush and no one ever came'). After only forty-five minutes a ten-man army patrol who were several miles wide of their intended destination meandered down the track. Trip wires set off thunderflashes, flares lit up the night sky while the fusillade of fire was so intense that it was surprising that a Pongo did not die of heart failure. They were so taken aback that all of the ambush team had emptied their first magazine before one of the 'enemy' got a shot off in return. The proper enemy had planned to make their appearance at 0300 but with the ambush site compromised the batch returned to their harbour delighted at the prospect of an extra two hours' sleep.

Usually the men left behind in the harbour to guard the batch's Bergens are considered to have proffed – until Ashby founded the 'FRV Club' which decreed that henceforth those left behind at the

Final Rendezvous should seek to make themselves as uncomfortable as humanly possible. Thus it was that on returning from one Night Navex the batch found a shivering Shaggy wearing only his underpants.

The preparations and orders for the dawn attack on the small dam again showed the difference between the YOs and the Cloggies. Andy Harker – he had been given the command appointment by Wolsey who, competitive as ever, was determined to show how much better his boys were – was so bemused and confused by the orders he was given that he completely rewrote them before issuing them to his section commanders. Displaying true English ethnomania when confronted by a foreigner, only a few members of the batch remarked on the Dutchman's ability to give his orders fluently in two languages. Brian Adcock at least noticed it before adding, 'The company commander's orders took the piss out of the old adage of writing your orders on the pack of a fag packet – everything we had been taught seemed to be left untouched. On the night move from the harbour position they all had their torches on so they didn't walk into things or trip over twigs.'

Martin Wood, encouraged by the sight of an ally who was even less equipped than he to command men, said: 'The Cloggies made Tenderfoot look like a covert op and in fighting spirit showed the guile and tenacity of a Kit Kat wrapper.' The Cloggies' use of cover was another revelation – they preferred to walk along the brow of a hill, until they reached the top when they would mill around in a large group before getting out their torches to consult the map. Even Welsh sheep do not present such a perfect silhouette or target for a watching sentry.

It was not just the Dutch who screwed up. Chalkie Stovin-Bradford was in command of the fire support section covering the southern and only approach road to the dam. Having recced the ideal position in daylight he intended to lead his men below the skyline into a fire position fifty metres above the road but covering both angles of approach. 'About thirty metres from this road I was alerted to the fact that perhaps all was not going well when the words "Mr Stovin-Bradford, you fucking cunt" resounded all around the countryside,' he said in his debrief. 'It was explained to me that the Dutch Marines were located only fifty metres further up this road and might possibly mistake my fire team for enemy.

Upon strong advice I decided to move back the way I came looking for a new fire support position. I would like to stress at this point that *I was not lost*. I was however tactically extremely naïve.'

The attack went in successfully although the Cloggies' tactics surprised many, including Rob Lunn. 'Differences in tactical doctrine were shown by our NATO comrades in arms. Their legendary prowess in the scran queue was not matched by their tactical awareness: in all good Warminster manuals the ideal angle between assault and suppressive fire teams is given as 90 degrees whilst the Dutch prefer to assault head on into their fire support. Removing one's boots in tactical situations is apparently another RNLMC [Royal Netherlands Marine Corps] Standard Operating Procedure.'

The orderly withdrawal and 'reorg' (reorganization) brought Opal Star to a satisfactory conclusion though the batch were less than happy to discover that the Cloggies rushed straight to the head of the breakfast queue because they chose not to clean up first. The rest of the week was to be spent in an equally muddy mental environment, learning about trench warfare in the classroom. The only thing worse than learning about trench warfare is having to do it and that involves a delightful little foray on Salisbury Plain known to survivors as Busaco Ridge.

10

The Spirit of the Somme

He dropped – more sullenly than wearily,
Lay stupid like a cod, heavy like meat,
And none of us could kick him to his feet;
Just blinked at my revolver, blearily;
– Didn't appear to know a war was on,
Or see the blasted trench at which he stared.
Wilfred Owen, 'The Dead-Beat'

THERE IS A horizon somewhere out there but you can't see it any more. You know there is one because it was out there yesterday and the day before that. One of your oppos claims he saw it earlier but face it, he's been talking gibberish for the past half-hour. As for last week you can't say and anyway you don't give a shit. Last week this was all just pie in the sky stuff (just like the clouds up there that resemble a squad of abseiling Santas) – interminable lectures from Shagger Shaw, really practical stuff for a Marine officer to know – minefield rescue drills, infantry/tank cooperation, battle trench construction, troop and company defence tactics. You're being trained to be a troop commander. Your job is to yomp for ever and an extra mountain, then attack, not just sit here in this hole staring out at what was once a horizon. Oh Christ, there go the Santas again, they've landed and turned into the DS … they're inspecting the machine-gun trench, or is it the one with the anti-tank weapons?

You have never been so tired, sitting on this trainee Somme battlefield, somewhere in Salisbury Plain, lying, sitting, sleeping, shitting in this thing you hacked out of mud, blood and blisters with a little help from some corrugated iron – two earth coffins six foot deep by six foot long connected by a sleeping tunnel so tight as to give a potholer claustrophobia. You have to live in that dirty hell-hole and you hate it, it isn't half as comfortable as it would be rigging a bivvy in that little copse over there. The whole batch could disappear into that and the Pongos wouldn't notice for a week. Hating, yeah hating helps, it gives you a moment off from staring at the horizon that isn't there any more, waiting for tanks which are never going to come and if they do you'll probably think it's Billy Smart's Circus come to cheer up the lads. So you hate. Three things in ascending order of hatred.

First off you hate Matt Skuse. He's always been on the edge of being a swim-forty-miles-dagger-between-the-teeth merchant. Remember that time he was section commander on Eye Opener, walking along the path when he suddenly flung himself, apropos of nothing except a desire to show the DS he was a Welsh bonehead, into a ditch and crawled along it until he came up covered in mud and grass and water. No, you hate him because here he is sitting in a fucking trench staring at the horizon like the rest of you but he can hardly walk. The biff has a stress fracture of his foot but he insists on joining in everything, yomping along on his crutches. You hate Skuse because you're so damn tired and he keeps on smiling. He cannot be enjoying this, no one ever enjoys Busaco Ridge. Except Tanner.

You hate Tanner a bit more than you hate Skuse because Tanner has a command appointment. This means staring at that sodding horizon has some meaning to him. He's in charge so he's not so bloody tired, and when Shagger Shaw suggests something to him he nods his head because he understands, not because it's the only way he has to stop himself falling asleep. Tanner keeps sprinting over to your trench and whittering on about the predicted enemy tank attack and your first thought is, 'If they would only mark me as dead early on I can have a rest'; then you remind yourself that you're a Royal Marine officer and you laugh and then it's time for another go on sentry duty and you can stare out into the middle distance, swearing there used to be a horizon out there but now it's Les Dawson and Bernard Manning doing the can-can dressed in frothy pink and turquoise tutus.

What you hate most, what you really hate, is Pongos – horrible smelly bastards from Sandhurst, with voices that make the Boss sound like a coal miner; all over there to the left snug in their battle trenches and you're just a bloody adjunct on their exercise. You can imagine some smart stuck-up Guards officer saying, 'Oh we need some more young men to make up the numbers on the right flank. Could we have some of your lovely little Marine officers? Of course we haven't got enough JCBs, they'll have to dig their own trenches, but you boys like doing that sort of thing, don't you?' And you don't but you did anyway and that is why you hate Pongos, or you would if you weren't so tired from staring at the horizon that you're beginning to think Pete Joy's punch-drunk stare actually masks the only sane path to spiritual enlightenment.

You haven't left the trench in three days but you can live with the stench, you're used to that after Opal Star. It was wet then but this is worse as you can't yomp it off and so you just sit in this trench, freezing your bollocks off, listening to Skuse prattling on in forensic detail about one who wasn't smart enough to get away. It's so cold that you can't go to sleep so you start dreaming about the yomp into this hell, hoping that somehow physical memory will turn you warm. A long yomp, well, that's becoming second nature now, even if you were weighed down with enough ammo to start a war, lugging around GPMGs on heavy tripods, fixed anti-tank weapons and radios the DS promise will actually work this time. That was the easy bit. For once you didn't get lost coming in, even the blister on your heel stopped hurting after a while and that new non-Pussers chest webbing works a treat, so your Bergen doesn't feel as if it's resting on your belt prior to tearing half your arse out.

But then you got here and all the Pongo DS got terribly excited and showed you where to dig. So you chucked your Bergen on the ground and you unclipped your Pussers 'entrenching tool' which until now had proved more than adequate for burying gash, digging a latrine hole or even excavating that mortar trench that was deep enough to drown in on Long Knight. But you only need three inches of water to drown in and they want you to dig something deep enough for a bloody tank to roll over, so then you can leap out and shove a potato up its exhaust pipe or whatever you are supposed to do to disable a bad-tempered, centrally heated, armour-plated velociraptor with a fucking great gun manned by undersized, unwashed Pongos. So you start to dig before dawn and you keep on digging as the sun rises, burrowing away like a platoon of moles excavating lump after lump of rock the size of a football. You've been digging for twelve hours and it seems like half a lifetime and you realize that this metal thing you're digging with is fucking useless and then just when you've had enough you look over and see how the Pongos are doing.

And you see the Pongos are doing just fine, thank you very much. Standing around in schoolgirl gaggles watching while a bloody great bulldozer digs the trench for them – six scoops in under ten minutes and then they can move in to paint the walls with sheets of corrugated iron. A machine has done more in ten minutes than you have done in sixteen hours and you look at your hands and all you can see is a bottomless swamp where your palms used to be, a mess of broken blisters, caked blood, dried pus and dirt caked so deep you could be Trevor but you don't want to be reminded of him because you just know he's jacked it already and won't dig any more. So you look hopefully at the diggers and the DS tell you to keep putting your back into it, and you feel like crying because you've been digging for eighteen hours now and the fucking hole is still only four feet deep. Then dawn comes up for the second time and your spade is now glued to your hand by escaping bodily fluids and they tell you that the diggers will help for the last bit. That's nice, you think, and it is except it's not over yet, there is still the interior decorating to be done and you have to build the connecting tunnel between the foxholes.

So you try and bend the bloody stuff and the wooden stakes you put in as guard rails keep bending and your oppo looks at the roof and whistles between his teeth, mutters something about how it will never hold and you tell him to fuck off and then you start piling twenty-four hours of dug earth back into the middle of the trench. And you are so threaders, so flakers, you don't know what the words mean any more and you think 'at least now I can get some rest'. Except you can't because you're stuck in a bloody trench staring at the horizon for the closest thing to forever and you can't sleep because the bastards are making you run a one-in-three sentry routine – an hour on, staring at the fucking horizon and then a whole thirty minutes off. So you fall asleep and before you've stacked up half a dozen winks some cunt is shaking your shoulder and it's back to staring at the horizon.

Now you're beyond threaders and still you're stuck in the fucking trench, no patrols, no nothing, and the ration packs no longer look like the mud you're still digging through in your dreams, now they actually taste of it. And in another attempt to keep awake you've run out of the tepid brown shit that passes for coffee and so you really are starting to see things. Yes, you're hallucinating now, or you think that's what it is except half the time you can't actually put a name to the things you see. That was Tanner, not a brown bear on a unicycle. So to get some sort of grip on what's left of your reality you start to swap hallucinations. And Jezz says, 'Look, there go some penguins in tuxedos', so Paul looks out into the middle distance and says he thinks that is pretty normal behaviour for penguins. 'Yeah, I know that's pretty normal,' says Jezz, 'but these ones are different. They're breakdancing.'

About that time you get really depressed and start quoting Wilfred Owen war poems but something happens which is a great relief as you can't remember more than a couple of lines. Out there in the distance something appears that isn't a penguin or a bush masquerading as Les Dawson. Shit, it's a fucking recce tank, a Scimitar, and suddenly you don't need your bayonet to prop open your eyelids, you're so far beyond exhausted that it's like dancing in a dream. Then the assets start coming in, a brace of Tornadoes screaming as if Death was behind the joystick; skimming over your head, once, twice, three passes they make, arrogant falcons sweeping the ground giving you poor rabbits a chance to go to ground. On one pass some prat rattles off a full mag – sure, Rambo, you just know you bagged a fat zero. Then it's the turn of the hornets courtesy of our Crab brothers, the A10 tankbusters, nasty little monsters that can take out an APV with the flick of a switch. You get real for a moment, have a flash of precognition and decide that trench warfare is extremely dangerous, for these things have smart bombs and you are sitting in a very dumb trench.

Now you have to fight, there are tanks coming from everywhere – well, it seems like everywhere but there aren't more than a handful of them. Fuck, they are big and mean, especially when they decide to drive over your trench. Breaking all the rules of war – get your fucking head down! – you stand in the open foxhole and you watch this monstrous metal underbelly thundering towards you so fast that even if you could run away it would catch you and squash you like a bug. You dive into the tunnel just as it blots out the sun and then you pray because there isn't anything else to do now. As it goes overhead you can hear the four feet of earth you packed groaning and complaining; the corrugated iron splits in three places into jagged mocking edges, and the edge of the trench starts to crumble and then the monster's gone. Except you know it's not for

1. The batch in civilian clothes on 5 September 1991

Front: Lodge; *Second (from left):* Lunn, Collins; *Third:* Rowley, Bailey, Attwood; *Fourth:* Stovin-Bradford, Ostling (obscured), Henry, David; *Fifth:* Manson, Goldsmith, Jackson, Thomson (obscured), Joy (obscured), Baxendale; *Left side from back to front:* Woodall, McInerney, Harker, Corn, Robinson (Manson); *Back row:* (Woodall), Tanner, Ashby, Shetler-Jones, Parlour (Manson); *Right side from back to front:* Skuse, McQueen, Webster, Hussey (Baxendale); *Back row:* (Woodall), Tanner, Ashby, Shetler-Jones, Parlour (obscured), Parr (obscured), Adcock, Harris, Watkinson (obscured), Evans, Wood (obscured)

Colour Sergeant Jordan

2. Exercise Tenderfoot – early morning PT (*left to right*): Parlour, Tanner, Harker. Parr behind Harker, Shetler-Jones behind Parr

3. Exercise Tenderfoot – Andy Goldsmith enjoying early morning PT

4. Russ Corn at the morning kit inspection on Tenderfoot

5. Collins taking notes on Tenderfoot

6. Lunn after the yomp back to CTC

7. Matt Skuse cleaning boots in his cabin

8. Batch receiving orders on Final Nail. *Front row* (*left to right*): Ashby, Attwood, Adcock; *Second row*: Baxendale, Skuse

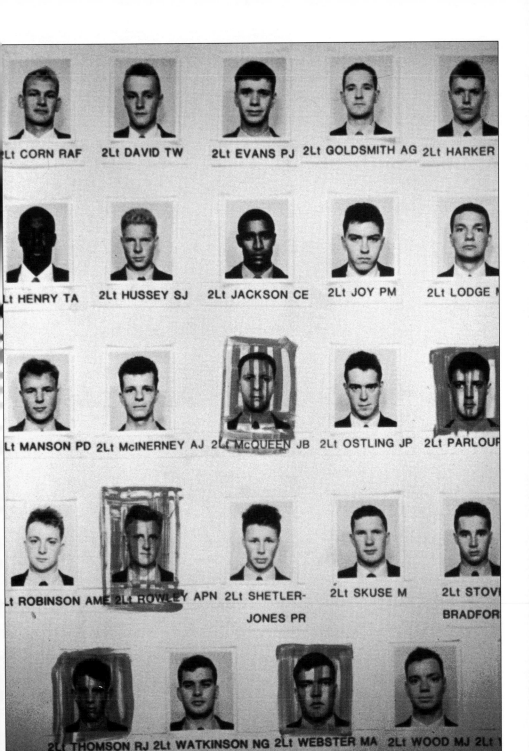

9. The batch poster – note the crossed-out names

10. IMF in the gym – Harker on the ropes

11. BFT – Jackson giving Attwood a fireman's carry

12. In the static tank. Adcock (*left*) and Harker are supporting Henry, (*behind*) Joy

13. The Mud Run. Attwood (*centre*)

14. McInerney on the Tarzan Course

15. Ropes over the static tank. Lunn (*right*) encouraged by Jackson

16. Busaco Ridge: Stovin-Bradford (*front*) and Lodge about to be run over by a
tank

17. Goldsmith, cigarette in mouth, briefing Skuse on Opal Star

18. Busaco Ridge – Jools Ostling

19. The Endurance Course: Lodge being pulled through the water tunnel by David. McInerney on the other side

20. The Commando Course. In the caves at Ashburton before the candles went out. *Front row (left to right)*: McInerney, Baxendale, Robinson

21. Pete Evans during the first Commando test – the 12-mile Load Carry

22. The third Commando test. The Endurance Course. Woodall (*front*), Harker and David crossing Peter's Pool

23. The Commando Course. Rob Lunn enjoying roping on Foggin Tor

24. Final Nail: Jezz Woodall clearing the *Ramehead*

25. The Thirty Miler: The first syndicate finishing, escorted by RSM Steve Perry. *Front (left to right)*: Skuse, Watkinson; *Second row*: Lodge, Baxendale; *Third row*: Ashby, Stovin-Bradford

26. The Thirty Miler: 'We've finished.' *Back row (left to right)*: Manson, Shetler-Jones, Parr, Corn, Harris; *Front row*: Sergeant Coyle, Mike Tanner

27. Mark Wolsey posing during Crash Action

28. Russ Corn receiving the Sword of Honour during Pass Out

29. Pass Out

2Lt. G. Parr RM 2Lt. B. Adcock RM 2Lt. P. Ashby RM 2Lt. R. Corn RM 2Lt. A. Harker RM Sgt. T. Coyle PW1

Mne. R. Keefe 2Lt. N. Watkinson RM 2Lt. P. Shetler-Jones RM 2Lt. P. Evans RM 2Lt. M. Tanner RM 2Lt. J. Woodall RM 2Lt. T. Harris RM CSgt. M. Jordan DL

Sgt. D. Phillips PW1 Sgt. T. Broomes PTI 2Lt. D. Bailey RM 2Lt. M. Skuse RM 2Lt. A. McInerney RM 2Lt. A. Goldsmith RM 2Lt. R. Baxendale RM 2Lt. P. Attwood RM 2Lt. T. David RM Sgt. W. Baxter ML

CSgt. P. Clements DL 2Lt. C. Jackson JDF 2Lt. Stovin-Bradford RM 2Lt. A. Robinson RM 2Lt. P. Manson RM 2Lt. M. Lodge RM 2Lt. S. Hussey RM 2Lt. R. Lunn RM 2Lt. T. Henry JDF CSgt. G. Foster ML1

Capt. D.G.D. McKinney MBE RM Capt. A.D. Shaw RM Capt A.M.S. Bailey RM Capt. M.A.R. Wolsey RM Col. M.A. Taffinder ADC Admiral Sir J. Slater GCB LVO Major M. Sturman RM
DS4   DS2   Batch Officer   Commandant   Commander in Chief Fleet   OC OTW
Training Officer   Capt. S.D. Miller Glosters DSI Capt. S.G. Newing RM DSI Capt. G.A. Pearson RM DSAO WO2 A. Tweed RM WSM

real because if that was a real mean bastard it would have straddled the top of the trench and ground from side to side until the whole fucking thing collapsed on top of you and your mates, leaving you all to drown in that coarse earth you'd spent two days shifting. And you think there are quicker ways to dig your own grave but by that time the tanks have gone and it's time to launch a counterattack.

At last you're out of the trench and you run screaming for ten yards before your head clears and those lessons you've been trying to remember for the past three days boot up inside the parts of your brain that can still function as a computer. So you counterattack and you retake a trench abandoned by some Pongo officer cadets, then you reorg with Tanner shouting at you and there's Skuse on his bloody crutches and you think 'couldn't one of the umpires have declared the gobby bastard dead' but then it's all over, you think you've won but if the truth be told you don't give a damn, though Tanner does, and you have to move out.

So you go on another long slog through the night but you're at the back of this infinite chain of Pongo officers who walk so slowly that you finally understand Coyle's hitherto unfathomable and irrational hatred for them. Then just when you decide to stop hating them for a bit they all get on a bus to go back to God knows where. Except you don't go back with them, oh no, you have to go back to that fucking trench and fill it in. By hand. So you crawl into the tunnel to pull out the short pickets before you remove the corrugated iron. And you pull out one and you never make the second because you pass out right there on the floor and someone comes in to kick you awake and you try another one before you crash out again. So you crash out for five minutes and someone kicks you and so it goes on and on. Then you get a break and you drop your spade and you sit down to pick it up and you wake up next to it a few minutes later with no idea who you are, what that is and why you are here. You fill in the trench all night and finally it's done and you get into the four-tonner for the trip back to Lympstone and you don't even remember your arse touching the floor.

And you sleep all the way back and you don't dream of anything because this week you've had all your dreams out there in the open while you were awake. When you wake up you're going through the gates at CTC and the first thing you see is Andy McInerney who's still got on his thousand-yard stare, the one he's been using all week when he's thinking about his girlfriend. But this time you really don't give a fuck because you're so tired and the first thing you have to do on Monday morning is a full drill inspection and you haven't got any clean kit.

Busaco Ridge was no fun. To Andy McInerney it was hell on earth. 'Busaco Ridge was my personal hate. I didn't know what was going on, I was stuck in a trench, the first forty-eight hours was solid digging, mucking out in a Wrigley Tin and filling in holes. I was just so tired, I wasn't able to get out of the trench, do anything, see anything. I didn't do a single patrol in five days, never saw over the horizon. As it was the army there were at least good assets, a mega air display but as I didn't have a single command appointment it was dreadful.' There were other problems too – he went into the exercise both physically drained and emotionally battered. The cause, as usual with members of the batch, was a combination of attempting to burn the candle at both ends and the middle, coupled with girlfriend troubles.

He may look and sometimes pretend to play the part of an old Etonian cavalry officer but in fact Andy Mac's background, which he does nothing to hide, is rather more prosaic. His father worked as personnel director for London Zoo before taking early retirement and Andy, the youngest of three, went to the local grammar school before reading zoology at Sheffield University.

'To get to go on expeditions you need post-grad qualifications, and all I had was an advanced A level in basic research techniques. I booked a year off after my degree and worked as an office clerk while I wrote out all my applications. It was pretty obvious I was going into the services.

'I've been forces pissed since I was about sixteen,' he says. 'I did an AIB for the Navy to try to get sponsorship as a pilot – I'd just been to see *Top Gun* – the rejection letter is still one of my prized possessions. At university I did a lot of TA which was just a paid drinking club. The Royal Marines didn't occur to me until two years ago – I did the POC, only because a friend had done it and I thought "if he can do it so can I". The Navy also appealed until I had a better look at it. I also had an offer from the 9–12th Lancers. I went on a POC with them but they were really slack. It's true what people say, soldiering got in the way of their social life. They were concerned with putting on this air of being a cavalry officer. I thought I could do well professionally – if not on the private income side – but I was worried my ideals would become corrupted and bend towards theirs after a while.'

Arriving at Lympstone he had the usual university legacy – a girlfriend, Andrea, with whom he had lived for the past two years. Just before Busaco Ridge he discovered he had a free weekend and induced a couple of batch mates to drive him up to Sheffield for a party. Not having a car and his determination to cadge lifts all over the country had led to Mac being pejoratively referred to as 'the Hitcher'.

'The plan was perfect on paper, the party was going to be great,' he says. 'I could see all my friends, surprise the girlfriend, have plenty of sex. Instead she walked into this formal dinner and ran out of the room crying – it was promising to be a good evening until then. Her reason was that every time we see each other she has to say goodbye within twenty-four hours, whereas before we had known every daily detail of each other's existence. She felt cut off, says she doesn't know what I'm like as a person any more, what motivates me.

'So I stayed up all night until the sun rose talking to her. It was very bad manners to the guys I was with, I had to farm them off on other friends,' he continues, displaying the somewhat blinkered view of relationships shared by most members of the batch. 'The next night we drove back to Exeter, went out to a nightclub and got trashed. Eight of us ended up naked on the stage, all of us pulled some girls and then it was straight out on Busaco Ridge which is why it was my nemesis. I had plenty of time to stare at the horizon, to sit and feel glum in a trench, but you can't feel so sorry for yourself when you are fucked. When we got back to camp I wrote to her saying, "If that is how you think, fine." '

It was not the end, of course, but there were still a few more good hands to play before resolution. And a few legs, too, but they belonged to Matt Skuse and Jools Ostling. Serious, if not life-threatening injuries are an inevitable part of YO training. The worst type are the nagging muscle tears and strains which have no outward manifestation but which, as was the case with Rory, get steadily worse because there is no time to rest the injury. Some YOs manage to dredge up a hitherto unrealized mental stamina to fight back from such injuries; more do not.

A stress fracture is a common enough injury for soldiers. 'Your legs,' says Tom Coyle sagely, for once refraining from gratuitous insult, 'only have so many miles' running with boots on.' Everyone is built differently but the constant pounding of heel and sole in boots which were not designed by an orthopaedic surgeon builds up a constant pressure. A series of small bruises or pressures continue to build up until eventually something has to give – a bone in the leg or foot cracks under the pressure. Anxious to avoid too many stress fractures the Royal Marines, to their credit, have done a lot of research into avoiding them, or minimizing the risks – hence the gravel covering on the Bottom Field – and regularly employ Simon Costain of the Harley Street Gait and Posture Centre to advise on injury rehabilitation and non-recurrence. From very early on various members of the batch put Sorbathane heels or insoles into their boots to reduce the pounding and many, as soon as Wolsey gave his permission, ditched Pussers issue for lighter, more comfortable ergonomically designed footwear.

The appliance of science is all very well but not very comforting when you have just sustained a stress fracture. The only cure is rest and that is one ingredient in very short supply in YO training. All the medics can do is wrap bandages around the affected area, excuse the man from doing BFT for three weeks, issue a pair of crutches and a couple of platitudes they know are impossible like 'take it easy' or 'put your feet up'. The worst part, psychologically, is that it does not look like a broken bone, and while the initial reaction from one's comrades is sympathy that is soon exhausted and the injured man finds himself teased, wound up and generally abused by everyone. He becomes the batch scapegoat.

'When Matt Skuse got injured he was tolerated, hobbling about behind the batch for a week or two,' recalls Andy Goldsmith, 'until one day we turned round and practically bit his head off. Everyone had got sick of his "Oh that's all right I'll just struggle along behind" playing the martyr. Sometimes the rapidity with which we could turn round and snap was frightening. It was just like a wolf bitch eating one of her lame pups.'

The problem for the injured man is that he can see everything he has striven for slipping away. The memory of Rory Thomson becoming more debilitated and slowly dragged under was still fresh for Skuse. Suddenly he was a member of the batch only on sufferance because he couldn't do what they were doing. It's OK, in fact something of a pleasure, to be excused BFT for a couple of days, but not for weeks. He can see that there are techniques to be learnt and mastered if he is to do it properly. Nagging away at the back of his mind is the worry that if he does not get himself back in boots soon, too much time will have passed and he will have to be back batched, which means joining the May '92 batch – close to another year of doing the same exercises again, and no matter how experienced he is, nobody would want to do Busaco Ridge again. Skuse, a man of not many written words, describes 'the broken foot and all the misery, the feeling of fucked upness that went with that' as his low point in YO training.

Matt's foot got better, though not completely, as it decided to show itself again at a crucial juncture. No sooner was he back up on two legs than the sick bay had to hand his crutches back out to Jools Ostling.

'I discovered afterwards that my feet were a bit flat, which put uneven pressure on them. The right one ended up with a stress fracture on the shin, from running in boots and yomping,' says Jools. 'It happened five weeks before Easter, they kept giving me painkillers which made it much worse, there isn't room in the course for an injury like that. I had two weeks off BFT but it wasn't enough.'

To some members of the batch Jools's injury seemed like a long overdue vengeance of the gods. Until that time he had never had a problem with the phys but his military performance had been on a steady decline since Christmas. His distrust of the middle-class nature of the Corps' officers had increased rather than diminished and he deliberately flouted the customs of the Officers' Mess by inviting recruits and other ranks to his cabin for a drink. He found it hard to hide his contempt for the less physically gifted YOs, like Lodge and Tanner, and increasingly followed his own training regime.

'No one should fail the phys because they start you at such a low level. I could cream guys like Lunn and Hussey in anything we did. I used to go down the gym every day and do all my own training,' he says, and then pauses as if this thought had just struck him for the first time. 'Maybe that is why I busted my leg. Overtraining. Months after it had come out of plaster, if I went running it came back. In the end I had to pull out of training all together, let it recover and start with the May batch just before summer leave. It did give me a good opportunity to learn more about strategy and tactics.'

Back batching solved one of Wolsey's problems for by now he had a much better handle on Jools's personality. Nothing remains a secret for ever in CTC and the stories of Jools's treatment of Jason McQueen had reached his ears by January. Wolsey is a man to whom physical things come easily, perhaps too easily, but underneath the arrogance is a compassionate side. To him bullying is intolerable; the weak should be allowed to confront their own failings and either overcome or succumb without malicious interference. From that moment on he wanted Ostling on warning and preferably out. The fact that he was screwing up constantly, as much as he was screwing around, helped. Because of the time it takes for the warning system to take effect it is just possible for a bad apple to slip into the YO basket and not be found out before he leaves Lympstone for a unit.

It may sound hypocritical when discussing the self-policing carried out by the batch, but in its own black-humoured way the YO wolf pack has honour. Above all else if you dish it out you have to be prepared to take it and Jools, hobbling around on crutches, was now vulnerable. The death-watch beetle forever calling time on the others now had little else to occupy him. His verbal targets were the same – Wood, Evans, Joy and whoever else was butt of the week. Funny thing was he never looked in the mirror, never saw the target tattooed in the centre of his forehead. For the first time since he came to CTC Ostling had lost the balance of power. He was no longer one of the strong, his future lay in the hands of those who were once weaker. How forgiving would they be?

Mike Tanner, for one, had had enough. He could read the prevailing wind and see that Jools was out as far as the batch were concerned, but he didn't want to see Gav Parr dragged down in the mud with him. 'Jools seemed to get a bit silly about it. He started off really keen but after his injury he lost all enthusiasm, his only pleasure in life became picking on other people. He nearly took Gav down with him. Gav Parr is an excellent soldier, a good bloke as well, and didn't need that.'

Gav had enough problems already. He was still lurching along on Commandant's Warning but the Training Team's negative opinions were beginning to mellow. He now spoke to Wolsey regularly seeking guidance and survival pointers. He in turn was coming to terms with what being an officer entails, the top of his head was enlivened by some hairs with the potential aspiration to become curls.

'When Jools Ostling got injured people were quite keen he shouldn't come back,' understates Matt Lodge, usually generous to the San Andreas fault when describing his colleagues. 'I don't deny I found Ostling difficult, not initially but as time went on. I got on with and had a tremendous respect for Gav, but Jools and Gav were not good for each other. I know Gav still thinks about going, he feels a bit persecuted by the hierarchy for his previous mis-demeanours at Dartmouth. He is well liked within the batch, he pulls well, is a very unselfish team player and popular as a result.'

By this stage most people were aware that Ostling's behaviour was based on insecurity and that to cover his own shortcomings he would divert attention on to others. Even Pete Evans who detested him decided to forgo blatant revenge. Instead the batch set about freezing him out of their lives. 'It's difficult to talk to anyone when they are going down, there isn't anything you can say to someone on the way out. I'm amused by irony and it is a case of just rewards, so a lot of people are breathing a small sigh of relief. I won't say he wielded that much power but he was a bloke it was difficult to get on with unless you really went out of your way to do things his way,' said Andy Goldsmith, before making a typically cynical prophecy. 'To start with he's done most of the exercises already so he'll probably end up as lord of the roost with May batch.'

'Ostling was indeed the chief persecutor and it was noticeable once he was injured how quickly the character of the batch changed,' says Pete Joy, who had suffered much and while less inclined to charity was considered in his appraisal. 'Everyone sud-denly seemed more relaxed. Even those who'd shared in Jools's ridiculing sessions and a number of YOs remarked what a pleasant batch it was to be in now that Jools had gone. He wasn't an "evil" guy, he was simply good at acting a particular role. In truth he didn't enjoy training any more than I did and had almost no real friends. I only regret I didn't shut his mouth with a fist back in Week 9 or so.'

It is a subtle process but the batch were used enough to render-ing the recently departed non-people, so adapting their behaviour to a physical presence was not that difficult. They always spoke to Jools in the bar, still went out with him, but somehow it was as if he had become their younger brother − always hanging around, forever underfoot but never fully understanding what they were talking about, never really part of the gang. By the time the batch came back from Easter leave Jools was the Mess equivalent of Banquo's Ghost, walking the corridors lamenting his lot, breathing poison into ears that were no longer inclined to hear. Not gone, not quite forgotten but no longer dangerous. Or so they thought.

The Games People Play

If you know the enemy and know yourself, you need not fear
the result of a hundred battles. If you know yourself and not
the enemy, for every victory gained you will also suffer a
defeat. If you know neither the enemy nor yourself, you will
succumb in every battle.

Sun Tzu, *The Art of War*

FROM THE VERY first day of training Matt Lodge was carrying a
monkey upon his back, constantly gibbering away in his ear – the
knock, knock, knock of doubt, questioning whether he could
handle the physical challenge. It was a personal battle he was
determined not to lose, though two of his bottom teeth did give
up the unequal struggle and fell out, leaving a grin that resembled
that of a cheeky street urchin from the cast of *Oliver*. Despite
working hard at the ropework in the gym he did not enjoy life on
the Bottom Field and as the time approached for the BFT passout
the smile became a frown which even regular visits from Amanda,
who had taken a job in Exeter earlier in the year, could not
smooth out.

On the other hand, to a man who can do one arm pull-ups on
sheer rock faces the Bottom Field held no terrors. During BFT the
batch were continually being told to do three circuits of the Assault
Course, at the end of which they had to crawl through a tunnel.
There are five tunnels to choose from but no one ever uses anything other than the bottom two because that would involve a little
extra exercise, like running a few more yards. Except Phil Ashby
who would dive into the very top one, crawl halfway along and
stop. Having counted slowly up to one hundred and forty, which
he had worked out was the equivalent to a relatively fast circuit,

once or twice – depending on how idle he felt – and then reckoning that most people were going round for the third time he would crawl out and nonchalantly join in again.

For the BFT passout the YOs have to do a thirty-foot rope climb, complete the Assault Course in four and a half minutes, fireman carry a similarly shaped and sized colleague (Parr and Tanner, Jacko and Attwood, Lodge and Lunn) also wearing fighting order two hundred metres in under a minute and finally do a full regain over the static tank. Come Thursday 2 April Ashby sailed through. Lodgie however had worked himself up into a bit of a mental state. Brow furrowed in concentration he moved uncomfortably and when the time came for his go he took off like a startled rabbit. It was going fine until he came to the half regain; the tension in his arms turned them to unyielding rock, his coordination went, and try as he might he could not pull himself back up. Three times he tried, three times he failed – each time his fighting order weighed heavier, but he never gave up trying again and again until eventually Toby Broomes told him to stop. His time had run out and all that he could do now was exhaust himself.

Matt was gutted. 'It must have been nerves,' he repeated over and over. 'I have never had a problem doing the half regain before.' He passed it easily enough the next day but it was to leave another question mark of self-doubt hovering at the back of his mind. Matt Skuse, still recovering from his stress fracture, had to wait until after Easter leave when he passed BFT easily, while Jools Ostling with his leg in plaster also had to wait his turn.

Being in plaster did not stop Jools and other self-appointed members of the batch police force from keeping the pressure up on Martin Wood. He was approaching the end of his third month on Commandant's Warning and had become the focus for constant sniping. He suffered most at the hands of the batch, but in their eyes it was deserved, as he failed to give proper orders time and again. That made him Harker's particular *bête noire*. 'If Wood is at the end of the receiving line after the Thirty Miler I won't take my green lid back if he is to get one too,' snarled the Yorkshireman who forgives little, but incompetence in the field not at all. 'I always leave his briefings feeling I know more than he does.'

People would do ridiculous impersonations of Wood, portraying him as some kind of whimpering cretin. After visiting the tank museum at Bovington, Wood got on the bus with his suitcase to be greeted by Ostling saying, 'Don't bother to unpack that, you'll be needing it soon.'

'Some people did give Martin and Pete Joy a hard time, trying to help them on their way,' says Brian Adcock. 'Someone put a note up on the board saying "Fuck off Martin Wood" – you would like to think intelligent blokes could do better but by then it had stooped to animal instinct and the stronger personality would always force through what he wanted. I'd like to say I didn't join in but someone will probably contradict me. I wasn't into persecution because I suffered from it myself when I was thirteen. I had just changed schools and I did well on the sports field with boys a year older than me but naturally I let everyone know about it and so I got bullied.'

Just before the batch went to Cyprus for a week of Adventure Training, Wood was withdrawn from training. 'He just wasn't learning as quickly as he should do, information wasn't going in, he wasn't able to assimilate it, to show he had learnt anything,' says Wolsey, explaining the decision. 'His reaction was not at all surprised; he told me, "My previous boss had always said he would be amazed if I passed and I guess he was right."' Wood's reaction is pretty typical of the man – a shrug of his shoulders, a nonchalant 'I gave it my best shot' and it was back to the girlfriend in Exeter, concealing what he really felt. Knowing the axe would fall eventually he had laid the groundwork and had been accepted to do postgraduate work at his old university.

Wood had never fitted into the batch. He was a fantasist, infatuated with the romantic idea of being a commando, but either incapable of understanding or unable to make the real commitment which being an officer entailed. Contrary to his protestations he found it hard to accept his failure. Two months after he was thrown out of Lympstone he bumped into members of the new May batch in Exeter and, according to Jools Ostling, told them he'd been stalking them out on Woodbury Common during their Tenderfoot exercise, claimed to have crawled around their bivvy bags and joked that he was now going to be a mercenary in Bosnia.

'In training people are judged on their military prowess,' noted Tanner. 'There never was any period you thought "he's a good bloke, he's just crap in training". Martin Wood was doomed from the beginning, he might have been the world's best bloody character but he was never going to get anywhere because he couldn't prove himself in a society that only proved itself by being good in work.'

With Wood gone that left only Gav and Pete Joy on Commandant's Warning. Gav had climbed a long hard route back and for all his devil-may-care image was determined not to fail. Whereas Joy avoided Wolsey 'like a leper', Gav had learnt from his earlier attempts to ingratiate himself with the Team and instead concentrated on learning his fate – and some good moves – from the Boss. Just before they went to Cyprus Gav was told his warning would be extended until the end of August. Believing the same thing applied to Pete he told him the good news.

With the Commando Course only a month away, beckoning him like sanctuary, Pete was not taking any chances. 'The day the batch left for Adventure Training in Cyprus we sat Progress Test #3. The night before I had shut myself in my cabin to revise for this test and only found out five minutes before it began the next morning that the rest of my colleagues had spent the previous evening frantically studying two copies of the selfsame test kindly provided by the May batch. My exclusion was probably an over-sight – with thirty people in two rooms frantically looking up the answers, it would have been every man for himself. Worse, this paper was full of things we had not covered – how to construct a helicopter landing pad for example – things Sept. '91 could have only found out by a rapid reading of the observer sections of our hefty manuals. When we went to Cyprus I was a very worried man.'

The batch's attitude to all written work, essays and tests was that of a co-operative. 'The course written tests were originally designed for eighteen year olds who had just left school, so for most of us the tests were not that intellectually taxing,' says Matt Skuse. 'If you ask a graduate to learn fifty facts he can do it pretty easily, he has been trained to do that. Sometime they would flaw you with an obscure mnemonic for stoppages on a GPMG or GRIT (Group Range Indication Target, a classic fire control order). At least with signals tests one did have to learn and remember things but tactics were so simple. You did have to work for it but whether by accident or design the batch were kept very busy the week before a test so the revision would begin at 11 p.m. the night before.

'The simplest solution was to pay a visit to May batch and

inevitably someone had smuggled out either the test questions or the answers and once you knew that you were pretty well home, because there was very little variation from course to course. In the past it has been known for members of other batches to attempt to sleep with the secretary to get the questions,' he grins, 'but our batch – even Neil – absolutely refused to do this because the secretary was a man.'

For essays on non-batch subjects they developed a sophisticated tutorial system to aid the weaker. Depending on the subject, one of the batch – Ostling on economics, Lodge or Lunn on international affairs – would give a brief five-minute pen picture spelling out the basic issues, which everyone would note down and could then expand upon. When Wolsey set the essay topic 'What is it that gives a batch its spirit? Are your batch mates the type you'd expect to find in OTW?' Goldsmith composed this conclusion: 'In summary the construction of a cohesive batch can only be achieved not by mindless conformity but instead by the individual efforts of each of its members.' This was then distributed to everyone else so that the final fifty words were identical in each essay. The Boss had read through a dozen essays, scratching his head at this strange coincidence before he realized that his batch did indeed have a lot of spirit ... and a sense of humour to boot.

On occasions snap tests were deliberately intended to be too difficult, failure an excuse for a beasting. In January Wolsey decided that the boys were getting a little above themselves – 'I can't imagine who they got it from,' he grinned – so during Eagle Eye he had the Team busy scouring the newspapers for the obscurest questions they could find. He had forgotten about Rob Lunn with his first class degree in international affairs from the LSE. Rob confounded them by knowing, among other things, the Spanish name for the Peruvian Shining Path guerrillas (Sendero Luminoso) and even spelt the name of the Serb president correctly, enabling him to pass a current affairs test specifically designed to make the entire batch fail. Not that it made any difference, for when the batch were taken out for their midnight beasting Rob went along anyway.

'I was in the shit either way,' says Rob, 'so I just went along for the ride. They dropped us from a four-tonner miles from camp with instructions to make our own way back. Actually I ran back all the way and quite enjoyed it.'

'We all failed the current affairs test except Rob Lunn so we

were all paraded at midnight to hear the bad news,' recalls Rory
Thomson. 'Everyone had the feeling something was up so we had
packed all the necessary survival tools — Visa cards, torches and
maps. Lunn was given the option of going back to his cabin but
chose to stay with the batch. There were three four-tonners and
the worse you had failed the further you were dropped from camp.
We were in the last lot and as we stopped Shaggy swung on to the
roof and the rest of us milled about outside so Wolsey couldn't see
there were only nine of us. The DS searched the back of the lorry
but they didn't look on top where he was hanging on, then he
jumped down into the back of the truck otherwise the sentries at
CTC might have shot him. We started running back while he got
his car, came back out and picked us up.'

Such hi-jinks appealed to their Course Officer. While he could
not be seen to approve of such initiatives, he always knew more
than it might have appeared. More of a problem was the cocky
swagger with which his charges strutted around camp and he
resolved to cool their collective ardour with a batch dunking in the
static tank.

Certain YOs were already close acquaintances of the static tank.
In the first ten weeks the Team had joked that Shetler-Jones should
take out a season ticket. However as Shet appeared to be physically
indestructible, impervious to pain, cold and discomfort, it was not
an effective deterrent for him. Others were desperate to avoid it —
even during his last days at Lympstone Trevor Henry would shudder if he passed within ten metres of the tank. His horror dated
back to just after Easter leave when Wolsey had dunked the entire
batch in the freezing tank for half an hour.

'You have been criticized by various members of staff for being
slovenly, sloppy and arrogant. You are therefore going to be punished,' Wolsey announced before turning to Watkinson, the Duty
Student. 'Parade the batch in three ranks inside the static tank in
ten minutes' time.'

At the appointed time Wolsey arrived at the tank to find the
smaller members of the batch already up to their necks in the
water. He leapt in to join them, expelled a whoosh of air and then
held up a piece of paper saying, 'I have seven different points of
complaint that I have received about you. We will stay in the tank
until you can tell me what they all are.'

Some of the complaints they got quickly enough: poor turn out in the Mess, dressing contrary to regulations, bimbling around the camp, not paying attention to outside lecturers ('but sir, they are so boring'), being late for detail, 'being arrogant little fuckers, sir'. Running out of ideas and starting to get pretty cold they then started to hazard guesses about things Wolsey didn't know but was interested to hear about – the time they had females in the Mess without permission, treating Mess staff poorly. They got six right, by which time Adcock and Robinson had gone blue with cold; Trevor had gone into panic mode (being a lousy swimmer) and after the first five minutes had had to be held upright by Adcock and Harker, while David was beginning to find the weight of Wolsey's shell too much but dared not drop it. After thirty minutes they gave up the unequal struggle and instead started to tell jokes to keep themselves conscious. Chalkie, who had to lean his head back to keep his mouth out of the water, won the prize with a particularly revolting punch-line about John McCarthy and Terry Waite.

Not wishing to kill anyone Wolsey finally let them out, although he appeared to show no signs of cold whatsoever. 'Are you wearing a wet suit, sir?' demanded Adcock between chattering teeth. 'No, Mr Adcock. I'm just tougher than you are,' he lied, for as he confessed later he was wearing 'a very thin wetsuit which meant I was as warm as toast'.

(YOs enjoy – if that is the right word – the delights of mud runs and long immersions in the static tank far more than recruits. In military training the dividing line between 'disciplining' and 'bullying' is often indistinguishable to the uninformed observer. Recruit troops can only be taken on a mud run with the Wing Commander's permission and under the supervision of a PTI, while only individuals can be immersed in the static tank. The *pour encourager les autres* principle now only holds true for officers. 'Pretty well anything goes for YOs,' says Wolsey. 'We have more of a free hand to treat them harshly. Putting the entire batch in the static tank can be seen as simply testing their resolve!')

Life in the military often requires lateral thinking, the ability to get around the system in order to get anything done. Wolsey is a past master at it and like any good teacher wishes to impart such knowledge to his pupils. The batch trip to Cyprus was a perfect example.

'The trip to Cyprus was a good ruse. I discovered there was money in coffers that needed spending and I secured enough to get air tickets to do some adventure training,' he says. 'We stayed in the Officers' Mess in Dhekelia. It was a pleasant and relaxing break before the Commando Course started. I wanted also to show some of the more pleasant things the services have to offer, the facilities that are available so that they would learn how to tap into this vein and when they go on to lead their own men can tap into it for their benefit too. You teach them how to access it and they go and do the same.

'Every day we were doing a PT session followed by climbing, water skiing, parascending, windsurfing, helicopter abseiling from two hundred feet up – there was a slight military angle, a bit of drinking and a lot of enjoying yourself.'

That is something of an understatement, for the town of Ayia Napa in Greek Cyprus is a favourite holiday destination for Scandinavians, about the only people in the world who take having fun and drinking to excess as seriously as a bunch of YOs. 'Some people were coming in from nightclubs at 5.30 in the morning having just enough time to take off their glad rags and put on PT rig,' says Wolsey. 'At times you could smell the alcohol on their breath. There was a lot of trapping, or at least I hope so, as I told them "go and have a good time". There was only one small problem discipline-wise, no one got into serious trouble except when Skuse was late for PT. He arrived looking very sorry for himself.'

'I woke up on the wrong side of the island, twenty miles from the PT session,' confirms Skuse. 'I hadn't even had sex because I got so drunk I passed out. All I remember is she had a missing tooth and I spent ages spelling out the letters on her tattoos. We got a taxi from this club, then a lift in a minivan and then on a moped. In the morning, for some reason, she got really stroppy so I got the hell out and found myself standing by this lonely hut on a dirt road with nothing but scrub around in every direction and I didn't know where I was. I walked three miles, got a lift and got back four hours after PT. Paul Attwood was the Duty Student and I asked him if Wolsey had asked if everyone was there.'

In such cases the batch Duty Student was in a tricky situation. He always knew if someone was absent, but the rule of thumb was that unless he was asked a direct question he would not volunteer this information and therefore would not have to lie or turn the absentee in. At the same time he would detail another YO to try and find the missing man. In this case Attwood, asked if everybody was present and correct, had had to admit, 'No sir, Skuse isn't here.'

'So I went over to the Officers' Mess where Wolsey was having lunch and excused myself,' continues Skuse. 'He told me: "You've made a cunt of yourself, haven't you? If you can't handle getting pissed up and turning to for work the next day, you shouldn't do it." "No, sir." "All right, dismissed, you're on my shit list now." "Thank you sir."'

Harker later described Cyprus as 'the longest, most intense sleep deprivation exercise I've ever been on'. It was full of incidents, not all savoury, usually fuelled by an excess intake of alcohol, though somehow nobody ever managed to top the episode of the Sennybridge Chuck-up. That was the legendary occasion when on returning, somewhat inebriated, from the pub two members of the batch had inadvertently thrown up over the sleeping form of a third. The next morning, he had equally accidentally defecated in the miscreants' boots. It was simply an unfortunate coincidence that the gentlemen had pulled on their boots before eating their breakfast.

Humour was generally good, which may not have been unconnected with the absence of Jools Ostling, who was obliged to stay behind in CTC, and whose comrades could not be said to have missed him. Sometimes things got a little out of hand. 'Gav Parr and myself had one particularly fractious occasion,' says Brian Adcock. 'He was pissed up and sleeping on my bed. I pushed him off on to the floor, he took a swing at me so I pushed him down again and Bob Rob had to stop me from ramming a cricket stump up his nose.' Shaggy and Neil also ended up exchanging blows. 'The two most passive, pacifist guys in the batch – both complete and utter weirdos,' recalls Tim David. 'One night they both got pissed and tried to kill each other. For a while we were laughing too much to separate them.'

Andrew Goldsmith and Billy Baxter, realizing that they were both walking cripples, took to comparing injuries over the odd beer. 'I have had a few physical problems which I thought would not let me into the Corps,' admits Goldsmith, before commencing a litany of complaints that would have an orthopaedic surgeon reaching for the aspirin. 'In '84 I dropped a weight bar and took off my right knee cap, sliced off the top, and threw it round the back of the joint. They had to put that back, I had a lot of physio, it still operates but grinds in cold weather. Two years later I took up karate and had my left knee kicked completely out of joint, a side-ways dislocation: when I landed I compounded the injury by frac-turing the outside of the joint. That was reset, I slowly recovered until I started to play hockey and found I had lumps of cartilage floating around in the joint. I had three operations, two of which weren't successful. I still have a lump floating around which seizes up – I'll be running along, go to swing my leg and suddenly the knee won't bend and I just pile over. It has always made me ner-vous jumping around assault courses, waiting for the knee to buckle, it makes nasty noises and aches like hell.

'The last two vertebrae in my back are fused together as the result of an industrial injury caused lifting heavy weights, further compounded by playing rugby. I went to see an osteopath who basically said "well, you're fucked" and tried to break my joints loose. There was lots of cracking and no luck. It makes load carry-ing uncomfortable – if I put my Bergen on I can't bend over to pick my rifle up, I have to bend from the knee. I can do the job – I just have to do it slightly differently, and if that means laying my weapon across my boot before putting the Bergen on so I can flip it up and catch it, so be it.

'I'm a bit of a wreck but fortunately these things never all come together. If they happen next month on the Commando Course, I'm finished.'

Many blondes were trapped, though the prize for the most pub-lic place to commit a private act was won by Dan Bailey and his Finnish partner inside a phone box in the middle of Ayia Napa's town square. That evening Bailey had no need for the most com-monly used form of transport – hired small motor bikes – but it was hard to get the Jamaicans off theirs and into the bars. 'One early evening,' says Chalkie, 'Trevor was cruising past us when he turned round to say to Jacko "Look how cool, man!" Smack. He drove straight into the back of a Land Rover. There was nearly a major pile-up as the rest of us fell off our bikes laughing.'

Wolsey went one better. He celebrated the birth of his first child, Millie, by passing his bike test (very easy and cheap in Cyprus) and buying a Harley Davidson from an Army officer. Amelia Wolsey had been born on 24 March 1992. 'Fortunately it wasn't a particularly busy part of the course, at least it wasn't during the Commando Course,' he said, forgetting who actually bears children. 'I didn't find it any particular pressure as I have broad shoulders, it added another dimension to what was going on.' Funny how selective the memory of Royal Marine officers can be. In fact it was his wife Fiona who remained ridiculously calm throughout, while for several weeks before the baby was due Mark took to carrying a bleeper with him wherever he went, toying with it nervously in the Mess or local pubs, or scratching nervously at the slowly healing scar under his right eye. The arrival of Millie also allowed the YOs a new insight into the character of their batch officer.

'Before she was born he used to joke that if the baby turned out to be a girl he'd drop her off a bridge,' says Mike Tanner, 'but you have never seen a more proud father. I remember Fiona pushing her around in a pram and the Boss just couldn't keep his eyes off her. It showed us that beneath all that arrogance he is really a nice, caring guy.'

In Cyprus there were other quieter, more reflective moments. Phil Ashby, Shet, Brian and Pete Joy sat in the garden of the Mess all evening drinking brandy sours and just talking through the night. Fortunately Tom Coyle was drinking a different bar dry and so never heard one of Ashby's ruminations that would have confirmed the sergeant's oft-voiced suspicions that Ashby was an undercover CND operative. Phil expressed a somewhat fanciful wish to be a Greenpeace Raider – 'I'd probably see more commando action than I will in the Marines,' he said ruefully.

'It is surprising how rapidly an individual loses his place in the batch,' mused Pete Joy. 'Collins, Parlour, that Northern bloke – half forgotten names. Even Andy Rowley, once the life and soul of the batch, has now ceased to exist in its collective consciousness. These names are only jokes now, to add to the lexicon of Pussers terms we all now spout. Batch spirit is an exclusive entity. Sadly it excludes girlfriends and many of us have already chosen which to hang on to.'

For Pete Joy, to this day, that evening remains one of his happiest memories of training. He was at peace, relaxed and ready to tackle the Commando Course.

12

Yomp or Die

I am giddy, expectation whirls me round,
The imaginary relish is so sweet,
That it enchants my senses.

William Shakespeare, *Troilus and Cressida*

'STANDING IN THE corridor drinking G&T in the last few seconds of "normal" activities on Friday 29 May there was amongst those members of the batch still awake, a sense of anticipation not unlike that felt by six year olds waiting for Father Christmas,' recalls Andy Goldsmith. 'The batch was in good humour, good physical condition and ready to accept anything that didn't actually require death. We had got wet enough earlier.'

Fresh back from Poole a scant few hours earlier they had paraded at 1600 hours to be met by a stern-faced Wolsey who said: 'Once again you have been criticized by various officers at Lympstone for which you are going to be punished. Therefore I want all of you to go and submerge yourselves in the static tank and parade back when you have done it.' Upon their bedraggled return Wolsey noticed that Steve Hussey had dry hair. 'Mr Hussey,' he said softly, for Wolsey seldom raised his voice, 'exactly what did I ask you to do?'

'To submerge ourselves in the static tank, sir,' came the bemused reply.

'Mr Hussey, what is the dictionary definition of the word submerge?'

'To fully immerse in water, sir,' said Hussey, the penny dropping as the faces of his comrades around him either dropped to their boots or glowered at him. 'Attention to detail, gentlemen,' said Wolsey. The whole batch was then ordered to re-submerge themselves in the static tank before being allowed to change and return for their brief upon the Commando Course.

'Well, gentlemen, I can assure you of one thing,' Captain Wolsey announced, 'whatever you may have been told by other batches about their Commando Courses yours will be very different. All that has happened so far is teaching, from now on you are going to be tested. The physical content will be relentless and you will be tested to the full. Your course begins at 2359 hours tonight from when you will be on one hour's notice to move. Your kit is to be ready at all times, standing by, for whatever detail you are given; the idea is to simulate as close as possible the chaos of war, so you won't know what you're doing or where you are going until you get there. From now on you are to expect the unexpected, be prepared for the unknown element in everything and the subsequent dislocation of your expectations.

'I expect the telephone on your corridor to be manned at all times and it will be picked up within three rings. Failure to comply exactly with instructions will result in severe penalties being incurred which may involve nausea and sleep deprivation. That is all. Gentlemen, good luck and good hunting.'

So the time has finally come upon the batch. Thirty-four weeks of training and it comes down to this. Four weeks at the mercy of the Boss and all the schemes he has been cooking up with the Team since God knows when and all you know is that at the end of it you have to pass five Commando tests to win that green lid and that four of them will come in the last three days. Dislocation of expectation has already begun and how. Batch 'int' (intelligence), which follows such sneaky routes as grilling the waitresses, who are employed by an outside catering firm, as to exactly when they are booked to eat in the Mess, or sneaking a look at the Training Programme in OTW, has for once failed miserably. For a start they had all been under the impression that Exercise Sea Urchin in Poole (an introduction to landing craft and SBS procedures) would last until this evening and that the Commando Course proper would not start until midnight on Sunday. As they file out a few are cursing the telephone calls they are going to have to make to girl-friends – bang goes their last cuddle for a month. Most are simply excited, finally feeling they are on the Course.

That morning there were twenty-seven members of the batch intending to start the Commando Course. From midnight there will only be twenty-six and Gav Parr – as ever – is on his very last chance. 'I was given an ultimatum: perform to the standard expected of a young officer or look for a new job,' he said to his mates in the Mess that night. For Pete Joy there were to be no more chances. As of now he is out, binned, and will not be taking the Commando Course. Joy took the news very badly.

'The group identity had always required frequent sacrifices of stragglers – people like Rory Thomson and Martin Wood, and also McQueen, were mercilessly ridiculed and certain YOs openly gloated when they left. It made them feel more secure, you see. I too got my share once I was on warning and therefore "fair game",' he recalls, suffering to the end from an inability to see himself as others saw him and from a certain naïveté. 'This is particularly hard when you cannot go home at night to recharge your batteries. Rather than reply in kind I opted to sit things out, drove the two hundred and thirteen miles to my girlfriend in Leicester most weekends and waited for the sanctuary of the Commando Course to arrive.'

The Commando Course had become Pete's Holy Grail; he believed that if he could survive that long he would get his green lid, and with it, magically, his confidence and self-respect would be restored. From then he believed the switch would turn back on and he would complete training – albeit at the bottom of the batch, not towards the top as he had once expected.

'Unfortunately,' he continues, 'I didn't get there. Although I was finding training a demoralizing experience, wrapping was not an option. Quite apart from my sense of determination I had not seriously considered any other job and in the middle of the worst year on record for graduate employment it hardly made any sense to throw myself on the dole queue owing the Corps £12,000 in sponsorship repayments. Also I didn't want to leave under the cloud of warning without my lid and give Taffinder and Grice [the Wing Sergeant Major in OTW] the satisfaction. I knew that if I could stay through Week 39 I'd be home and dry, with the pressure off. I had no fear of the Commando Course from a physical point of view. According to Gav I was to get an extension on Kommandant's [sic] Warning for another three months from Week 34. The reason the powers that be changed their minds says quite a lot about OTW and those who run it.'

The final knot in the noose Pete had been plaiting for himself since November was ironically an academic one. On return from Cyprus he discovered he had failed Progress Test #3. 'I found out I had failed by 1 per cent with 59 per cent, while my brother officers' average mark was some 90 per cent – though Trevor Henry who had seen the previous papers somehow contrived to fail as well. When I was summoned to Colonel Taffinder's office on 29 May, the fact that I had failed a progress test *on warning* was the chief item against me. It's funny to think that had I been able to recall that the capital of Georgia was Tbilisi I'd probably be commanding a troop in Comacchio or Commando Logs today. That is the honest truth.'

Perhaps but unlikely. 'There were several single grounds on which he could have been removed from training,' says Wolsey, 'one of which was his sheer liability in carrying weapons, which is after all the bread and butter of being a Marine. The number of times that Tom Coyle went up to him and gave him one of his best bollockings telling him he was a cunt for doing what he did, but if the guy still doesn't understand you can do so much and no more.'

The truth was Pete had been on the way out since he lost his rifle on Dartmoor back in Week 9 – a major indiscretion but one that could and would have been forgiven had he switched himself back on. After all the Corps had invested a certain amount of hard cash and considerably more judgement, now found to be wanting, in making him a UCE in the first place; it was in their interest for him to succeed. Pete's problem was that he could not cope with confronting his own failure; he looked in the magic mirror and believed it when it told him what he wanted to hear, told him he was up to the job. He did not look inside what he saw and realize that the only one who could stop his free fall from mediocrity into failure was himself. Undoubtedly his increasingly fragile confidence was dented by the warning system, and he suffered from being trapped in a system that wanted him out and was not really interested in resurrecting him.

'The warning system seems to me something that should be looked at. The Corps loves to picture itself as an encouraging supportive organization in training but a YO on warning gets exactly the opposite treatment,' he recalls from bitter experience. 'Left to stand outside the office for anything from one to two hours he's then called in to be given the thorough verbal pulverizing the Commandant, OC and Batch Officer have spent all this time preparing. [It may have seemed that long but Colonel Taffinder insists nobody was ever kept waiting for more than 40 minutes.] I didn't find this sort of treatment very inspiring. It seemed to me bullying, cowardly and counter-productive – the way to deal with a hardened juvenile delinquent, perhaps, but no way to motivate a Young Officer with any pride. An informal talk over a cup of coffee would have stood far more chance of rescuing my motivation – but that's not the military way and Taffinder and Wolsey lacked the imagination to think or see that. All the warnings system achieved was to put extra pressure on people who have their hands full as it is.

'Gav Parr was only on warning for being Gav. Objectively he should never have been on warning and since the batch knew it it didn't affect him too badly. In my case it turned temporary problems into ongoing ones. But at the end of the day if the Corps ends up with more than a 50–70 per cent pass rate for YOs it's not training them hard enough. So during my final interview, trying to argue to be allowed to continue, I opted not to grass the rest of the batch up for cheating the progress test even though I was given plenty of cues to do so. To do so would have kept me there but after six months on warning I really didn't give a damn whether I stayed or left, either way.

'My motivation was ultimately my own problem and if I couldn't perform as required, for whatever reason, when others could I didn't deserve to pass,' he says. 'Looking back it was a strange combination of circumstances, attitudes and sheer bad luck that caused things to turn out as they did for me. Knowing I had to serve until November '98 – the rest of my twenties – in return for the £12,000 I'd had from the Corps (with no option to repay after passsout) was pretty daunting once I found out how mundane and authoritarian life at CTC was. It really didn't seem much of a deal.

'However the green lid was important to me because it had been dangled in front of me for years, since before I went to university. I may not have done well during training but I certainly suffered a lot during it – mentally and physically – and felt deeply cheated when, after all that pain and sweat, I was withdrawn the day before the Course began.'

Joy's first spirited and then pleading requests to be allowed to complete the Commando Course took Wolsey by surprise, but Taffinder who wanted him out was adamant. Wolsey had no idea that it was so important to him, but then as far as he and everyone else in OTW was concerned, Joy was only there because the warning system required that it take five months to get rid of him. 'In the small print, strictly speaking, you have to pass the Progress Tests and exams,' says Wolsey, a trifle uncomfortably. 'If you are on the highest form of warning therefore the situation is slightly grim, so what you can ill afford to do is fuck anything up overtly. If I was on warning I would be one of the guys mugging up on last year's test if I had it available. There was a standard pass mark of 60 per cent, it is quite a simple test and there is no excuse for failing it.'

The batch, while not as openly contemptuous of Joy as they had been of Wood, were relieved. 'It's impossible to go through by yourself, you need the support of the blokes around you,' commented Mike Tanner, issuing an epitaph. 'It will be bloody uncomfortable and you would not enjoy yourself. Pete Joy tried to be a loner but once you start letting the batch down, making a fool of the batch because of your own individual stupidity, people soon start to get pissed off.'

That evening, except for one solitary cabin, the top floor was an ants' nest of activity, a hubbub of anticipation rippling along the floor. Every time the phone rang twenty-six YOs jumped three feet in the air and rushed out of their cabins yelling 'What is it?' At one minute past midnight the phone rang once more. It was picked up halfway through the first ring. Everyone was already rushing to action stations before the caller identified himself. It was Bob Robinson calling from the bar asking if anyone was thirsty and would like to join him for a drink. At this stage his comrades were prepared to treat this as a joke and did not force him to eat his own Bergen.

Shaggy had been busily preparing himself, but to little or no avail. 'Keep on a psychological high, expect worse than is likely to happen and it'll all seem easy, that was my intended solution to the rigours of the Commando Course; I got off to a bad start as all week at Poole I was under the impression that the Course did not actually begin until Sunday night. In reality by Sunday night we appeared to have been yomping for an eternity ... but that is getting ahead of myself.

'Alphabetical order meant that once again I was second in the batch, this time to man the phone for a short stint of half an hour.

It didn't seem worth going to bed only to get up at half past twelve so I stayed up and read. By one o'clock nervous anticipation meant that I no longer felt tired so it took the best part of an hour to drift off. At least I wasn't too fast asleep when the dreaded knock finally came: I rolled over to glance at my alarm clock, realizing I'd only been asleep for ten minutes. Perhaps it was another joke.'

Not this time. Wolsey had decided to begin the Commando Course with a bang – or rather a blister. At 0430 the batch were to undertake the only compulsory test not to take place in the final week – the Load Carry. The YOs had to carry a Bergen weighing at least 70 lbs, in addition to their fighting order and weapon, twelve miles in four hours. In the past this test has generally taken place during the first Commando Course exercise, 'Crash Action' – once again batch 'int' had failed miserably and while none of them had been lulled into idleness by the relaxed approach of the past few weeks, suddenly the corridor was alive in the depths of the night, chattering with adrenalin spiced up with trepidation. The YOs had already learnt one major lesson – eat at all times and as much as possible even if this involves starting with the earliest breakfast of your life.

'I find breakfast hard to eat at the best of times,' grumbled Ashby, over Pussers Set Fry. 'At 3 a.m. I am only able to eat greasy fried eggs and even greasier sausages which are at least lubricated enough to slip down my dry gullet.'

Over on the football field the far side of the main Exmouth Road the Team waited for the YOs to assemble. In the pre-dawn haze a fine white mist scuffed the surface of the grass and the shadowy figures, knees bending under their Bergens, silhouettes of Quasimodo, faces still indistinguishable in the murk, gathered in their twos and threes around the goal posts, from which hung the weighing machine, a limbless body swinging on a gibbet.

A couple of the YOs were a few pounds under the regulation weight so were ordered to shove in a couple of rocks. Andy Harker, ever suspicious, was five pounds over so that just in case they did not return to the Mess he had all the necessities for surviving in the field with him. His was a deliberate choice, unlike Stan Harris and Andy Mac who in missing the full detail that it was to be a load carry also turned up ready to deploy to the field. Their curses were to be heard echoing over Woodbury Common for the next three hours. For the duration of the Commando Course their blue berets were dispensed with and they wore khaki cap comforters – 'just like real commandos in Second World War movies', remarked one of the more romantically inclined YOs.

The batch were accompanied by Colonel Taffinder who despite the early hour feels compelled to engage all and sundry in conversation of varied and arcane interest. Will a woman ever be able to win a green beret? The general consensus appears to be that physiologically most women will have insuperable problems with this particular test – yomping miles under a heavy Bergen. Taffinder agreed but as Commandant of Lympstone would be happy to let one attempt the All Arms Commando Course.

'All I can remember about the Load Carry is a boring conversation with the Commandant about what he fed his camellias with,' says Dan Bailey, 'though at the end my feet felt as if they had been microwaved under a four-tonner.'

It was a beautiful morning to be out on Woodbury Common; only the fluttering, billowing mist, playing hide and seek amongst the gorse bushes, prevented an awesome view all the way to the Atlantic Ocean. Not that anyone has the inclination to admire it, for a brisk pace had been set. At the halfway point they collapse gratefully to the ground, though nobody removes his Bergen for it requires too much extra energy to put it on again, and consume large gulps of water. A combination of sweat, mist and exhaustion have turned Trevor Henry's hair to a speckled grey and white so he looks like an old man, tired eyes in pale face. Stovin-Bradford is having problems with his feet; his shins were already tender and, concerned about aggravating them and provoking shin splints, he placed some Sorbathane soles inside his boots. The Load Carry was not a good time to start messing about with new kit; by halfway the extra lift had caused both the top of his foot and the back of his heel to rub on the leather. By the end of the yomp the result was 'one shredded foot'.

Nor was he alone. Attwood and Woodall had also picked up some vicious blisters by the time they yomped back to CTC. The test had been completed in three hours thirty-five minutes, a very healthy time but at serious cost. Taffinder noticed that various members of the batch were wearing non-regulation boots and chest webbing. He pointed this out to Wolsey who was extremely pissed off. Eight hours into the Commando Course and the batch were already ignoring the letter of his orders.

'From now on all tests will be conducted wearing Pussers kit,' he snapped, pausing before adding ominously, 'Your penalty will be issued at a later date – when I have decided what it will be. Your next stand to is at 1400 hours for your introduction to the Endurance Course. Until then you are free to do any last-minute admin and personal chores.'

When Wolsey marched off, some of the batch took his advice, hurrying into Topsham to buy last-minute essentials – foot powder, plasters, emergency rations and lots of Mars Bars. Others like Stan Harris retired to bed 'for two and half hours in an attempt to forget my recent ordeal'.

'There are those YOs who believe yomping is a state of mind. I firmly believe it to be a state of feet,' says Goldsmith, angry over this unnecessary bollocking. 'It was therefore less than pleasing to note that those members who had supplied themselves with light-weight walking boots and in doing so had secured the entire batch penalty points walked easily to the showers afterwards without the now familiar heelless hobble of the rest of us. Walking with sore feet most definitely is a state of mind. It takes concentration to seek out and use parts of the appendage which normally don't touch the floor in order to ease those parts that normally do. The satisfaction that the Load Carry was at least complete dwindled somewhat the next morning under 110 lbs of battery deadweight and concrete rocket simulators.'

While the Tarzan Assault Course is the most fabled – and photogenic – of all the Commando tests, the Endurance Course is the hardest. To cover the six-odd miles in under seventy minutes in fighting order does not seem unduly hard on paper. It is however an individual effort; while comrades can urge you on and DS can run beside you, there is no obligation to finish in a group. But there are a couple of little hidden treats – being soaked to the skin within the first five minutes and at the end of the run having to put six out of ten shots into the bull of a target on the thirty-metre range. Fail that and you have failed the whole Endurance Course. That might not sound at all difficult if firing a weapon with a telescopic sight, but the SA80 is not the most robust of weapons and the firer is only allowed to pull through the barrel once to clean it, whilst wading through mud pools and crawling along tunnels can lead to bits breaking off and unexpected failure.

The Endurance Course starts on Woodbury Common, a four-mile walk from CTC. You have to crawl through a series of tunnels, sometimes inches deep in water, wade Peter's Pool (which can vary from thigh to neck high depending on the weather) then through the Water Tunnel where you are completely submerged, pushed and pulled through a six-foot concrete tube. After years of training runs the route is obvious to anyone, the red clay hillsides have been worn down ten feet in some places – a slippery treacherous ravine with sliding pebbles underfoot. The tunnels vary in difficulty but the bigger you are the harder it can get, as the sharp rocks and pebbles gouge into the knees, the pouches catch on the shrinking narrow walls of the 'Smartie tube' and the little guy in front is always going much faster. Through the last one and it's only another four miles back to camp with stagnant water swilling around inside your boots tenderizing already tender feet.

All the YOs had completed the Endurance Course during their POCs but spirits – notably those of Adcock, who was forever on a fruitless hunt for the woman of his dreams – were raised as they were accompanied on the run-through by half a dozen lady aerobics instructors being shown round by a very smug PTI. However for those with blisters caused on the Load Carry the water proved agonizing. 'It proved to be exceptionally painful on the blisters I'd acquired on the Load Carry,' says Paul Attwood, normally the most sanguine and fit of men, 'and so I had to travel back to camp in the Sherpa. The first real day of the course and already I'm in the Sherpa so my spirits are not high. Day One was complete, we covered twenty-two miles and had four hours' sleep. How I hope this is shock treatment and not a gentle intro.'

It was both, for Exercise Crash Action was to be worse still – one of the few compulsory serials on the Commando Course, a 'yomp or die' exercise that incorporates the Load Carry across Dartmoor. This year, though, the batch were heading for Wales and the Brecon Beacons. Not through the Brecon Beacons. Over them. The 70-lb Bergens of the Load Carry were soon to appear light. Now that the batch were deploying to the field they had to pack all the necessary accoutrements for war: spare radio batteries, ammo, rocket launchers, mortars, rations, more ammo. The average Bergen weighed in at over 100 lbs, some stretched to 125 lbs – the equivalent of carrying a medium-size jockey on your back, or in Lodge's case almost his own body weight.

The state of Attwood, Woodall and Chalkie's feet was already far beyond that of normal Marine blister treatment. A favourite trick – inserting a needle and thread through the blister and leaving the thread inside so the fluid can drain out slowly and the air enter to harden the skin – only works if you can have a day or so off yomping. Others had visited 'Dr' Billy 'The Butcher' Baxter to resort to the tinc benzine treatment. An old Marine standby, it is no longer practised by the medical officers down in sick bay, probably because it contravenes all known UN Charters on Human Rights by being a cruel and unnatural punishment. All the fluid is drawn out of the blisters – some of which can be the size of a hand palm – with a hypodermic syringe. Tinc benzine, a yellowy brown caustic agent, is then injected back into the blister. The effect is not instantaneous but as the victim moves his crippled foot around to allow the liquid to flow throughout the blistered area the pain starts; a few minor warning prickles of discomfort are overtaken by a streak of agony driving at 150 mph straight up the spine into the cerebral cortex. People have been known to jump, from a sitting position, to the ceiling. The distress is so extreme that by the time the brain reacts by manufacturing enough endorphins to dull the pain, the second adrenalin rush has also worn off. The great advantage of tinc benzine is that the caustic agent immediately sets to work hardening the tender skin on the inside of the blister. Within a couple of hours it is as if the injured area had been calloused through weeks of barefoot jogging and the man can go on.

Preparing for Crash Action those YOs not suffering unduly prepared preventative measures, winding zinc tape around toes and heels sensitive to rubbing. 'The tape basically screws up your socks, but that is a small price to pay for healthy feet,' explains Brian Adcock, before asking, 'but why do people have such soft feet at this stage of the game?' Such DIY medicine was not really suitable for Chalkie who had scraped his foot raw, while the other two had blisters around the heel as well as underneath the soles. Their wounds were covered in a plastic sheath to promote healing while preventing further infection and some heavy painkillers issued.

'After the Load Carry fucked my feet up this was a seriously low point for me – worse even than the first yomp back from Tenderfoot,' says Chalkie. 'I wasn't sure I'd be able to complete the Commando Course because the buzz going round was that you had to finish that first yomp on Crash Action otherwise you got thrown off.'

'The state of my feet meant I experienced some of the worst pain since I started. By the time we got back I could feel myself slipping into an all-time low,' adds Jezz Woodall, his physical condition compounded by stress and worry. 'On the move to Brecon I took a painkiller and slept most of the way up, waking to find the pain had dulled considerably. I must have watched every step I took on that yomp. This was the first time I have had an incapacitating injury during training and it was a depressing experience.'

Until Crash Action the batch thought they knew how to yomp. After it they certainly did. It was a beautiful day – too beautiful for as the sun rose, so did the temperature and so did the need for water. There were twenty-two kilometres to cover but even the first eight on a gently undulating track through the woods along the banks of the Talybont Reservoir took longer than expected. Then the climbing began.

Even Andy Harker, who views a Marathon as a gentle training run, considers that day's yomp to be the hardest thing he has ever done. For Gav Parr on a vital command appointment he had the added worry of knowing this was 'get it right or it's goodbye time'. While personally as strong as an ox Gav had to motivate the weaker members of his section, for their failure would reflect on him. For Chalkie, Paul and Jezz every step was like walking alternately on to a bed of red hot coals, then into a freezing pool and from there on to a bed of nails. Chalkie solved the problem by doubling his painkiller dose until he alternated minutes of agony with others where he appeared to float six inches above the ground.

The first climb up above the reservoir into the hills was relatively gentle, but already some of the Bergens were listing to one side, dragging the balance, the rhythm of the walk and the carrier's temper with it. Says Tim David: 'I along with the others had to learn to ignore pain, ignore the temptation to stop for a rest, even ignore the yearning to shift the Bergen about on the shoulders.' Many an occasional walker, in their lightweight boots and day pack, hove into sight staring with amazement at the sight of the YOs whose packs from a distance seemed bigger than they were, struggling up hillsides that could easily be traversed around.

Even the batch's black sense of humour, usually the very last thing a Marine lets go, suffered as the feet grew wearier and the local Welsh insect life grew bolder. 'It was said during rest halts,' says Goldsmith, 'that any military skills course that concentrated on judging distance, camouflage, stalking, map reading was sadly lacking and should instead feature walking on the outside of your foot, having your spine compressed, sleeping on gradients and being eaten alive by winged carnivorous ninja which patiently examine each part of your body until they find the square inch least soaked in repellent.'

They could see the climb coming for two miles. It towered above them, a little cairn at the summit challenging, sneering, mocking their efforts. Unlike most climbs this one got steeper the closer you approached, the deeper the straps of the Bergen dug in. Then you were into it and it seems to go on for ever. The difficulty is keeping your balance: lean too far forward and the weight on your back pushes the trunk forward and the soles of the boot can slip on the loose rock, too far back and it's good night Charlie. For about fifty metres the climb is literally a goat crawl, on all fours, until grey with exhaustion they reached the top.

But that was not the end, not even the middle, for the lesson today was pain – real pain and how to endure it after the tank has been reading empty for a long while. This is the time when grown men break down and cry, and if not now later, for it will happen to all and only then will they be strong. Some men can cry internally and feel better for it; others will do it in private, but do it they will.

The path is flat again now and the batch are soon strung out along the ridge. It is a breathtaking sight even to those for whom every breath is agony – dangerous too, for the path, little more than a single goat track, meanders along the edge of cliffs with a straight drop hundreds of feet down on one side where to fall could only be fatal. Some are straggling now, knees buckling under those cement-filled plastic tubes that pretend to be anti-tank weapons, the cord strap from the GPMG a slow-acting garrotte on a neck burning pink in the sun. Eventually six hours into the yomp Henry and Jackson are offered the choice of ending their misery in the back of the Signals Land Rover. Jacko is busted but he does not want to go – it's writ large on his face – he wants to find the courage to go on for those last few miles. Not Trevor, though. Given half a chance he'd throw his Bergen in the Neuadd Reservoir and collapse into the bracken; he looks at Jacko, pleading with his compatriot to come with him – and so it goes, and they go, national honour winning over personal.

Onwards the rest struggle, foot over foot getting slower all the time as Pen-y-Fan approaches. The route takes them to within one hundred metres of the summit. Someone even suggests they detour up to the top, no one laughs and on they yomp, time stretching slower with each faltering step. In the past if the batch have been late for an RV Wolsey has dispatched the four-tonners further down the track. On this occasion realizing that while all of them will literally yomp until they die or their feet fall off – whichever is the sooner – he ordered the RV brought closer. Naturally enough the YOs believed that was just another trick, that the trucks will drive off as soon as they come into view. In fact they don't really believe they won't be thrown off somewhere else, until they are actually dropped at their bivvy site.

By the end of that first day, according to Pete Evans, six members of the batch were all but crippled. It was only sheer bloody-mindedness, a refusal to countenance the possibility of failure that had carried them through. Chalkie, Paul and Jezz champed at the bit for the next two days but were confined to gentler duties like being on sentry or signals duty. Pete had expected to be among them since 'I've never been strong on yomping' but the fact that he was using his own Bergen and, as a civvy, had walked the route before, had meant that he found it much easier psychologically. Indeed throughout the rest of Crash Action, smaller yomps followed by 'rather forced serials' in the area of Sennybridge passed off almost as an anti-climax.

Wolsey did not mind at all. As far as he was concerned the batch had proved they could hack it under extreme conditions. 'There is no point in completely crippling them to prove a point. There is still a long way to go and much to do and I am not prepared to let blisters destroy that for anybody. A couple of days live firing in Okehampton will cheer them up.'

13

Dislocation of Expectation

Our greatest glory is not in never falling but in rising every time we fall.

Confucius

WHEN THE BATCH returned to Lympstone – which amidst much derision the int cell had correctly predicted – Gav Parr had reason to be cheerful. Crash Action had been make rather than break: he had led a successful troop attack, and his orders were well up to scratch. Matt Sturman told Gav, 'Well done, if everything goes according to plan you will be off warning within the month.' Being off warning might appear a formality but given Gav's ability to land in hot water nobody, including him, was celebrating quite yet. Particularly with the Tarzan Course beckoning.

The Tarzan Course is aptly named – an aerial assault course, all ropes and wires, monkey crawls, baby crawls and throwing yourself into a net. It is the first thing visitors to CTC ask to view and yet it is a long time before a YO or a nod gets to swing on it. Those YOs with a view from their cabins over the estuary look down at it every day and from a distance can only wonder what the fuss is about; why is this bunch of trees protected from the rest of the camp by a very high wire fence? (The answer is self-protection. Unless properly supervised by PTIs the Tarzan Course is potentially very dangerous, particularly to inebriated Marines who think they are invulnerable. Foolhardy civilians wishing to prove their manhood on the Tarzan Course are firmly told 'No, we can't get insurance.')

The Tarzan Course is not very difficult, provided you have been trained to do it properly and do not suffer from acute vertigo (if the latter is the case a career in the Royal Marines is probably not ideal). Most people could get round it in a leisurely fifteen minutes, but to pass out the YO has just four and a half minutes for the Tarzan Course and twelve and a half minutes for the combined Tarzan Assault.

The fun starts on the Death Slide – Tom Coyle's particular favourite. The YO clambers up a forty-foot tower accompanied by catcalls from his batch mates and abuse from the PTIs. (To a man PTIs get an even more perverse pleasure than usual from shouting at: a) YOs and b) anybody on the Tarzan Course. This may be because: a) they are sadists with an evil sense of humour who hope one day to give someone such a shock he falls off the baby crawl or b) as advanced students of Marine psychology they have discovered that nothing works as well at shifting an exhausted man half crucified on the climbing nets as screaming 'you fucking useless cunt ... sir'!) At the top he loops a rope around each wrist and slides down feet first. There are two tricks to remember: hit the ground running and don't let go too early. Coyle did once and dropped ten feet straight into the most vicious bed of stinging nettles in Devon.

From then on you are off and running, a rope swing, punch through the net leading with your right hand, grip and climb. Tanner and Lodge hate this bit – it's too early to have got their rhythm going and the adrenalin is not pounding. The Tarzan Course is a great leveller: big men suffer on the net climbs, the smaller can get into real difficulties on the baby crawl which involves crawling along two taut wires – where if the man behind is quick (or the one in front is slow) and is still on the wires stretching them out beyond your reach, this wrenches the groin muscles. Then comes the walk, balancing on the climbing ladder. Then you run along a narrow plank and leap the gap at another net, the object being to leap as high as possible and punch through to cut down the amount of climbing. Then it's flip over the top of the net to shouts of 'keep one hand on either side of the top, you cretin', down the other side, swing a rope over a wooden bar, drop down without breaking your ankle and that is the Tarzan Course over.

Now go and do it again in fighting order with an SA80 attached by a brace of bungee cords to stop it falling off. Except that never stops the barrel gouging a hole in your right buttock and the telescope beating the retreat against your scapula. Just time to get it comfortable because this afternoon you are running the Endurance Course again.

The second visit to the Endurance Course is no longer a gentle introductory jog. It is always started in syndicates of three because you need three men, one pushing, one pulling and one submerged, to get through the water tunnel, but from that point it is every man for himself. For this run through, however, the syndicates are ordered to stick together and muddled up so that the fastest (Harker) will be shackled by the slowest (Henry, Tanner) but will also jolly them along by setting a faster pace, proving they can do it.

The last stretch into CTC is a narrow country road that always seems longer than it should do. It is known as Heartbreak Lane. Mike Tanner found out exactly why. He collapsed through heat exhaustion less than half a mile from the finish. 'All I know is I was running down the lane one minute,' says Tanner, 'and the next I was in the med centre with a tube up my bum and someone trying to shove a thermometer up there as well, stripped naked with water being poured on my head. I'd put everything I had into that run so I was really worried. Then I worked out it was simple fluid and energy loss so the next time I will be able to do it in a reasonable time. But straight afterwards I was thinking if I don't pass that what will I do? This is the most worried I've been in months.'

Many of his mates and the Training Team were very concerned too. The Team were united in their opinion that Tanner would make a brilliant troop officer but they can only help so far. 'We can't run the fucking thing for him,' says Coyle, 'but we can push him along when he flags.' It is a subdued Mike who prepares for the night's covert operation against suspected terrorists operating out of Torquay.

The Commando Course is Wolsey's baby – the one time on the course when he has a virtually free hand. He had toyed with seeing if he could jack up transport to the Falklands or Gibraltar or any-where overseas for some of the exercises. The batch appeared to believe he would and were speculating on anything from the Himalayas to Yugoslavia for some serious hands-on experience. 'It's too easy,' he says, 'just to do things the way they have always been done. Set Crash Action on Dartmoor enough times and soon that is set in stone and it will always be there, so any element of surprise is taken out. My job is to train these men for armed combat and in war the element of surprise is always there, hiding behind the next building or over the next brow. At the same time you have to keep their interest up by setting realistic scenarios. Preparing for a Russian invasion with T72 tanks trundling up the M4 simply isn't believable any more.'

The batch were circulated with various photographs of known terrorist gun runners believed to be operating in the area and to be landing arms in a secluded bay. Gav, Russ Corn and Bob Rob were sent aboard *My Fair Lady*, Andy Shaw's pride and joy, a sailing boat he has refurbished by hand. They sail out to the bay, pretend to be on holiday and wait aboard – entertained by Shaw, his girlfriend and a bottle of Scotch – keeping in constant touch by radio. Meanwhile others were sent out in plain clothes to check the local pubs for any of the suspect faces. With hindsight it was agreed that while it was good idea to send Pete Evans – who does not drink – to scour the hostelries, it was a bad idea to send Bob Baxendale anywhere near a pint mug. 'It would look odd to any watching terrorist to see someone like me not drinking,' he excused himself not altogether convincingly, 'and it is Saturday night'. While Bob had a couple of pints and failed to spot any baddies (who did however spot him) the rest of the batch practised their boat drills in rigid raiders (unsinkable, glass-reinforced plastic boats, able to carry up to nine Royal Marines through high surf at speeds up to 35 knots) in the calm waters of the harbour.

It was a quiet night in the bay but the raiders made scarcely any sound as they came ashore at 0200, the engines throttled back to nothing and the tidal drift carrying them in. The batch were all ashore and in position within five minutes, the only access road in and out of the bay covered by one section and the whole beach within easy shot from a low cliff. They waited and they waited; tonight there were to be no Pongos blundering about.

At last as dawn is breaking two four-wheel drive vehicles come down the road, stopping every few metres, sniffing for any sign of trouble. Half a dozen men and three women, carrying a variety of armaments from an old Bren Gun to assorted Browning 9 mms and a brace of MP5s, step on to the beach. They are signalling out to sea when the warning shout comes ... No one ever heard what the voice said – crack, bang, the terrorists scattered and a fusillade of shots rang out. A man and a blonde woman made a break up the road, they covered all of thirty yards before another burst of automatic fire (it must have been Tanner) at point blank range brought them to a perpetual halt. Then figures in fatigues were moving towards the bodies, covering each other, eyes fixed on the weapons not the dead; each firearm is removed, emptied and counted out. This might be fun but all the YOs knew that within a couple of years this scenario could be for real.

Wolsey is delighted, the batch are elated. Even more so when he tells them, 'You have until midnight tonight – the rest of the day off, make the most of it.'

Less than twenty-four hours later, the phone rings. They are to be ready at 0700 for a six-mile speed march. Speed marches in training are always conducted by a PTI as the intention is to maintain a constant average speed of ten minutes a mile irrespective of the distance covered. The Commando test is a nine-mile speed march but in theory it should be possible to maintain approximately the same speed over longer distances. A speed march is always conducted as a squad so the difficulty is working out the correct pace. The man at the front, on the right hand side, is the pace-setter so it is essential that his stride be equally easy for Gav and for Steve Hussey. An early attempt on a Four Miler with Lodge as the pace-setter was not a success.

'I remember the outrage when I was the right-hand marker and people were dying at the back from taking six-inch strides,' he laughs. 'But it was just as bad if they had someone like Shaggy or Brian who take one step to my two. Eventually they took the biggest and the smallest out of the squad and made us traffic guides because of our stride length.' (Speed marches always take place on the road. Both at the front and the rear of the squad will be three traffic guides all wearing a bright orange vest with the legend 'Caution Marching Troops'. Every time they come to a crossroads one guide will stop traffic on each side and then trot to catch up with the man at the front.)

Generally on a speed march the PTI will slow the pace to a walk going uphill; once the flat or brow has been reached he will increase it to double time and then up to a fast jog. The object on the Six Miler is not to finish in fifty-five minutes but as close to sixty as possible; theoretically the men will then be in better shape to attack or undertake any other military operation required. Today, however, Toby Broomes is not familiar with the chosen route and subsequently the pacing goes wrong. At the halfway stage the batch is behind the time and are forced to jog uphill for much of the way back to CTC. The forced pace is particularly gruelling for some and by the finish – three minutes over time – virtually everyone is hanging out. Once more the Team looks concerned. Having rid the batch of its last two problems on warning, Wolsey is now looking to get everybody (Henry included) through the tests but Tanner's ability to run is a constant worry. It's not that he cannot run, and his stamina is inexhaustible, but his pace is slower than the rest, 'more dignified' he might say, 'like a supertanker' others have sniped. At least there are no recurrences of the blisters that blighted Crash Action.

The rest of the day was spent on survival lectures – three different ways to build a shelter in the woods, various ways to make a fire to cook the food you catch by tickling trout or snaring rabbits. The demonstration was originally slated to take place up on Woodbury but Dai Phillips reported back that morning that his carefully constructed hides had been destroyed by local vandals or children – 'I don't believe he ever built them,' sniffed a suspicious Billy Baxter, 'what a jack!' Dai's demonstration of how to prepare a chicken for eating in the wild was not enhanced by the specimen he'd caught, with extreme difficulty, in the freezer compartment of his local supermarket. The sight of this slowly defrosting lump of white feather-free flesh was bleakly comic and when Dai demonstrated the art of removing the bird's insides by pulling out a plastic bag of rock-hard giblets the batch collapsed in giggles.

Nor was his attempt to kill a rabbit with an 'SBS pea shooter' a success. A dead bunny, the victim of a hit and run driver, had been rigged to sit up – it looked like Sooty after a night on the gin and tiles – with a detonator shoved up its fluffy backside. The idea was that when Dai shot it with his pea, Andy Harker hit the switch and the rabbit blew up. Not this time. Despite a direct hit the creature stared balefully back at Dai who eventually gave up. Thirty seconds later when everyone had turned away there was a small explosion; they all turned round to see bits of bunny decorating a bed of nettles.

Dai had more success with the trout (courtesy of Safeway fish counters) that was slowly cooking away in a clay survival oven, heated by a couple of burning twigs. There is a permanent survival exhibition on display in the trees behind the Tarzan Course. This was much more successful and the prized delicacy was consumed in seconds. Obviously there were no YOs present during the Feeding of the Five Thousand as Tanner alone would have consumed all the loaves and fishes.

The afternoon was given over to unarmed combat training in the gym. Suffice it to say none of the YOs was close to challenging Steven Seagal or Jean Claude Van Damme as a martial arts expert, though Skuse appeared to take an unhealthy enthusiasm in bending McInerney's fingers over backwards. And someone did ask the instructor if he had any infallible tips on how to pick up girls.

That evening Wolsey continued his personal crusade on 'expecting the unexpected'. At 2000 the batch paraded in possession of their waterproofs and helmets. For once they looked completely confused as they got into the four-tonners. All the way down the A38 towards Plymouth, speculation was rife. Maps smuggled into the trucks were consulted, with YOs hanging out the back to report where they had got to. Eventually the four-tonners left the dual carriageway near Ashburton and drove up a small leafy lane where they stopped by a farm gate. The YOs unloaded, still wondering where they were, and when Wolsey told them to put on their waterproofs – 'it's wet where you're going' – the speculations continued as they walked through the gate, through the farmyard and on to a path through the woods.

They were led into the lee of a shallow cave where each man was issued with a two-inch candle stub, which was duly lit. Then in single file they walked to the end of the cave and disappeared into a narrow passageway. For two hundred metres they walked, crawled and scrambled until it opened out into a larger cave. Wolsey and Billy Baxter counted them all in and then led them down a slippery slope into a larger cave. Then Wolsey ordered all the candle stubs to be blown out, before clattering up the slope and turning off the torch – leaving the batch in the blackest pit they had ever been in. The Team had equipped themselves with a couple of night vision goggles – expensive pieces of kit at £2,500 a pair – but in order to share them around they had left the head pieces behind. This was a mistake for it meant that they did not have their hands free since one hand had to be holding the goggles in place.

The original scheme had been to bring the batch to the location in a bus with blacked-out windows and then lead them blindfold into the caves where they would stay for some eight hours. The Team would then sneak back in wearing the night vision goggles to watch, eavesdrop and see if anyone panicked. Lack of time made the entry as planned impossible. The YOs responded to this unexpected turn of events by lighting one candle that was not handed in and Wolsey was forced to show he was still around by yelling at them to blow it out and collecting all the candle stubs. They complied and responded by singing a few raucous choruses of some obscene rugby song, though a couple did look a tad concerned before the lights went out, for this is a very alien environment. After a while most settled down comfortably and coped with sensory deprivation in the most effective manner – they got their heads down to catch up with some zeds – while others chatted *sotto voce*. After a couple of hours all was quiet so Wolsey decided to stir things up a bit. Sadly his attempt at a mouselike approach was ruined when he slipped down the muddy damp rocks, his muted 'oh shit' warning those still awake that something was going on. They were not however prepared for his firing two blank 9 mm rounds in the cave next door. Those sleeping awoke instantly, disoriented for a moment in the blackness.

It took another forty minutes to leave the cave system as they had to do it in the dark, holding the hand or ankle of the man in front, aided in their task by audible cues, muttered imprecations and obscenities as knees, foreheads and funny bones regularly collided with rock outcrops. It was night outside but not as pitch dark as inside the caves. Everyone was filthy dirty, covered in the chocolate brown slime of the caves, and back in camp they all looked as if they had been doing a night surveillance operation concealed in a pile of dog shit. The bar was long closed but there was washing and personal admin to be done before the morning phone call comes.

And come it does: by 0530 the batch were settling down to sleep in the back of a coach bound for Portsmouth and God knows what. The only thing they know is that they have been told to wear their blue boilersuits. The day's lesson was to be fire fighting on board ship at HMS *Phoenix*, a Naval shore base where they also train divers. In essence it was a day out for the lads. The sun was shining with the diver training canal looking especially inviting.

'OK, lads, we'll get you into some gear,' exclaimed a jolly matelot, with sandy hair, acne scars and tattoos on the other exposed bits of his body. The batch are all issued with Wellington boots, gauntlets and respirators. They have to share the special fireproof one-pieces that resemble a diving dry suit except that they're made of felt. *Phoenix* is designed as a training area for fire fighting with various metal superstructures, containing metal rooms that can be reached from the side or below depending on what type of fire they wish to simulate – engine room fires, oil fires, electrical fires, fires with loads of smoke, fires where the heat is so intense it would shrivel your nostril hairs if you weren't wearing a respirator.

Shipboard fire-fighting techniques vary, depending on what has caused the blaze, but speed is of the essence as dialling 999 does not bring immediate succour hundreds of miles out at sea. It is compulsory training for any sailor and the instructors are impressed with the speed at which the YOs get to grips with the basic techniques. 'They are obviously used to working as a team,' one instructor commented to Billy Baxter who grinned like a proud father whose offspring have just won the egg and spoon race. At the end of the day instead of heading straight for the showers to wash off the grime and soot, everyone just threw themselves in the water. 'It's usually a punishment,' said the instructor. 'You should see what happened when they went to Dartmouth,' replied Billy. 'They all went for a swim in the harbour. It was November and bloody freezing but it didn't stop them.'

'They were pretty good guys those instructors,' he says on the coach on the way back to Lympstone, then pauses for a split second, ' ... for matelots. For an outsider it is hard to fathom the relationship between the Royal Marines and their master the Royal Navy. Both acknowledge that Royals dislike serving on board ship but younger Naval officers enjoy the spark of life a Marine officer will bring on board. The latter tends to say what is on his mind whereas the ancient feudal hierarchy on board ship leads to a more formal relationship inside the wardroom than he is used to in the Mess.

The next morning saw the batch back out on Dartmoor up at Foggin Tor – the scene of that very chilly river crossing back in Week 10 – for a day's roping. Shaggy, a qualified extreme climber who admits he is more likely to die 'half way up a mountain than on active service', instead of turning his nose up at the activity was looking forward to keeping his hand in and particularly to sampling some of the M&AW (Mountain and Arctic Warfare) Cadre's less orthodox means of getting bootnecks to the top of a cliff very quickly.

They started with a bit of rope-climbing practice, just to keep the muscles in trim, followed by some abseiling. Anyone not following the ML's (Mountain Leader's) instructions to the letter was ordered to do a dozen press-ups – in the water. Baxendale and Shetler-Jones were soon climbing up in soggy combat jackets. Next they clambered up the wire ladders used for scaling cliffs. The technique is simple: you straddle them and climb up the side, but if the bottom is not properly anchored it can spiral out. When that happened to Corn and Adcock a certain concern was written across their faces – just the flickering of something that might be mild vertigo.

In a wartime scenario ladders and ropes would get the first couple of sections up in fighting order – Bergens can be hauled up later. For the rest the M&AW Cadre has developed a quick and efficient technique of getting men up to the top really fast – 'roller haulage'. This requires some very long ropes and a lot of faith. A section will grab a long length of rope on the cliff top, this will then be attached to a man at the bottom and the rope placed over a roller. The signal given, the section at the top heave and the man below literally runs up the cliff – all he has to worry about is tripping over the roller as he comes to the top or coming over too fast, taking off and being dragged head first through the rocks. Most YOs appeared to enjoy roller haulage and volunteered to do it again.

The next game – sorry, serial – was designed to teach the YOs when abseiling down ropes at speed that they must have absolute confidence in the brake man at the bottom. For many years they used to do a 'run down', which was exactly that – the man ran (pretty slowly) down the cliff face first with his hands clasped behind his neck! The brake man holding the rope can control the runner's rate of descent exactly; jerk it too sharp and he can be hanging off the rock face, twisting in mid air, face down, and none too happy. Many ML1s consider it to be something of a stunt that can actually frighten the subjects unnecessarily. On any mountain operation the word of the ML is final: it does not matter if the CG himself wants to do something, if the ML says 'no', no it is.

So despite Wolsey's grumbling, quieter than usual because Colonel Taffinder had come to see the day's sport – and walk his spaniel – the batch did the equivalent of the run down backwards. It still requires absolute faith in the brake man, except this way you cannot actually see the bastard's face. You stand at the top of the cliff, rope harness on, bottom over the sky, hands clasped at the back of the neck. On the instruction 'Jump' you launch yourself out into space. The tautness of the rope controls how far you drop before you come into the wall again, flex your knees and push off again. The farther out you jump the more trusting – or foolhardy – you are. Just to demonstrate how much in control he is Colour Sergeant Graeme Foster pulled sharply on his rope and Rob Lunn was hanging eight feet above the ground like a turtle on its back, boots kicking in the air but hands still behind his neck.

'I hope someone got a phot,' he grumbled later, for Rob is never happy at being seen as the butt of a joke.

Two nights later he was grinning broadly as two teenage girls and a gaggle of boys watched open mouthed as he took apart and cleaned his HK MP5. On his year off before university Rob went and worked in a school in New Zealand teaching rugby and various less important if more academic subjects, so he knows how to entertain schoolchildren. He could have told them a whole pack of lies about exactly what he and the rest of the batch were doing setting off charges of plastic explosive in a stream belonging to the school when the children were still having lessons. Sensibly he glossed over that as the Boss's dad was still the Headmaster of Wymondham College – a coeducational state boarding and day school – at least until the end of term. Andy Goldsmith, on the other hand, was swinging the lantern so hard it might have spilt, discussing other covert operations he had undertaken with many a nod, wink and surreptitious glance at his colleagues to see none of them was going to blow his cover.

This was a real Wolsey special, a three-day escape and evasion exercise in Norfolk for which he roped in the help of his father, to provide hostages, while his brother jacked up the enemy. The scenario was this: a group of terrorists in Colombia (a place Wolsey had visited on an expedition) had taken hostage about twenty British teenagers and were bringing them into the British Embassy before being given safe conduct out of the country. As all the available Special Forces were occupied elsewhere the Ambassador had asked for a troop of Marines under the battle-hardened Lieutenant Tanner to fly in from Belize to deal with the terrorist threat. Due to the somewhat erratic nature of local politics – nobody is exactly sure what the terrorists represent – it has to be a secret operation, so the Marines are to carry no identification, will wear blue boiler-suits and balaclavas during the operational phase and will not be using regular-issue weaponry. After the operation the men have to make their way to an RV for transport out of the country. In the event of something going wrong they are to split into groups of four and make their way to a backup RV point in forty-eight hours' time, avoiding capture and living off the land.

For the batch the best bit of all was being able to play with state of the art kit. All bar a handful were able to dump their SA80s in favour of Heckler and Koch MP5s or HK 53s (the HK 53 is a higher velocity weapon, taking .556 ammunition instead of 9 mm). This allowed them to spend hours taping two magazines together head to tail (meaning they can blaze off one magazine, then change over in one lightning movement – provided they have had plenty of practice). Section leaders were issued with the latest radios complete with hand mikes. Pete Manson, Andy Mac, Tanner and Chalkie all had Cougars clipped to their belts, the white wire trailing up to the earpiece giving the rather surreal look of a 24-hour plumber crossed with a US Secret Service man. Apart from Chalkie the section commanders were all armed only with Browning 9 mms but he had, as usual, proffed with an MP5. Andy 'Bubbles' Goldsmith, whose good humour, high spirits and perpetual cheerleading throughout the course have amazed everybody, was for once looking down in the mouth. Try as he might he could not get his MP5 to fire more than two rounds without jamming. He took it apart three times, cleaned everything that moves and all the bits that don't, before taking it to Tom Coyle for medical advice. That did not help either so he was forced to revert to his SA80 – 'at least I can fire it on automatic,' he grouched.

The thirty hostages will be held in the school sports hall and in lieu of the detailed floor plans that would be available in a real-life operation the batch inspect the ground beforehand. ('In a real hostage scenario there would be a building rigged out as close as possible and dozens of rehearsals would be carried out,' explained Coyle.) There are two main doors into the hall, and entry can also be effected through the skylights into the changing rooms. These however enter the main hall under a balcony upon which the YOs have to assume that an armed terrorist will be standing. As night falls the sections were all waiting in their places, one watching each door, the others on the roof.·

The terrorist role was being carried out by members of 7 Royal Horse Artillery, members of the Airborne Brigade with red berets but not pure Paras, commanded by Captain Simon Wolsey –

Mark's younger but bigger brother. Their camouflaged Land Rovers too have been under constant clambering from the boys and girls but only half a dozen had the chance to play terrorist and abuse the hostages. The entire school was lined up to watch the drama when three minibuses escorted by a local police car brought the hostages in. The Paras certainly relished their job, forcing their victims to adopt stress positions and keeping up an endless stream of abuse. It worked, for some of the hostages quickly forgot that this was only a game and started to believe it. Being forced to kneel with your legs crossed, your back upright and your hands clasped behind your neck for a long time while a thug brandishing an automatic weapon describes you as 'a piece of worthless shit' can do that.

Theoretically there was still a chance for negotiation. This ended abruptly when the terrorist leader, sporting a red bandana around his head and thoroughly enjoying himself, threatened to kill a hostage if his demands were not met instantly. Five minutes later he dragged out one of the masters and shot him on the spot. The assembled congregation broke into a spontaneous cheer! 'I didn't know he was that unpopular,' murmured Wolsey's dad.

Inside the boys' changing room the skylight was removed very quietly. The most dangerous part of any operation is getting enough men down into the building without being overheard. Tanner, naturally, was first man down. No sign in his eyes any longer of it being a game, he looked extremely mean, ready to take out anybody who wandered in for a piss. Half an hour later the hostages were looking pale, the terrorists had twitches on their index fingers.

Without warning the lights in the sports hall went out and simultaneously there was a succession of explosions, like a giant firecracker or the entire grid on a Formula One race backfiring in succession. It seemed to last minutes but in less than ten seconds the changing room doors were kicked open and the room filled with boiler-suited figures. (In a real scenario they would have thrown in flash bang stun grenades which blow out the eardrums and paralyse anyone in the room, slowing their reactions down for up to thirty seconds, giving the attackers time to shoot anyone with a weapon in their hands.) 'Get down,' screamed Tanner and the few remaining standing hostages – and one smart terrorist – did exactly that. There was a rattle of small arms fire at any standing figure, only one of whom gets off any shots in reply. The YOs moved swiftly amongst the bodies, kicking the weapons away before checking the corpses. One body's arm twitched, eight feet from Tanner, and without blinking he turned and one-handed fired half a magazine into the body which stopped moving for good.

As the batch escorted the hostages out of the sports hall into the open the terrorist who is hiding amidst them made a move to break away. A girl screamed and Tim David without so much as a shout opened fire at close range. The entire school cheered again as the body hit the gravel. One of the girl hostages, a blonde sixteen year old, started to cry with either relief or shock at witnessing such a clinical dispatch. 'It seemed so real,' she wailed.

Another girl followed the 'Stockholm Syndrome', a well-established psychological pattern of falling in love with, or at at least fancying, one's captors. She gave her phone number to the Para whom Tim had shot, with instructions 'not to call me until July because I'm taking my O Levels until then'. The batch were green with envy when they heard about that. 'After all, we rescued her' was the common consensus after discovering how very pretty she was.

'Never mind,' interrupts Tim David, ' I enjoyed shooting that terrorist who moved ... and making those girls cry – girls never get scared of me.'

Two hours later at the RV nobody was surprised to discover that they had to go to ground for the next forty-eight hours – though not simply go to ground for they were to spend their time criss-crossing the MoD land to various RV points, all the time being hunted by Simon Wolsey's Paras in Land Rovers and a company of Royal Marines from 40 Commando. They were left with nothing except their weapons, the boilersuits they stood up in and any minimal survival tools they might have had in their pockets. They were given no food and expected to stay within the boundaries of the Standford Training Area.

Heading off in six different directions, Chalkie and his cohorts soon stumbled across a deserted building. After a brief recce they entered, built a fire and settled down for a warm carefree night's sleep, ready to start off fresh – if hungry – in the morning. Batch legend also has it, though no one ever admitted it, that one group walked into the nearby village and persuaded a middle-aged house-wife to cook them breakfast. Wolsey would not have minded for he knows that survival may depend on breaking the rules.

For other groups a warm night meant that they were not too shattered by the morning when the hide and seek really began. Shaggy led Rob Lunn, Andy Mac and Shet on their first four-mile move. The blue boilersuits could be seen from miles away so movement had to take place where possible twenty metres back inside tree cover. The first sighting of some suspicious khaki-clad individuals had them diving into the densest part of a wooded marsh, which proved all but impenetrable. Surfacing again muddy but unbowed they spotted Mike Tanner four hundred yards away heading towards a different RV. The first part was accomplished easily enough, though the final 200-metre dash to the RV had to be made across open ground in direct contravention of the textbooks. Billy Baxter was not pleased at this but after bollocking Ashby he gave them the coordinates of their next RV.

Shaggy should never have spotted Mike Tanner's syndicate but then Mike should never have let Trevor do the map reading. 'There we were yomping across Norfolk getting bloody hungry, me, Bob Rob, Skuse and Trevor,' says Tanner. 'Bob and I had been map reading and asked Trev if he wanted to take a leg. He said, "I'll take a leg but I don't know how to read one of these things." Thirty-seven weeks into training and he still can't read a map – I'm sure he won't even when he leaves training. Trev is just a liability, useless at everything.' To be fair Trevor was not reading the map when they were pinged by the RHA, but if he had been they might have been in Cambridge.

Harker and Watkinson's syndicate was the first to get captured, much to the former's displeasure. The Airborne trussed them up and were preparing to dump them in a nearby bog when they spotted another syndicate breaking across the open ground. It was not to be Harker's day: that evening they walked straight into a troop of camouflaged Marines who did not give them such an easy ride. Their wrists were bound tight behind their back so the blood drained out and they were forced to lean against trees in stress positions for hours. According to the reports they later fed back to Wolsey Neil particularly found this a distressing ordeal. 'There was tears in his eyes,' reported a corporal to Wolsey proudly. 'It was probably just the pain coming out,' answered the Boss loyally. (Mark Wolsey's original plan had been to subject any captured YOs to some serious interrogation techniques to see how they would stand up to it but – to prevent any ill treatment of men under training – such things are now allowed to take place only if supervised by trained interrogators and, most importantly, with permission all the way up to the top of the red-tape tree. After making a few jovial references to getting hold of some rubber hosepipes and electric cattle prods, he abandoned the idea and left it to the men on the ground, who have their own personal and idiosyncratic ways of dealing with captured prisoners.)

Andy Goldsmith, as befits a former horny-handed son of the soil, had camouflaged himself and the rest of his syndicate so effectively that they escaped detection for thirty-six hours, lying doggo in woods and copses as the RHA drove past and Marine patrols passed by within feet. Sadly they could not evade capture after one passing patrol actually trod on Goldsmith's back. The exhalation of surprise and pain might have shocked the man in the boots but an incapacitated Goldsmith and his oppos were easily rounded up.

Ashby's syndicate, too, nearly got away with it when they walked into a copse and stumbled upon a camouflaged RHA patrol. The plan was to bomb burst – everyone just run in opposite directions – but when Shet was rugby-tackled to the ground the others, having misunderstood the parameters of the game, surrendered. 'A shame,' commented Wolsey RM. 'The others could have got away or even turned round and attacked the Para to rescue Shetler-Jones.'

Adcock and his merry men – Stovin-Bradford, 'Gazza' Attwood and Stan Harris – did exactly that when they were pinged by an RHA Land Rover. Instead of surrendering they fought back, overpowered and took a great deal of pleasure in tying up the men in the red berets. Being rather hungry they stole their ration packs and were considering taking the Land Rover as well. 'Unfortunately we didn't know whether that was in the rules,' Adcock grinned triumphantly, 'we wanted to and there was a general view that we should have driven it to the nearest pub.'

At the end of the serial the batch were transported back down to St Martin's Plain Camp outside Folkestone for their final exercise before the Commando tests. Once again it was to be a surveillance exercise against terrorists, conducted mainly in plain clothes. First they had to spend a day practising live firing drills – what to do if they were driving in civilian cars and encountered terrorist roadblocks. When three or four men are armed with Brownings and MP5s the general rule seems to be 'get out of the car and run like fuck', but the actual techniques are classified. The same cannot be said for Mike Tanner's ability to shoot a rock six feet away, with a pistol he had already informed the Team was unloaded. The bullet ricocheted ten feet over Baxendale's head. Mike was mortified, for an ND (negligent discharge) is worse than dangerous, it is highly embarrassing and expensive. Wolsey later fined him 'a lot of money'.

Rob Lunn was in command of 'Green Beret', juggling plain-clothes operations in town and a couple of military OPs, a complex multilevelled task requiring good comms and clear thinking. Rob has the latter in abundance, but he also has a short fuse. Parr and Corn were shadowing a terrorist suspect from the jetfoil port in Dover into a café; the tails were moving well, overlapping, talking to each other passing by, working as smoothly as in any cop thriller. Everything was fine except that the radio shadow meant the Cougars were not working properly and kept losing touch with the base. This happens – indeed had done so throughout training – but it infuriated Lunn and his subsequent briefing was even more brusque than usual.

'Rob's communication skills will always be found wanting in a lot of ways,' says Adcock; 'he snapped something at the batch instead of going the right way about it so we all laughed at him.'

Despite all the comms problems, both personal and mechanical, the terrorist suspects were successfully tailed. The outer OP which had been watching a white hut on a deserted track from the comfort of a very prickly bush finally reported life and the ambush went well – though not for the terrorist suspects. The batch, now back in khaki denim, packed their Bergens and were dumped in a field in the middle of Salisbury Plain to await further instructions.

At ten minutes to midnight they received orders to move. Eight YOs were given UV (ultraviolet) torches and told to stand on opposite sides of the field at 100-metre intervals. The rest were told, 'You will be picked up at 2359 by an RAF Hercules flying without lights. The plane will land, turn around and taxi back to pick you up.' The Hercules was all of twenty seconds late – you heard nothing, saw less for there was no moon that night and suddenly it was there, a droning sound and this black shape appearing out of the southlands, a giant bat on the hunt. The Herc landed smooth as silk with not a light to be seen, except for a ghostly green neon refraction from the cockpit bouncing off the pilot's night vision goggles. It turned around by the last man, Adcock, and taxied back to the waiting batch, swinging around 180 degrees. The ramp at the back whirred down, opening up like a sperm whale's jaw preparing to gobble up a giant squid. The batch moved quickly into the belly of the beast, slinging Bergens on to the floor and making themselves comfortable in the debris, and by the time a panting Adcock thundered inside, the ramp was slowly rising and the plane moving off.

The pilots doubtless had a great time, flying the forty minutes back to RAF Lyneham without lights, skimming the ground at five hundred feet. Most of this was lost on the batch, who though as thrilled as kids at a birthday party could not actually see very much. Harker promptly went to sleep while Tim David tried to interest people in his exploits flying – 'I went solo before I could drive, you know.'

The excitement of such a pick-up and flight was momentary for now there was but one set of tasks left to face. The hardest, most Herculean, of all. The Commando tests. God willing this time next week all of them would be wearing green lids.

Green Lid or Bust

The woods are lovely, dark and deep.
But I have promises to keep,
And miles to go before I sleep.
Robert Frost, 'Stopping by Woods on a Snowy Evening'

THE DAY STARTS rudely enough at 0400 though for most of the
batch it has been a long slow night, an insomniac mixture of slow-
burning adrenalin, anticipation and fear fuelled by the constant
need to piss. Ever since the Nine Mile speed march finished at
0900 the previous morning everyone has been preparing for the
morrow, readying themselves for the big one, stuffing their faces
with huge plates piled high with mountains of carbohydrates (no
dietary niceties here), rice and chips, pasta and chilli con carne and
hunks of meat all squabbling over the same china. The intake of
liquid has been continuous. Look anywhere around the batch dor-
mitory and all you see is young men taking constant small swigs at
huge bottles of Coca-Cola or arguing over the merits of Isostar and
other energy-inducing drinks.

Tim David expounds his theory of liquid intake, fortified and
honed by his experiences racing mountain bikes. 'I shall drink at
least two pints of Isostar before we start and then concentrate on
water all the way through. On the long haul water's best because
there isn't really time for the bodily salts to replenish and if you
take too much glucose you get a quick high followed by a
depressed trough.' David had bought £50 worth of Isostar at a
bike shop and sold it on through the batch – it does not taste of
much, a synthetic medicine for the sports fixated, a comforter for
the Thirty Miler.

Palpable tensions have been bubbling away all afternoon, but

they brew up to a head during the European Football Champion-
ships semi-final. Outside it is warm but most feel more comfortable
inside watching a portable TV precariously lodged above an upper
bunk. The room has taken on the muggy comforting stench of the
locker room – perspiration, both ancient and modern, vying with
boot polish, gun oil, the sweet, sticky odour of the Real Thing and
the all-pervasive aroma of feet, pampered with powder, bound with
zinc tape, lovingly wrapped in dry socks but feet, cheesy feet, all
the same.

The batch are still trying to absorb the implications of Gav Parr's
announcement that he finds Kylie Minogue in a pointy bra to be
not only ravishingly beautiful but a sex goddess to boot, when
Chalkie goes off to replenish his glass, temporarily vacating his seat,
which is promptly bagged by Andy Harker under 'the three-second
rule'. Harker who has already done a Thirty Miler has no worries
at all but this conspires to wind up an already tense Chalkie and the
upshot is an increasingly heated argument – somewhat akin to children bickering over a toy when there is another perfectly good one
next to it. Harks, whose nose and cheeks have been scorched pink
by the unseasonal June sunshine, surrenders no ground; his roseate
complexion turns choleric and his pale thick, bushy eyebrows
which meet in the centre of his forehead in a single unyielding
platinum line give a sharper physical edge to the native bluntness of
his speech. He is not budging, or at least pretends not to, and most
people would not dream of tangling with the fittest member of the
batch, whose only publicly professed ambition is to join the SBS.
Chalkie, however, is made of sterner – or is it stupider – stuff. His
threat of violence elicits no response so he grabs Harker in a neck
lock and pulls tight, then tighter.

Those of the batch watching the soccer are momentarily dis-
tracted and proffer various suggestions along the lines that this sort
of behaviour isn't really on – though nobody moves to break up
the spectacle, probably because they are enjoying the sight of
Harker going white with anger. Eventually Chalkie, realizing that
Harker will only leave the seat when he loses consciousness, and
maybe not even then, lets go. Andy is furious, stands up and looking down on Chalkie spits, 'You ever do that to me again and I'll
kill you.' Unable to apologize even if he wants to, Chalkie laughs it
off, braving it out in front of his mates but watching out of the corner of his eye as Harker moves off, stiff backed, towards his bunk in

the far corner, where he sulks for the next hour. The atmosphere is gloomy for a while after such a display of unseemly behaviour but before long the sarcastic sense of humour that governs Marine morale exerts itself once again. Baxendale cracks when he leaves his bunk: 'Leave my bed alone, the three-second rule is no longer in operation' and soon Chalkie's chair is being treated as if it were a royal throne, upon whose hallowed, anointed surface the posteriors of poor folk may not even brush.

The Thirty Miler will start before dawn so all is quiet by 2130, though the bunks sound in perpetual motion; bodies toss and turn, or get out of their bags with a clatter of ancient springs to urinate once again. One bunk does not move at all. Its occupant has not moved since midday, face buried into the pillow, hiding himself from the world, pretending it does not exist and that maybe, just maybe, come sun up all will be all right again. The batch have tiptoed around Trevor Henry's pit as if it were an electrified compound, out of bounds to avoid causing its solitary occupant unnecessary pain. Trevor is beyond threaders. Having already blown two out of the first three Commando tests he has been told by Wolsey that he will not be allowed even to start the Thirty Miler.

Nor will one other YO, but for very different reasons.

Although the first two Commando tests – the Tarzan Assault and the Endurance Course – are actually run at Lympstone, the batch moved up to Okehampton Training Camp on Saturday afternoon. 'They need a chance to relax and prepare themselves mentally, and they can't do that at CTC,' explains Wolsey. 'There are too many distractions there and let's face it while I hope they have enjoyed the Commando Course it hasn't exactly been a rest cure. Some of them just need to do nothing but lie around recharging their batteries for a day.'

Okehampton Camp is perched on the edge of Dartmoor, one mile and one very steep hill above the town. It has hardly changed in years, the same creosote brown wooden huts, used by everyone from school cadets to the Pongos and Marines doing exercises on the Moor. To discourage men from going down into town the Corps have their own dining room with a well-stocked bar, TV and video. The batch love being at Okehampton Camp for the food, which while it may not win any awards from Egon Ronay, is far better suited to their purposes than the Officers' Mess in

Lympstone. Their purpose at every meal is to consume as much fuel as fast as possible. The average breakfast might consist of two packets of Alpen, a pint of milk, followed by poached egg on toast, bacon (in true military style this is a giant rasher of which the top half is invariably burnt and the bottom under-cooked pink), sausages, beans, tomatoes, fried egg on fried bread and even more toast.

On Sunday morning after breakfast Wolsey decides to take the batch out for a 'gentle jog to stretch your legs'. His definition of a slow warm-up is not generally shared as the run starts at 0900 and he sets a cracking pace up the first hill, which stretches for a very long mile. Soon he leads them off the road on to a track where loose shingle can turn an unwary ankle. Tanner is lagging a hundred metres off the pace, a position he keeps all the way, neither falling behind nor catching up. 'A good warm-up,' chortles Wolsey, fifty minutes later, refusing to believe he has covered seven miles until a map is produced. However, he has learnt one thing from the run. If they begin the Nine Miler at the bottom of that long hill the long slow climb could destroy morale, stamina and timing before they have really begun. That afternoon while the YOs are lounging around, Dai and Toby Broomes go out in a Sherpa to measure the right distance, starting on the flat.

Not everybody enjoyed the pleasures of Wolsey's little run. Bob Baxendale was fast asleep in his bunk when everyone got up to do their half-hour of warm-ups and stretching. Skuse shouted at him, got an affirmative grunt in reply, so went out. Bob just turned over and went back to sleep again. He was still there snoring away when they returned and, as soon as he realized that the Team had not noticed his absence, was extremely smug all day.

That Sunday the YOs appear outwardly calm but the internal organs are fizzing with tension as if they were awaiting their orders to go over the top at the Battle of the Somme. Few want to talk about the morrow, preferring to burrow themselves into writing all those letters they have avoided for weeks, browsing through the Sunday newspapers or like Matt Lodge reading a thick novel begun in September which he is still no more than a third through. In the afternoon, while others watched England making a spirited fight back in the Test Match, Goldsmith was busy chatting up some sixteen-year-old girls staying in camp on their Duke of Edinburgh Award Scheme. Their teachers hovered anxiously in the background clucking around as their charges ogled over a rapidly increasing number of bare-chested YOs posing contentedly in the afternoon sun, preening like peacocks but only fanning their tails at half mast for their minds were on bigger game.

Brian Adcock might have been around the camp in body but his spirit was elsewhere. Except when he was watching the cricket he preferred to be alone, either writing letters or just sitting out in the sun, lying in his sleeping bag outside the barrack room. Normally a social animal, he was at his most contented lying out there next to Andy Harker, as if both knew where the competition was, while the rest of the batch got their warlike spirits stimulated by videos of *The Eagle Has Landed*, *Who Dares Wins*, or laughed themselves sick over *Blackadder Goes Forth*.

Outwardly supremely confident Brian keeps pushing Harker to admit he will be going for a record on the Tarzan and Endurance Courses. Brian can be enigmatic at times, that polished veneer of immense self-assurance countered by a nagging personal doubt that he almost acknowledges but cannot accept because he has never had to confront it. He is driven by an obsessive need to compete and a contradictory desire to be seen to be holding back with the rest of the boys. A triathlete and international water-polo player Adcock is superbly fit; his only physical weakness seems to be the tendency of his hands to go blue when immersed in cold water for a long time. God knows how much body fat he possesses but it must be less than 10 per cent, leaving his face a cadaverous thing, a skull with bulging forehead and blue eyes deep set under a ridge of bone.

That last Sunday evening seven of the batch slept out under the stars. Complaining about the uncomfortable metal bunks, they moved the mattresses outside. Not that it helped Tanner, who long after the others were asleep was still lying up on his elbow, his face blank with worry and his mind going over and over the tests with no respite. Or Brian, who was prowling the galley with Shaggy until past midnight.

Early on Monday morning in the washrooms the batch prepared in their different ways for the first test. Most had showers, all shaved carefully – having to avoid nasty razor nicks on the pimples that seem to sprout with the food and discomfort – while Bailey, as if going on a first date, takes immense care to make sure his platinum hair is primped and pushed into position. Neil Watkinson looks in the mirror and tries to adjust his cap comforter – after six weeks it still resembles a pixie hat rather than a piece of military headgear. 'His military career will not be a long one,' bitches Russ Corn to no one in particular.

The first stop at Lympstone is the 30-metre range where the batch have to zero in their SA80s for the afternoon's Endurance Course. After completing the Endurance Course in less than seventy minutes you then have to pull through the rifle once, then fire ten shots – five kneeling, five standing – of which 60 per cent have to be on target, otherwise the fastest time in the world won't help. (This principle runs throughout the tests: at the end of any physical exertion the YOs should still be capable of performing as soldiers.) The tensions start to show on the range, with those who have to wait grumbling about the length of time being taken by those ahead, McInerney and a couple of others having completely to disassemble their weapons. Pete Evans has gone off to get a totally unnecessary haircut but as Duty Student he has the keys for the range hut, which contains the spare targets and the phone, which rings plaintively but unanswered.

That unheeded bell is tolling for Gav Parr but eventually Colour Sergeant Foster comes down to tell him to see Wolsey. He is to report to the Commandant at 1015 to be formally taken off warning. He leaves the office, his face breaking into a huge beatific smile like a kid presented with an early and unexpected present.

10.30. It's time for the Tarzan Assault Course, first a run through without kit, then for those who want it one with. PTIs (always referred to as 'Staff' because you can't tell what rank they are) are in strategic positions around the course from which they scream helpful advice. The YOs are pissed off with this by now, they know what they are doing and do not need or want to be screamed at – on Test Day that is simply another uncalled for distraction. Both Toby Broomes and another PTI have been winding up Adcock about what time he's going for. 'I'm going to go for the record,' he announces to anyone who is interested, while Russ Corn shakes his head as if to say no good will come of this sort of competitive behaviour.

Adcock is slightly worried by the Tarzan Course; he might even have a deeply hidden fear of heights and is always circumspect in his approach to anything more than his own height off the ground. Trying to be helpful Ashby suggests he try a two-handed vaulting technique on the second net (the correct technique is to throw yourself into it right arm extended, punching through, then climb up and swing over the top with one hand on either side of the top horizontal pole). In order to save a couple of seconds Adcock puts both hands over the top, and ignoring PTI screams of warning swings over. His hands fail to grasp and his forward momentum carries him head first on a twenty-foot drop. His forehead hits a bolt on the way down, puncturing a sinus, and he dislocates his wrist so badly he has to have screws inserted later. Blood is pouring from a deep hole in his forehead and he is quickly whipped off to the sick bay in the waiting ambulance.

Matt Lodge was having his own problems even before Brian hit the deck. For him, with his short stumpy legs and seemingly frail body, the Tarzan Assault Course was the true nightmare. He had failed that initial BFT passout and once earlier on the Tarzan Course he had died on the net, his arms literally seizing up. Being small – 5' 6" – may have its advantages in some of the Endurance Course tunnels but on the Tarzan it is the opposite. On the rope ladder walk his arms are at full stretch and if any extra tension is applied he is flying in the air. The baby crawl is hard too: on the first run through there was another body behind him as he crawled across and the extra tension caused the wire to stretch, pulling a muscle in his groin.

Hobbling back to the start in tremendous pain he saw Adcock about to start his ill-fated run through, yelling up to him for advice on some specific groin stretches. For half an hour, he is running, stretching it, bending himself double in an attempt to alleviate the pain. It works. But then he is a tough little bugger and the Tarzan Course is not going to stop him now. He finishes it with a good half-minute to spare; so does Mike Tanner. Each is delighted for the other, perhaps only they know how much each has dreaded this moment.

'I was always apprehensive about the Commando Course, right up until this moment,' he says, 'and Brian hitting the ground didn't help. It took a bit of the shine off for all of us.'

Brian's Commando tests are over before they have even begun – goodbye to any record breaking. He is left sitting in the hospital while the batch all successfully complete their runs. He is deeply upset but knows 'it was my fault trying for those extra seconds. I am fairly pissed off. I know I'm not permanently injured but my main concern is that I don't get back batched and spend more time in the Lympstone hell-hole.' By the following evening he is back up at Okehampton, a sorry figure in his sling and bandaged head, but for all his personal distress Brian proved himself to be a team player and devoted all his energy to cheering the others on.

Wolsey is, of course, furious – annoyance mixed with parental concern for he is very fond of Adcock, whose demeanour reminds him of his own youth. Now even before the first test has started his chance of having a 100 per cent pass rate has been shattered. Henry's failure to complete the Endurance Course is merely confirmation it is not to be his day.

Poor Trevor, there is nothing wrong with his fitness – in PT rig he is as fast as anyone there; but put weights and a rifle on him, tell him it's a Commando test and he goes to pieces. He passed the Tarzan Assault Course with a good forty-five seconds to spare though he virtually expired atop that final thirty-foot wall, gulping in huge breaths of air as if he were a drowning man, breathing so fast you doubted his heart would ever catch up. On the Endurance Course he lost it soon after the water tunnel, despite being accompanied throughout by the not overly sympathetic Colour Sergeant Foster. Although during the syndicate run through he had been only thirty seconds outside, this time he is three minutes away at the seventy-minute cut out, his face drained of blood, dissolving into battleship grey. At the end Foster and Coyle grab hold of him, trying to shake some sense from his mouth which is only issuing forth snow-white spittle, shouting questions at him, throwing buckets of water over his head to cool him down.

In contrast Andy Harker's Endurance Course run was well nigh perfect. Tim David, no mean sprinter himself, was with Harks until the water tunnel, 'after which he just took off. I thought I'd done a pretty good time but he could have been out of the shower before I got to the range.' Harker's time was just under fifty-two minutes, believed to be an all-time record, though no one seems to know exactly what the fastest time is. It was certainly the quickest time for a number of years and Wolsey had to admit that it was faster than the fifty-four minutes he had managed in training.

Matt Skuse had a horrendous run in, right from the moment he came out of the final tunnel and turned his foot on a pebble. The pain continued and increased on the run back to Lympstone. By Heartbreak Lane he was in agony and crossing the footbridge he screamed out, 'I've broken my fucking foot again.' Fortunately it turned out to be a bone callus, though he was favouring it for the rest of the day. That was the extent of the injuries though Steve Hussey complained of sore shins. Tanner came in with time to spare – though not a lot – and professed himself satisfied. The Thirty Miler he knew was not a problem – hell, Mike Tanner can yomp all day – but the morning's speed march could be.

'Yes, there are times when I find phys really hard,' he says. 'It's not that I want to give up or I'm completely knackered, I just can't seem to run at a particularly fast pace, it's slower than everyone else's. The Boss says, "You don't seem to be that tired but you don't seem to be able to keep up either." I'm never screaming for air but my legs don't seem to keep up with my brain.

'I have never believed I won't be able to cut it because at the end of the day I really believe that most of it is mental rather than physical. Other people on the batch are better suited genetically to the tests than me but at the end of the day it is mental. I want it and I will do it.'

The Team, too, are determined that Tanner, Lodge, Lunn and Hussey, who have all shown up as possible problems on previous speed marches, will make it. The simplest plan is to push them out front as traffic markers where the rest of the squad are perpetually pushing them from behind and various members of the Team can take it in turns to apply personal encouragement. And Henry? 'He doesn't have to pass and basically we don't give a fuck,' says one of the Team. 'He'll blow out long before the finish.'

So it came to pass. Before they hit halfway Trevor was trailing by four hundred yards and all the frustrations that the Training Team had had with Commonwealth officer cadets came to the fore. Foster told him to get in the Sherpa and he refused, pleading 'No Sergeant, please give me another chance, I can do this thing', his arms outstretched, locked hard to prevent him being pushed into the back. Eventually Foster just hurled him in face first, chin crashing through the plastic mugs and the jerry cans. Undeterred, he tried to crawl out the front door.

At the next water stop he sat hunched in the back of the van, eyes looking at his feet but seeing nothing. Trevor's failure was all in the mind. As with Pete Joy winning the green beret was incredibly important to him – so much so that when he was confronted by the reality of it, his mind froze, paralysing his body so that it could never work, decreasing the pain threshold so that each step became a long-running, agonizing exertion. For Trevor the battle was lost even before it began. It did not help that he was so petrified of the cold that he insisted on wearing a thermal vest and long johns for all the Commando tests, so in that most un-English warm June he overheated, his body boiling over like a car radiator in the perennial Okehampton traffic jam. Trevor might have done better had Matt Sturman actually carried out his half-expected, half-threatened bottom inspection, a surprise search for non-Pussers undergarments. After Mike Tanner collapsed on the Endurance Course run through, Sturman had banned lycra cycling or running shorts from being worn under khaki denims on the grounds that they could lead to overheating and dehydration. Many of the batch objected to this edict on the grounds that they helped reduce chafing along the inner thigh and wore them anyway.

The route of the batch speed march took them through the middle of an exercise involving 40 Commando. Their humour was further increased at the sight of Paul Redding (who had moved to Taunton before Easter) who was having a few problems organizing the company haybox lunches. Tanner was in front of the main squad – between them and the traffic markers. After hearing the noisy demise of Henry, Mike pushed his flagging step further and faster but at the five-mile mark as the hills got a bit steeper so the gap between him and the squad closed inch by inch. His jaw, always so belligerent, began to slacken, his eyes to lose their focus. 'Come on, Mike, keep it going,' cried the squad as one, but within five minutes the advantage had dissipated, the gap had closed again. Wolsey realized that unless he did something Mike would fall behind the main batch and might never catch up again.

'I was hanging out six miles into the Nine Miler and if there was ever a point when I was really struggling, that was it,' says Tanner. 'Wolsey ran up behind me and shouted, "Come on, Mike" – he used my Christian name which meant a lot anyway as I had learnt to respect him a lot over the past nine months and until then he always called everyone in the batch "Mr" – then he put his hand on my back and started pushing me along. To me that meant a hell of a lot, it wasn't just a physical push, it was a real mental kick up the behind. A bloke I admired, and he wanted me to finish it. I'm not saying I wouldn't have passed it but he helped a hell of a lot at the moment I needed it most.'

From then on it was all downhill for Tanner and as the others realized that he was through the barrier, you could feel their spirits soar. It helped, too, that the last three miles were downhill but they finished with so much time to spare that the traffic markers were all pulled in and the entire batch marched into Okehampton Camp in the best order – and step – they had managed for months. There were three minutes left on the clock.

Matt Skuse's left foot was holding up fine, though Steve Hussey was still suffering with his shins. They did not appear to be improving and there was the unhealthy and nagging worry that he might be developing shin splints. 'I'll just have to get through it tomorrow,' he says, grimacing as he rubs his legs. 'I've got nearly twenty-four hours to rest up.' In the afternoon Brian Adcock discharged himself from the sick bay, insisting on being with his mates even if he cannot do the Thirty Miler. Secretly perhaps he harbours the belief that Wolsey might let him do it however shitty he's feeling. He is patently in no condition to do so, his arm in a sling and a large gaping hole in his forehead. He is, at least, in good humour and the batch's penchant for savage jokes at the expense of the halt and lame is, for once, voluntarily muted. They all know Brian can do it, always could do it and there but for the grace of God go they. His presence, while sobering, is a tremendous morale boost. Brian is pulling for the team and that means a lot to everyone.

The Thirty Miler begins just outside the bottom gate of Okehampton Camp, where a stream gurgles past between boulders and grassy banks, chattering and giggling away at the insanities of man at attempting such a thing, especially so close to dawn. At least the morning is clear, no sign of the mist that hung above the speed march like a shroud. Bad weather can screw the plans and timetable totally, turning an endurance exercise into one demanding time-consuming map reading skills and – if the weather really clags in – a survival exercise which there is no chance of passing.

The batch are divided into four syndicates, one seven strong, the other three of six, each escorted by a member of the Team or an officer along for the ride. The syndicates set out at ten-minute intervals. The first off comprises Lodge, Stovin-Bradford, Watkinson, Ashby, Skuse and Baxendale plus Wolsey, clutching a long wooden staff 'to help belabour the stragglers', and Matt Sturman. Everyone is wearing Pussers fighting order, pouches weighing 22 lbs (mainly of lead, plus assorted provisions, water, isotonic drinks, chocolate etc.) plus the SA80 slung over the back. Each syndicate also shares a safety Bergen, weighing some 50 lbs, which contains a 24-hour ration pack, a radio, one change of clothes and a bivvy bag, enough for the YOs to survive if Dartmoor turns the climate on its head. Baxendale has drawn the short straw and has the Bergen for the first thirty minutes and it's uphill all the way.

Everyone is wearing denims, a cotton shirt and boots. The weather has been warm and the forecast is bad – bright sun in a cloudless sky. Nobody wishes to overheat and any rains will be a bonus. The game plan is simple: keep up speed march pace for as much of the thirty miles as possible; the long steep climbs slow the pace down to a walk but the flat and downhill are there to be run. Except on Dartmoor there is no flat.

The last five minutes until the start at 0530 are fidgeting, twitching agony ... like race horses waiting outside the stalls you just want to be off. Seven hours away lies a green beret with your name already written inside it. You start at a cracking lick set by Chalkie – the old 'Seven Bellies' Stovin-Bradford seems a lifetime away – straight into that fast Marine walking pace, which can cripple a civvy. The hill stretches for maybe three kilometres and this time unlike Sunday when Wolsey took you all running up it – apart from that idle bastard Bob Bax – it's a rather nice stretch of tarmac road. Once the first brow of the hill is cracked the pace picks up further and the running begins, stretching out the limbs.

After the first twenty minutes you leave the track and head straight uphill, picking a tortuous route pioneered by acrobatic sheep, over rock and bouncy scrub that gives under weight. At this stage the route is taken with some circumspection; later there may not be time for such things but everyone is concerned with the dangers of turning an ankle. Matt Skuse is under some pain already from his left foot – the recurrence of his stress fracture: while it does not seem actually to have broken again it hurts like fuck. After two hills and a sharp jog, Bob Baxendale is slowing under the weight so two of the guys come alongside chatting and encouraging him. Throughout the day there will always be someone accompanying the Bergen bearer, a combination of moral, physical and spiritual support.

At the top it is swap-over time and Watkinson – who shows an extraordinary ability to fall over on the flat during a speed march but the agility of a goat on hills – takes over. Next is a straightforward downhill jog, followed by a long steady climb along the contours of the hills to the first unmanned checkpoint. Your target, Ashby points out with some glee, is the cleavage between two tors that resemble a girl's nipples. Forty-five minutes into the day the plastic butt plate on Watkinson's weapon pings loose; with a muttered 'shit' (instantly disproving Tom Coyle's theory that the closest Neil has ever got to a swearword is 'damn') he continues on without breaking stride. Skuse looks briefly for it but immediately shouts forward that it's as hopeless as looking for a needle in a haystack. Neil then inspects the butt, still on the move, and realizing that it has just worked itself loose, he hands the weapon over to Chalkie who fixes it amidst many imprecations on the weapon's antecedents, the defence minister who green-lighted it and the idle fuckers who assembled it in delicate tones and inferences doubtless learnt from Uncle Tom Coyle.

You reach the left nipple a good ten minutes ahead of schedule and the next three kilometres look easy enough on the map – grassland heading gradually downhill. However, as is so often the case, the map masks the reality for the grass conceals a bog. The dry summer weather means that it does not come pouring over the boot tops, but the marsh grass acts like a sponge dragging the energy out of the calves, sucking the legs dry, meanly taking more energy out of your muscles than the ground actually covered in return. Then you are heading downhill, along narrow sheep tracks a foot wide with Chalkie and the Bergen picking up a tremendous head of steam behind you. 'Gangway, Bergen coming through,' he bellows, thundering through like a rogue elephant, and suddenly you're into the first checkpoint, a circle of standing stones.

Sergeant John Atkins is scurrying down with a full jerry can of water. He was not expecting anyone quite so soon but you can see the second syndicate hard on your heels already. Twenty minutes up on the time now and Ashby does not give anyone more than a minute before it is off again, jumping across a stream and another slow climb up to the corner of Fernworthy Wood.

At first glimpse on the map Fernworthy looks like a simple skirt around the edges of a neat wooded area. In fact it's a real bugger, a steady climb to the top of one hill and then a rollercoaster dip back down; straight down on a 30 per cent incline and straight up the other side; then a fast run on a treacherous surface down to another stream, followed by a slow climb up through gorse and bog. Running down a steep hill can be more tiring in the long term than walking up it for the heel is perpetually acting as a brake, forcing your toes up into the top of the boot, rubbing voraciously on tender skin, bringing the blisters in to bear early. You can almost feel Harker's hot breath between your shoulder blades as he pushes the second syndicate along. So you crank up the pace and achieve a decent speed down the final decline, only turning your ankle once where a sheep had cunningly scrabbled a hole.

Going up through the gorse Matt Lodge has the Bergen and his legs are small. He is showing signs of flagging and as you start the gradual downhill jog into Bennett's Cross he bares what is left of his bottom teeth and emits an exhalation of anger, of exasperation accompanied by a facial contortion that Mike Tanner might envy. This grimace creates an adrenalin surge and you cruise into Bennett's Cross well ahead of time and still five minutes ahead of the second syndicate. While it is only a race against time and it doesn't matter if you are overtaken, what would that do to syndicate morale – especially the weaker members?

At the twelve-mile mark Bennett's Cross is a major meeting point with several cars and vans and a dozen people to offer support and encouragement. Colour Sergeant Foster hands out lashings of 'limers' (orange squash) and everyone realizes that the CG, Lieutenant General Sir Henry Beverley (the closest thing Royal Marines have to God), is standing over there with Colonel Taffinder but you can only gasp and drink some more.

A two-, perhaps three-minute breather and you are off again, handed over to the tender ministrations of the Commandant and the RSM. 'This is where we make up some time, gentlemen,' bellows the RSM (actually he is is speaking in normal tones but it sounds as if he is bellowing – somehow it always does with RSMs). 'The next leg is some eight kilometres and we aim to do it in forty minutes. You're going to hate me for it now but thank me later.' Instead you hate him for it right away.

The route is easier, tracks through the woods, light going except for when there is too much cinder and the heels slip. The RSM insists the syndicate do it in formation like a speed march which handicaps both Lodge and Ashby, as if tying them together in a three-legged race, but any sign of lagging is curtailed by a barked order.

The RSM keeps his promise and you reach the next checkpoint in the promised time, so you stop hating him about an hour later. (RSM Steve Perry adored running legs on the Thirty Milers. Tragically six weeks later while running on a recruit Thirty Miler he collapsed and died of a heart attack. He was only 42.) Ashby's fine, but then he always is. Skuse typically has decreed his foot to be no longer part of his body and therefore it cannot hurt any more, but you have reached that point – after four hours – where the mind is fine and the brain is sending all the right signals, it is just that your legs are failing to respond. The walking pace has dropped and the jogging is now a tremendous effort – move those legs! – and the pace is small, taut and tight. After a five-minute rest at the checkpoint – don't sit down because if you do the legs will stiffen up – and chewing on a Mars Bar for instant glucose gratification, you start off again.

This is the time when failure either triumphs or is overcome. Simply going through the motions you jog on, picking your way somewhat nervously on the long rubbly track down to the main road – another sign of incipient exhaustion – lagging behind the second syndicate, where even Pete Evans is holding his own. The main road should offer relief for a couple of miles but it doesn't; instead it mocks you, cars whizz past taking an exaggerated detour around the syndicate. You can feel the clock ticking away as you run on the spot – downhill, uphill, the flat – your comrades all forgotten and the miles grinding inexorably on. Crash. Bang. You have just run straight into the wall and there is only one person who can get you over it.

The first part of the road to the Hexworthy checkpoint is a gradual decline but for the first time you are truly alone and feeling it, feeling sorry for yourself. You do not hear, do not see any of the others. It is a beauty spot, a winding lane, covered by the leavings of a herd of cows, trees and bushes that curl over the peak of the road guarding a secret from the clouds. You find the tears rising unbidden in the throat, welling at the corner of your eyes, a rash of goose pimples over the shoulders – perhaps it is post-glucose depression, perhaps the confrontation of frailty – but there you are running along, tears trickling down your cheeks, saying out loud: 'No, I will not fail now. It is too late to stop now.'

The sight of some idiot civvy with a video camera makes you pull yourself together and then the apotheosis comes, as it so often does, in a moment of near farce. At the bottom of the valley where a wide deep stream curves underneath a stone bridge, the sun which had graciously spared us his presence for most of the day is beaming down, reflecting off the water in a most inviting manner. 'Fuck this,' you say out loud, startling a rather daft wood pigeon sporting a thin band of white feathers round his neck as if he were the local vicar, 'I don't have to do this if I don't want to. Why don't I just jack the whole thing, take off my clothes and have a leisurely swim in the pool?' And you laugh and so does Andy Goldsmith who is having the selfsame thoughts at the selfsame time. Later you find out many others did too.

With that laugh you cracked through the wall. Gnawing at a Mars Bar which tastes more like gristle or deer tendon than choco-late, alternating with slugs of water, you start the climb up to Hexworthy. Half your mind is left splashing in the stream, the other half is giggling at the very concept. The hill is steep, with hairpins that curve right back on each other, and at least as tough as the Fernworthy climb. Even the pub is closed – for ever if the sign on the door and the lack of buyers can be believed – and then you have made it to Hexworthy. Time has been lost but there are still two hours left in which to crack Ryder's Hill, he of the six false summits and the heartbreak ridge.

Throughout this long gradual climb, you're picking your way across, sliding and slipping off tufts of grass. It goes on and on, one false ridge after another; you know they are coming, but it's still a hard grind, made worse by the sun who has now emerged in all his blazing arrogance. It is 1030, the temperature is soaring through the mid-seventies, the sweat soaking your shirt through with not a chance to dry out.

What you are suffering, though, is nothing compared to the final syndicate who have been having problems from the off. Steve Hussey has shin splints, which means that every time his boot hits the ground, pain shoots up his leg from ankle to thigh. Within the first hour they reach a simple decision: if Steve tries to carry the safety Bergen it could finish him off, but that means that each of the remaining five will have to carry the Bergen three times, which will slow them down drastically. Sergeant Dai Phillips, who is running with them, offers the use of his day sack, so they split the Bergen, putting the radio in his day sack so that two of them are carrying about thirty pounds extra rather than one with fifty.

Morale is not improved over the final yomp across Ryder's when they are accompanied by WSM Colin Grice. He is being a by the book prick. Paul Attwood who is map reading puts it away for ten minutes and walks next to Steve, encouraging him on through that grass that sucks and pummels and drains the energy from his legs, leaving only the hurting. The group drift a couple of hundred yards off the direct line whereupon Grice gives Paul a bollocking and orders Dai Phillips to give him an extra map-reading lesson the next week. The Sergeant Major follows this morale-boosting behaviour by pinging Rob Lunn for a haircut and yelling at Dan Bailey towards the top of Ryder's Hill for cracking jokes – 'this is a serious exercise, not a laughing matter ... sir.' Several hours and beers later Paul is still fuming about the unnecessary nature of his comments – 'I'm not a fucking child!' – and for the whole syndicate it tarnished their achievement.

From the top of Ryder's to the finish is still over three miles but you know the battle is won as long as you can keep rolling along. Steve Hussey's syndicate have cut it fine but it is only a constant jog on the spongy Dartmoor tracks, jumping over the bare white rocks that nudge out of the clay soil, a perpetual reminder to the unwary foot. Down the last hill, through the gate and the track becomes tarmac and the rhythm of the run increases with the consistency of the surface and as the end approaches so do the emotions in your throat. But Royal Marine commandos do not show such emotions and you are all determined not to emulate the example of the last May batch.

Some of them had literally made it with seconds to spare, their syndicates straggling out in individual bundles; some had parents watching, even running alongside shouting encouragement to little Johnny. Having completed it they proceeded to hug and kiss each other – 'like footballers, not Royal Marines', sniffed interested observer Mark Wolsey. YO Sept. '91 got his message. Every syndicate arrives trotting down the road, in perfect order three ranks deep, two across. So much dignity on display, at once both defiant and elegant, faces red, streaked with sweat and perhaps a surreptitious tear, shirts soaked but chins held high; the relief on Hussey's face mingles with the pain from the crunch as his heel hits the road and the cheers of the spectators and those who have already finished echo and fade, echo and fade their triumph back over Dartmoor.

This is what they have been sweating for – the green beret. And it is presented to them in a small open field in the most informal ceremony imaginable, by a man dressed in a beret and camouflage fatigues, distinguished from their own only by his shoulder flashes, a crown over crossed baton and sabre.

When the CG presents each man with his green beret the batch display little emotion, a fixed expression on each face, with twinkling eyes above it. When they smile for the camera a few display nervousness, but not Charlton whose white grin could be a beacon for ships on a starless night (Henry is nowhere to be seen throughout the ceremony). Similarly when the awards are dished out there is little surprise when Harker takes the Lumsden Trophy (best performance on the Tarzan and Endurance Courses) and that for displaying the best physical fitness in the batch – he has not even returned to his position (all in alphabetical order) before he is called out again. Away to the side a momentary cloud passes over Brian Adcock's face, a mixture of distress and sadness leavened by a drop of jealousy.

Stovin-Bradford gets the award for most improved physical fitness – 'I always thought you had a chance, Chalkie,' whispered a colleague, before adding sardonically, 'until after Easter leave when you seemed to be letting the beer run to your belly once more.' The Commando Medal – 'for the YO displaying the best batch spirit on the Commando Course' – is awarded to Ashby. This surprised the batch somewhat as Wolsey had asked them to vote for that award: in the main they had voted for Goldsmith and Lodge but he had decided to give it to Ashby. (On one of their recces during Green Beret, Wolsey and Coyle had discovered Goldsmith fast asleep on sentry duty, which cost him any chance of the Commando Medal.)

Mike Tanner, too, had a prize at stake, an important wager with Gav Parr. 'After I finished the Thirty Miler I had a bet that I would be under sixteen stone. When we got back to Lympstone I ran straight down to the gym and weighed myself. I was sixteen and a half stone and I thought, "Mike, after a month of extreme effort, that's the lowest you are ever going to go."'

At five in the evening the batch are to be found celebrating in the Turf Inn with multiple beers and a massive barbecue – so hungry that the usual meat quantities had to be doubled. A few are limping, the odd hobble is sighted but quickly vanishes as the first three pints rehydrate aching empty limbs and the next four start to get them pissed. Matt Lodge turns up with Amanda, who causes some stir as she appears to lack a visible panty line. Shaggy's girlfriend Anna is down because she is off to spend a year studying Arabic in Egypt but she must have had a few because she appears fascinated when Dai explains to her down to the last firing pin what weapons are carried by a Royal Marine troop.

Now the YOs have their green lids – Henry is absent, while Brian takes the jokes about his disability well and leaves the evening with the new nickname of 'Robo Nod' – the Training Team are very relaxed with them. Billy Baxter gets raucously slaughtered, Dai never stops talking – most of it rubbish – Coyle empties a barrel of lager and expands further his observations on Pongos, Graeme Foster somehow ends up being pursued by a bunch of YOs on to the mud-flats and stripped naked. The RSM remarks cattily when a barge-load of (primarily old) women arrive on a barge trip from Exeter, 'Here comes the May batch', to be greeted with much applause. Wolsey just sits there drinking his Murphy's, his face a mask behind which his emotions play hide and seek. He smiles frequently, sometimes the smile of an indulgent father, sometimes one of relief, and once in a while there flickers behind his eyes a waterfall of sadness.

They laugh and they drink and they drink and they laugh. It is just past the longest day of the year and twilight is meandering into midnight when Andy Goldsmith leaves the batch, leaves his beer and his cigarettes on the table. He walks down to the beach where an ancient lifeboat hulk has been rotting its way back into the earth for years. He affects to scrutinize it but he does not see it. Nor is he looking at Lympstone, straight over the estuary, the lights in the Officers' Mess winking on one by one, acknowledgement perhaps of the YOs' achievement.

Andy wants to be alone with his thoughts, to be solitary for a while. He stares out to sea, seeing nothing, hearing even less. Around his mind is whirring both question and prayer, neither understood nor answered. 'Now what?' he says again and again, 'What can I do next? What is there left to do?'

From the wind comes no answer, the sea offers no succour, no solution. The mud offers but a raven's wink. He stays there a while, contemplating the void, hoping for a sign. At last it comes. Not a whisper from the water but a bellow from the land.

'Oy Goldsmith, it's your shout!'

Heaven Knows I'm Miserable Now

> You may not believe it now but there will come a day when
> you get up in the morning, put on your green beret and it
> won't mean anything, it will just be part of your uniform.
>
> Billy Baxter

THERE WAS LITTLE thought of the future as the batch splintered off throughout Britain for a long weekend. All who still had them fled straight to the bosom of their girlfriends, to repair the serious dents in some supposedly solid relationships caused by the all-pervasive demands of the Commando Course. 'A whole month of summer wasted,' grumbled one girl, her worst fears realized by the July downpours that followed. Matt Lodge, once looking so secure, was now teetering on the brink. Tim David was rushing up to London to find exactly what Lisa's being a nanny in Clapham involved, before the batch's sexual fantasies took over; Chalkie wanted pampering and bullying in roughly equal proportions; Andy Mac split for Sandhurst where Andrea had started a TA course, much against his wishes.

'The Commando Course was a month when we didn't know what we were doing, being picked up by Hercules in the middle of nowhere,' recalls Mac. 'When I first got the beret, I thought that was it, I'd not thought beyond this last month at all. It feels funny wearing a green beret. First of all it's a big shock in that people actually salute you walking around the camp – there is a very big difference in the manner in which it is done, a bit of real acceptance, they seem to mean it now.

'Having finished the Thirty Miler I didn't think "I must be rufty-tufty now", I just felt a bit knackered. I thought about this three years ago, set myself a target and as you achieve each step along the way they seem smaller as goals, the hurdle you jumped looks smaller. I had a great weekend, celebrating. On Saturday night I went to a party with all my old friends, I got blind drunk and ended up wading through a pond and clambering across a marquee in my dinner jacket. But on Monday I came back to CTC feeling a sense of anti-climax.'

Andy Goldsmith felt the same way. 'It took two days for Baxter's prophecy to sink in, for me and for the vast majority of us. I wandered around for a long time feeling despondent and wondering why. As soon as we walked off the Thirty Miler everyone was talking about doing a "P Company" [the Paras' training programme, renowned for its beastliness]. I have to do something else, next challenge please.'

It was as if a huge post-coital sadness were visited upon the batch. The game over, the chase won, the hunter was now blooded; the beret that had seemed so all-important was now just something they put on every day. They were now part of an élite club but all the suffering they had endured to join it was fading away in the memory banks. They were no longer special, no longer the ones in waiting; now they were the grown-ups who would soon have a real job to do, real men to command. The new May batch were wandering around like headless chickens – which made them laugh, as much at recent memory as at the blue-bereted YOs; but they could also see developing in them that slow coalescence, the forging of batch spirit and unity, detect the feral innocence of the developing wolf pack. It seemed as if their batch ardour and vivacity had migrated the day they won their green berets.

'Until we cracked the Commando Course everyone was bound very tightly together, trying to achieve a common aim,' says Mike Tanner wistfully. 'A lot of energy was concentrated on speculating who would be next to drop out, but there was a strong batch tendency which wanted everyone to get through. After we got our lids, that broke away and we lost concentration, lost focus.'

The first week back was not too bad in that after two turgid days being introduced to the intricacies of Service Funds there was another visit to the Senior Service at Dartmouth. This was not so riotous as their November trip, which had involved the introduction of a captured sheep into a formal Naval dinner; the baring of some hairy backsides in a public house and a subsequent complaint leading to Rory Thomson and Tim David being confined to CTC for three weeks as punishment. It was however a surprise to Jason McQueen who, having been at the Naval College for all of eight weeks, came into his cabin one night to find three of his former colleagues in his bed, two more hiding inside the wardrobe and a sixth sitting in the sink vainly trying to camouflage himself as a piece of soap.

'I was glad to see them,' he smiles. 'I was having a much easier time at Dartmouth, Lympstone had prepared me for all the kit inspections and I was doing pretty well. Actually despite just getting their green berets they were reasonably subdued – for Marines. They cheered up after a while and went off to use a very expensive model of a ship in a perspex case – they cost about £5,000 each – as a sledge.'

Real depression set in on Monday 6 July, when they began their Range Qualifying Course, seven weeks of misery, fortunately broken up by the Lympstone Summer Ball and three blessed weeks of leave. The RQC is too long to keep the interest of young men who have just been stretched to the limit and it has been trimmed for subsequent batches. The aim of the course is to qualify them to be able to take their men live firing, to set up ranges, following all the safety procedures, checking that the arcs and extreme range of fire do not threaten livestock or humans. Skuse and Lodge – among others – were to admit a year later that they had found the qualification vital in their first job but at the time they too bemoaned the many nights spent doing range traces, cutting out plastic shapes only to find they were a millimetre out.

After three weeks, morale was hovering around the zero mark. 'This course is killing us, robbing us of all drive,' moaned Chalkie as he and Tim David tried desperately to get it right at the third time of asking. 'You can't come off the Commando Course and go into range traces. If you fail this course it doesn't really matter because in a unit there will always be a PW1 – like Coyle or Phillips – to supervise, so all we'll ever get to do is sit around reading the papers or trying to turn Shingle Man into even more of a bugger.'

'We know that war is supposed to be turgid and boring and that nothing happens for weeks but it has to be better than this,' interjects Tim, whose confidence has increased steadily throughout training. Once he was frightened and happy to hide in the middle of the crowd; now while he eschews centre stage, he prefers to inhabit the fringes, sniping at the unwary with sharp, well chosen and timely putdowns. He is depressed because the batch rumour brigade have come back with a gloomy prognosis about the available postings. 'The short service people have been told that the chance of getting a troop in a Commando unit is nil, so we've all wrapped on that idea.' The rumour was to be proved false but not for another two months.

Because they are bored and feeling pissed off members of the batch are getting at each other. They are all in it until Pass Out so any self-policing element is now redundant but the tactics can still be used against anyone who is believed to be getting above himself. There are no Lords of Discipline, no secret courts where wankers are adjudged guilty and sentence of exile or death passed – never have been, and anyway the Lord High Executioner has himself been back batched. But there is still judgement by your peers.

Andy Harker is one candidate. Since the Commando Course he has retired into his own phys world, pushing himself to the limit and further with each passing day. Ten days after the Thirty Miler he took part in a Royal Marine 87-mile run along the coastline from Lympstone to Poole and his syndicate won in record time. Never much of a social animal, he has withdrawn from the batch. Now he never goes out with anyone and absents himself from any voluntary group activities.

However, despite his eccentricities Harker is soon replaced as target of the week by the oleaginous Mr McInerney. 'Mac is now being cheesy and getting on everyone's tits,' gripes David. 'He's now known as Big Mac Cheeseburger and before long the whole batch will call him that and he'll calm down. Someone gets carried away, doesn't realize that he is pissing others off. Andy Mac is doing it right now and eventually will get the message. Either Lodgie will have a quiet chat or me and Chalkie will use our own methods, the batch lets everyone know through fair means, no one has got punched yet.'

McInerney's elevation to Hamburger Hell started over dinner *chez* the Commandant. At some point every member of the batch will be invited along for an informal evening meal, as they are to Matt Sturman's. 'At the meal,' says David, 'he was coming out with these incredibly cheesy comments. Like when the Commandant mentioned he had grown the raspberries for pudding Mac is talking to Sarah Taffinder and comes out with "I don't know where you got these from, Sarah, they're just great – lovely and fluffy". The Colonel goes "Thank you, Mr McInerney" while Gav and I are sitting around the corner going [he smacks his head for emphasis] "Christ, I don't believe he said that." Eventually Colonel Taffinder leant forward, smiled and said, "By the way, Mr McInerney, you still pass out on November 6th – like the rest of the batch."'

The RQC was boring but any problem the batch had with it was primarily of their own making. Wolsey had never made any secret of the fact that he considered the course to be a waste of time when everything necessary could have been gleaned in three weeks. This attitude had been communicated to them and it did not help that they all realized how different and special their Commando Course had been and were in a state of acute Wolsey hero-worship. Their generic arrogance had not been damped by long spells standing in the static tank and when they met their range qualifying course officer Captain Malcolm Norman of the Duke of Wellington's Regiment they could not stand him. For a start he was a Pongo and they were wearing their belligerent 'don't screw with me I'm a Commando now' attitude as proudly as they wore the T-shirts Gav had printed up with the logo '*YO Sept. 91. Too Sexy for the Tank*'.

Mike Tanner, who is not a man given to disobeying the commands of senior officers, recalls the course with a combination of consternation and horror. 'If there was an all-time low for the batch it was on the RQC. We were getting messed around by the OC of the package who was an army officer; he was trying to beast us and give us speed marches, stuff like that; he tried to make us work on our days off because he thought we were slouching around. That caused a lot of morale problems and by the end we were as close to a mutiny as I've ever seen.

'We were originally given a day off after two weeks of doing range papers. It was a Sunday and he decided to have a competition of military skills instead: everyone had to submit a programme of how they would arrange it and the best design was to be instrumented and we were all to be put through it in groups of five. Originally we thought he could not be serious – judging distance, camouflage, it was stuff we had covered on Tenderfoot. I think it was done simply to impress upon us the fact that he was in command.

'So we did this bloody thing and found ourselves in the middle of a live-firing artillery range with all these live rounds whizzing over our head. It had to be Endexed, called off. He was in the middle of a valley and everyone was in groups all around up the hill. Endex came over the radio and the next minute everyone was jumping up and down yahooing; people shouting over the net, "Yeah, brilliant, it's called off", and he was on the other end. He was down at the bottom and could have heard us cheering without a radio so he just walked away. He'd been getting loads of pisstaking behind his back up to this point. It was pretty much a mutiny really – it must have been embarrassing for him – but we didn't need all that rubbish from a man without a green beret.'

Another man without a green beret, Jools Ostling, had now joined the May batch. The lack of a lid put still greater distance between him and his former batch mates. Phil Ashby for one never quite knew what to say to him. 'It's as if we've left him a long way behind, he's a reminder of a past life where we no longer exist.' However Jools was still not immune to causing a bit of mischief. It was always an accepted part of the batch sense of humour to suggest to their friends that absentee girlfriends were consistently sleeping with other men; it was another thing to fan the flames of rumour over one living in Exeter.

Everyone knew Matt Lodge and Amanda had been having problems for a while but rumours began to circulate that she had been spotted in the company of another Marine – not even an officer. One version had it that she had been spotted by a member of the batch being chatted up by a Marine, either from MT or a chef, when he was out walking his dog. Ostling then claimed he and Gav had seen them together in Exeter at the cinema.

'It was,' says Skuse sadly, 'one of those wild rumours that circulated until everyone knew about it but no one would bring themselves to tell Matt. Rob Lunn was told that he ought to mention it because as one of Lodgie's closest mates he knew him well enough but Rob said, "No way, it's none of our business." I reckon Jools played it very cleverly; we were bored so he got the rumour moving, and then finally he got drunk and barged in on the pair of them.'

'She was out of order,' insists Ostling. 'Everyone was saying Lodge's girlfriend is doing the dirty but no one told him. Eventually me and Gav got very drunk and barged in on him, told him what was going on; she was there at the time. He came out and said "No, she's not", she came out and said "No, I'm not." Then he shut the door and asked her, "Why are they saying this?" "Oh he's just a friend," she said.'

This dramatic and noisy turn of events had woken half the corridor from their range traces. Jools, perhaps realizing that he had gone too far in openly accusing Matt's girlfriend of being unfaithful, had a massive attack of the guilts. He turned to Goldsmith who had come out of his cabin and yelled, 'I don't believe I did that, go on hit me, I deserve it, please go on hit me.'

Goldsmith, who like various other members of the batch had been waiting many months for such an invitation, tried to play it down. 'You're pissed, Jools, go to bed.' But he wouldn't and the shouting went on for another five minutes with Jools entreating Goldsmith to punch him out. Eventually Rob Lunn shouted out: 'For fuck's sake Andy punch him, then we can all get some sleep.'

'Go on, I deserve it.'

Whack. Crash.

'I don't believe you did that,' came the plaintive wail from the floor.

'You deserved it.' Goldsmith's punch was delivered for Matt Lodge. Unfortunately it might have come too late to save his relationship.

The Lympstone Summer Ball is traditionally the time when the September batch rule the roost. They have their green lids while the new May batch are still finding their blistered feet. As the days grew closer the main panic seemed to be whether their Mess kits would fit properly or whether the tailor would muddle up Rob Lunn's trousers with Russ Corn's jacket. The YOs all dress in scarlet Mess jackets, a low-cut black waistcoat, starched white shirts with studs instead of buttons, black bow-ties that have to be tied – clip-ons are considered to be beyond the social pale and 'only for idle civvies'. The jackets are cut high above the backside, to reveal firm athletic bums in navy blue worsted trousers with red stripes running down the seams.

The military as a whole revel in formal balls and dinners for it enables them to escape from the conformity of khaki into exotic dress uniforms dating from an era when men were allowed to, indeed expected to, preen like exotic tropical birds. This means that in their uniform finery they often upstage their lady guests and any civilian friends are put firmly in their dinner jacketed place. The Officers' Mess was transformed; up went a giant marquee that still was only big enough to feed the four hundred and fifty guests in two separate sittings. The theme was the Wild West so the front of the Mess was transformed by artfully cut logs into Fort Lympstone where the cannons still looked at home. The ball was officially opened – bizarrely, many thought – by a mock Wild West gunfight performed by a local club, instead of the more traditional 'beatings' performed by members of the Royal Marines Band. This shoot-out was watched with professional interest by the assembled officers who to a man commented on the poor quality marksmanship and old-fashioned tactics displayed by the dying cowboys. 'No wonder Custer lost at the Little Big Horn,' remarked Wolsey sardonically.

Neil Watkinson was the only batch absentee, away at a friend's wedding – having missed one in his first weekend of training, he was not going to absent himself again. This was a feeling all his comrades understood: training was coming to an end and it was more important than ever to rescue civilian friendships as the batch began its slow slide into dissolution. Chalkie and Bob Rob had invited down a couple of friends from Southampton University who proceeded to tell endless stories about their appalling behaviour on rugby club beanos. Compared to some of the antics in training these no longer seemed that bad. Andy Rowley, too, made his first formal appearance since January. He insisted that there were no regrets and that he was far happier teaching PT at King's School, Wimbledon. But at times there appeared a wistful glimmer in his eyes and he was very determined to remind Wolsey of his athletic prowess.

'Well, Mark, how's the phys?' he said loudly, stressing the 'Mark' in front of those members of the batch listening in, who still, to this day, address him either as 'Sir', or informally as 'Boss'. 'I always could beat you on a run.'

'Quite right, Mr Rowley,' came the reply. Later Wolsey could not resist remarking to a friend that he reckoned Rowley was regretting his decision to quit. 'I expect he always will ... and, incidentally, he only beat me once by a matter of seconds.'

Those girlfriends who had survived were all there. Mike Tanner with his Helen; Chalkie and Katie, who did not look like an Abbey National branch manager; Tim David arguing with Lisa about the morality of war, a discussion he lost hands down; Steve Hussey and Emma who somehow had ridden all the storms with equanimity, while Matt Lodge and Amanda were still trying to. Trevor and Jacko were 'threaders' because the two dates Jacko had invited never turned up. 'Look man,' said Jacko to the distressed Trev, 'I spoke to them this afternoon and they promised they were coming. What do you want me to do, drive round to their flat and hammer on the door? Let's have a drink.'

Gav made up for the Jamaicans by turning up with two dates – schoolgirls he had met while invading their boarding school for a dare. His behaviour towards them was that of a perfect officer and gentleman, a source of great amusement to all the senior officers watching. For Bob Baxendale the night was to have unforeseen consequences. He had been passionately in love with a girl who had gone travelling to Australia, but they had parted over the summer and he was very depressed about it. By dawn he found himself first dancing with and then dating a beautiful American model, five years his senior, brought along by Andy Goldsmith's Rachel, an Exeter nurse.

The summer ball was to be Jools Ostling's last public appearance. He was not happy in the new May batch. Being off phys had enabled him to brush up on his tactical and other military skills that had been letting him down before his leg injury but the class structure he saw everywhere in OTW was really getting to him. 'Sturman came into my room one day when I was injured and asked "how's it coming along?" So I just spoke to him as I did to people in my rowing club who were thirty-five years old – they might have been high-flyers in the City but you could talk to them with no divide. After he went out Sergeant Major Grice came in and shouted, "You don't say 'yeah' to a senior officer. It's 'yes sir'." I started to get more and more angry three weeks before summer leave, wondering whether it was worth it.

'I knew I could do it easily, the phys was hard but I never had any problems being in the top part of the batch. I was looking forward to it in a way. I knew it would be easier because I would have started just after Long Knight with all the good exercises coming up. I was keen, I'd got on well with the new batch. Then I had a great holiday – I went to America, went scuba diving and sky diving. That was what I'd been expecting from the military when I went in and here I was getting it anyway, so I decided to leave. I decided I could get what I wanted without being in the Marines.'

Wolsey and Sturman who had been concerned – for different reasons – as to Jools's suitability were relieved. So was he, for underneath he too realized that striving to be a Marine officer had brought out the worst in his character, that he had hidden his own insecurities by trying to foist them on others. 'I've always been a piss taker,' he says, 'but I was definitely a bit cruel. The reason was that you did things to impress your mates, to be one of your mates; in a group like that everyone has to have their niche, there have to be people to have the piss taken out of them, and me and Gav were the piss takers, the sharp end of the batch. It wasn't very good for me, so I'm glad I quit.'

Two weeks after summer leave the Range Qualifying package was finished and the batch, with sighs of relief that could be heard in Cardiff, were back under Wolsey's control and indeed command for FIBUA (Fighting In Built Up Areas) – augmented by Marines up to company strength, which meant each YO was at least a section commander. Wolsey's company had to defend an MoD village built on Salisbury Plain for the purposes of training troops in urban warfare, house to house fighting and clearances. The attackers were 45 Commando at full strength.

Matt Skuse was in command of a screening force sent out to give the defenders early warning of any attack, to engage the enemy, thus disrupting their advance, forcing them to deploy early and reveal their tactics. His men were then to split up in small groups and attempt to make their own way back to reinforce the defence. It was an ambitious assignment that unfortunately for Skuse did not work out too well. It didn't help that Russ Corn, operating as one of his section commanders, chose to criticize his orders in front of a visiting brigadier. 'At Copehill Down I gave a complex set of orders to my troop,' recalls Skuse. 'There was a brigadier watching and Russ chose to stand up and point out the holes in them. I was upset because I never got another command appointment in training.

'Our job was to be a screen force, we ambushed 45's recce troop about dawn. I let them get really close then two young Marines lost their nerve, or thought they had been spotted and opened fire. All hell broke loose, we put down a great rate of fire and they dived on top of us, piled in for a scrap and we settled into unarmed combat. I yelled "Leg it" and everyone bomb burst in different directions. I lost one section commander and my radio operator was captured, which was a problem as he had all our signal frequencies for the day and the enemy then knew them all. I ran back to Wolsey and told him what had happened while others spread all over the place.'

Skuse had found himself up against trained recce troops whose job is to infiltrate and clear the way for the main force. They also had the advantage of night vision goggles to study positions, which the YOs lacked. Dan Bailey and his three Marines managed to avoid detection and evade capture by working their way around by a long route back into the village. It took them several hours but it was an impressive performance. 'It's a good experience for them for things to go wrong,' commented Wolsey. 'In training they seldom do because the object is to show people how it works, but they were up against professionals and it was an object lesson in not underestimating the enemy.'

Wolsey was less sanguine when admitting that officially his men had eventually been overrun. Competitive at all times and a renowned bender and twister of rules, he does not approve of them being twisted against him. 'In the strictest sense of the exercise, yes, we were overrun but there was much gnashing of teeth because 45 were also umpiring the exercise,' he says. 'Otherwise a lot of it wouldn't have unfolded as it did. Strictly speaking they would not have overrun us as we had such an infinite advantage in defending. We were picking them off before they got to the houses; then they wouldn't have been able to break in without being shot because all the houses were mutually protecting each other. The umpires kept coming in and saying, "This house has been taken, move back." Damian McKinney [the Lympstone instructor who set up the exercise] was always at loggerheads with the umpires, saying, "You can't fire a rocket into that house. They do not go round corners!"'

'The fighting lasted from 0600 to 1400 hours and we didn't really have enough ammunition,' confirms Skuse. 'It was 45's exercise, we were the enemy and we were there to lose but they pulled some fast ones like the time this troop ran up a ladder into a window and climbed into the house two hundred yards away – we'd have picked every single one off with our scopes.'

As a rule, Marines are notorious landlubbers so their next assignment – two weeks' sea training – was greeted with some trepidation. A few proffed greatly. Rob Lunn went to the Baltic, flew out there business class and was then on board a minesweeper during its goodwill visits to Estonia, Lithuania and Latvia. Gav and Chalkie flew to Denmark and sailed back to the UK stopping off in various fleshpots on the way home. Matt Skuse drove from his girlfriend Vicky's in Cardiff to Southampton where he boarded HMS *Birmingham* which promptly sailed back to Cardiff, did some firing of anti-aircraft guns out on the 'oggin' (ocean) and sailed back again. He had four days at sea. Andy Goldsmith was on a fishery protection vessel in the English Channel, he spent two weeks at sea bobbing up and down inspecting fishing vessels. Jezz and Steve Hussey took the train to Scotland, caught a helicopter out to their ship, and the first thing Jezz did within half an hour of landing on board was throw up over the wardroom table. Others were less fortunate, spending all their time on board ships in dry dock for the duration. As there were not enough berths for all the YOs, others were sent on an adventure training course in Wales.

Just before they went to sea Brian Adcock had taken his Commando Course reruns. This time there were no heroics from Brian, he passed the Tarzan Course comfortably, if travelling a little gingerly over the fatal climbing net, ran the Endurance Course in sixty-two minutes and the Thirty Miler in under six and a quarter hours. While hardly record-breaking times Brian had been feeling a little tired. The weekend before his tests he and five other members of the batch had driven up to Scotland in a minibus to run the Three Peaks, starting at midnight on Friday and finishing eighteen hours later.

The Robo Nod jokes were now finished with and it was time to reconvene as a batch for the last time for Final Nail, a two-week exercise designed to round off all those hard-earned skills.

Final Nail

God save me from my friends – I can protect myself from my
enemies.

English proverb

IT DOES NOT seem to matter which YO is awarded the Sword of
Honour, there will only be one person in the batch who believes
he deserves it ... and that is the recipient. It means the award is
always divisive, something Wolsey was fully aware of. 'In my batch
no one understood why it went to the eventual winner,' he says. 'I
don't like the whole idea of a batting order and would prefer when
I am writing to each man's new Commanding Officer just to say
they finished in the top third, middle or bottom third of the batch.
It should not make any difference if you finished eighth or
eighteenth.'

In recruit training the top recruit in each King's Squad is awarded
the King's Badge, which is sewn on to the left shoulder of all his
uniforms for all his time in the Corps. (Both Harker and Parr are
King's Badgemen.) On average in one out of every three recruit
troops, if the Training Team cannot agree on a clear winner, the
King's Badge is not awarded. The Sword of Honour, however, is
always awarded. Wolsey rationalized his choice of Ashby for the
Commando Medal by explaining that he wanted all the top three
YOs to walk away with something, saying at the time, 'Corn will
probably win the Sword of Honour, Harker has already won two
prizes and Ashby deserves something too.'

Russ Corn had probably set his sights on the Sword within his
first few weeks at CTC. A tall blond Yorkshire lad possessing generous ears upon which a beret could stand easy he arrived at
Lympstone from Cambridge University smart, ambitious, socially

adept, with a gift for diplomacy and an innate knack for manipulating people. Possessing most of the gifts of a natural leader, except perhaps the relaxed easy come, easy go, charisma that emanates from Phil Ashby, he made up for that with a bullish obstinacy and a tendency not to suffer fools at all.

Jason McQueen who left the batch in December was surprised when Russ got the Sword, for all he remembered was a very solid figure, notable for having a strong friendship with the independent Andy Harker, but not standing out from the crowd. Russ's career proves the old military adage that time spent in reconnaissance is seldom wasted. Arriving as a UCE he had the advantage of already knowing some of what was in store, so did not flounder under the erupting volcano of kit that all but drowned others – though reputedly on his four-week introduction before going to university he too had struggled constantly. He was fit enough to survive the early exercises strongly enough to be noticed and commended by the Training Team but by suffering horribly on the ropes in the gym he did not distinguish himself as a phys nut inside the batch.

From very early on, if his section was in bimble mode, whether due to a weak set of orders or the sheep syndrome when men just mill about aimlessly waiting for something to do, Russ would often step in unasked to take control and create order. This often seemed to happen just as a member of the DS or Team appeared from behind a bush. There is a knack and a certain amount of luck involved in being seen by superior officers and yet not appear to be metamorphosing into an anteater with a long and very brown nose. Russ always managed to balance both sides of the spectrum. Matt Sturman liked the way he did things by the book, while Mark Wolsey appreciated his ability to motivate others and still display an individual, arrogant streak the width of the Dales. He conducted himself very well at the first Regimental Dinner, impressing senior officers with a sophistication and social awareness lacking in some of his contemporaries who all got pissed first and conversed later.

A couple of the Team were suspicious, but then SNCOs always are. Tom Coyle reckoned he saw a bit of a jack lurking in there, but admitted that on exercise 'Corn looks for the solution, he does not court popularity and won't suffer fools gladly – he displayed great sense in nearly punching Collins once – he organizes his section without being appointed, fits in well, leads Navexes competently. The only question is over his physical endurance. But he will allow the man in command to make a duff decision, without querying it. On Eagle Eye he remained in his sleeping bag while Ostling fucked up.'

Russ himself was always aware of the dichotomy between being in command and being a member of the batch and having to support one's oppo. On Eye Opener back in November he recalls, 'One of the most worrying aspects was my personal reaction to the cold. It came as a real shock to find myself "switching off" despite a desire to stay alert. The idea of helping those around me became a genuine conscience crisis – to help, and prolong the cold whilst stripping down for the river crossing, or to make sure you survive the ordeal, then worry about others once back in dry kit at the other end. My personal belief is that it is of the utmost importance to remain up and running and only then can you help those around you. At the same time upon sitting back and watching, or having to follow others into whatever trouble they led us, I became less and less concerned about others' reactions and feelings and decided to get out front and do the job a little more effectively.'

Socially he quickly became a core member of the First XV ('Northern bastards' contingent) and a prime mover in their social activities. He and Pete Evans disliked each other on sight and as the months went on and Pete stubbornly stuck to realizing his ambition, detestation turned to hatred. 'At some point during training every member of the batch would have a drink and a long chat with every other member,' comments one YO. 'Russ would not have been seen dead drinking with Pete, and it was mutual. At times he used to rage about him to me with an intensity that bordered on the insane. Nor would he ever go on a run ashore with Matt Lodge who for all his physical shortcomings is an extremely fine and competent officer.'

'Russ would always tend to get his own way,' says Brian Adcock. 'In his own mind he was going to get the Sword right from the very start and no one was going to get in his way. The Team liked him from word go, so did Sturman which counted for a lot. He was a bit of a jack in that he had some shortcomings professionally but everybody did. At the end of training he sealed it without any doubt over the Three Peaks Race; he organized everything, wrote all the letters, we turned up and did it.'

To those who were not close to the top Russ's quest for the Sword had provided much amusement. 'One time in a classroom he got an answer wrong and a few of us took the piss,' says Jools Ostling. 'We were saying "The Sword, the Sword, there it goes, flying away from you." He wanted it so much he got really annoyed.'

'In training I always knew I was in for a shout and I thought it was between me and Shaggy,' insists Russ. 'When we found out I was genuinely staggered, which is difficult to say without sounding immodest. I wanted it, of course – who wouldn't? In fifteen months the Training Team will get to know you and the system scores you, you know how you are doing at various assessments, but there is always that uncertainty.'

The batch as ever eventually found out before time when Gav was in Matt Sturman's office for one of his bollockings and he read this signal with the top five placements on it. Even by Final Nail it was pretty obvious to most people in the batch that Russ was going to get the Sword, but he did not handle that knowledge with the quiet assured confidence one might expect; instead he continued to ram himself down others' throats. 'I finished eighth,' says Matt Lodge, 'but I knew from the start of BFT I'd never go any higher because of the physical side of things. None of the top five was ever wholly supportive of each other. The whole question of an order of merit got quite divisive towards the end. Mike made a few people take a step back because he let it be known he considered himself to be in the running ... and wasn't that far wrong. The batch looked at the obvious – the physical side – and thought "who's he kidding." But the thing that stuck in everybody's throats was when Russ stitched up Matt Skuse in front of the brigadier at Copehill Down on FIBUA. He didn't need to do it, he appeared to be Sturman's golden boy, his handling of the final presentation was bossy and authoritarian and didn't go down well.'

Competitiveness is encouraged throughout the Corps, especially in training, but sometimes it backfires and people can take it too far. It is not normal after one of your batch mates has given an O group in front of the DS and a visiting brigadier to stand up voluntarily and say 'But Matt, you missed this and this out.' It was a serious error of judgement by Corn which surprised the brigadier who later commented, 'When I went through training we used to help each other.' If such a thing had happened earlier in such public circumstances it might have cost him the Sword.

At the same time, from the moment Mike Tanner announced his candidature and threw his lid into the Sword pit, he set himself up as a butt, a scapegoat for the whole batch as everyone likes to see the mighty fall or fail. Mike was a prime target in that underneath that fearsome exterior beats a sensitive soul who will always leap at whatever bait is offered him.

'I can see why Russ was awarded it though I wouldn't have agreed personally,' says Mike judicially, now he has the experience of having commanded his own troop to back up his judgement. 'It is very difficult to pick from within any group; there are instances now when my boss asks me for opinions within the troop and I say, "He's a pretty good hand", and the boss says, "I think he's a total wanker." Sometimes two different people can misread the same situation, you don't always see the whole picture as a member of the Training Team.

'The Sword is important, don't get me wrong. I'd have loved it, done anything for it, but not to the detriment of others. Anyone would be foolish to say they didn't want it, it would be like saying you didn't want a million pounds. But I wouldn't have made a fool out of people like Matt Skuse. He was grossly misrepresented, one of the best leaders in the batch. He is one of the hardest working blokes, he never ever complained; if you asked Skusey as Duty Student, "I'm a bit pressed, can you get this done?" you could always rely on him. He got a lot of undeserved piss taking, he was a good leader who knew his military skills but wasn't prepared to stand out in front of people and take the piss out of them, which sadly seems to account for quite a lot.'

Perhaps because of the fallout after the Skuse incident many of the batch felt the Sword should have gone to either Shaggy or Paul Attwood. It also influenced Matt Lodge's immediate choice of career plans, his relationship with Amanda having foundered on the eve of Final Nail. 'The Commando Course proved the final hurdle in what had been a very extended relationship,' he says, avoiding any comment on the Ostling incident. 'She had moved down to Exeter and found it increasingly difficult as we were away so much. Basically it didn't hold and she ended up finding someone else. It all came to a head the day before Final Nail when I couldn't do anything about it. There is no question of attributing blame because I was away so much.

'Originally I wanted to go to 42 Commando at Plymouth, when I finished training, because of Amanda but when she went for a ball of chalk I decided to look further afield. I did not want to go up to

45 Commando. I did not make any bones about it at the time but I was unhappy about Russ getting the Sword. It isn't personal but I didn't want to work with him,' he says fibbing bravely. 'We get on fine and the chances are higher it will stay that way if I don't have to work with him.'

But first Matt and the batch had to enjoy their Final Exercise – two weeks based on the *Sir Geraint*, an LSL (Landing Ship Logistic) which resembled a battle-grey car ferry. In past years Final Nail had always taken place in Scotland on the Isle of Skye. Unfortunately the army officer in charge of the May batch exercise had omitted to obtain proper clearances for military use on some farming land with the result that the Marines had been told to take their muddy boots elsewhere for ever and a day. For YO Sept. '91 the whole caboodle had to be jacked up in double quick time in Wales and South West England. Any major exercise taking place for the first time is bound to have several unforeseen snags.

'The batch quickly christened it Final Herring,' says Matt Skuse. 'It was rather an anti-climax after the Commando Course. All we seemed to do was sleep or yomp aimlessly from one point to another. At least the Jocks made us feel good because they were dropping like flies.'

The YOs were joined on the exercise by a full company of Argyll and Sutherland Highlanders which meant that they were always in charge of men, if not Marines. 'On Final Ex my four days commanding the Scots taught me more than two weeks of class-room theory,' says Matt Lodge, rather more sympathetic to the Jocks, who after all were not wearing green lids. 'More hands-on experience would help, the more they can get soldiers in to use for command appointments the better we would be. They also con-founded Sergeant Coyle's expectations and lasted really well except on a couple of monster yomps.'

Final Nail is always 'strong on amphibious assets' (technical sup-port in the form of ships, landing craft etc.), and the idea was to base the troops on board the LSL, disembarking to do various jobs around the coastline, then embarking and sailing round to the next position to do another raid. It did not always turn out according to plan.

'We were dropped on this supposedly secluded beach and the Jocks were busy shedding their waterproofs and packing them into their Bergens,' chuckles Matt Skuse. 'Unfortunately it turned out to be chucking-out time in all the local pubs so all these half-cut locals came out and were milling around half pissed in the middle of a company of soldiers armed to the teeth. We had to pretend they simply weren't there, which was a trifle difficult with drunken lorry drivers demanding to know "Whatcha got there?" It didn't help that they couldn't understand what the Jocks said either.

'Then we set out on a 24-hour march in a straight line, with Jocks dying on us; eventually we turned around and marched for another twenty-four hours back again. Eventually we put down our Bergens, lined up in a long line and charged down this field setting fire to aeroplanes. I didn't fire my weapon once though there was quite a good fireball behind us.'

'The airfield raid was a bit of a cock-up,' concedes Wolsey. It did not help that Shagger Shaw, who was running the whole attack, took on too much responsibility which detracted somewhat from the point. Rather than letting the YOs have a fair crack he tried to control everything and ended up treating YOs who were troop commanders as section commanders so they did not have a proper role. Captain Shaw admits that when he gets into these exercises and people are running around firing, with explosions, bangs and lots of smoke simulating the chaos and din of battle, he sometimes sees red and gets flashbacks to the Falklands campaign. Suddenly it all seems so real, and shouting, screaming and cursing – too absorbed to stand back, guide and direct the YOs – he seems rather to be living it for himself.

Even the good humour engendered by a great serial – a raid on Pembroke Docks, where they came in at dawn in rigid raiders, blew up an oil refinery and split in good order – did not last long. 'The boats promptly took us the wrong way upstream,' says Skuse sarcastically, 'and we were dropped in a shitty, tactically unsound troop harbour for the next twenty-four hours.'

Then there was the ambush. Twelve of the YOs were in position from 2300, and the ambush was supposed to be set off at 0500 but the enemy eventually arrived at 0530 hours, minutes after they had packed up. Worst of all the fire position they had to hold was in a ditch, with their heads and feet up and their bellies slung down in the middle of the ditch. It felt as if they were holding a particularly excruciating IMF dorsal raise for six hours. When the order to pack up came over the net someone shouted out 'and stretch', to much accompanying mirth.

'The Final Exercise achieved its object but memory is eroded by time,' agrees Wolsey, 'and it didn't work that brilliantly. A lot of people thought it was shit and quite embarrassing. I felt for the YOs and things kept going wrong, like lying up in an ambush all night and the enemy not coming until two minutes after they left. In many ways that is an interesting lesson to learn and in Northern Ireland I've sat through dozens of ambushes and when someone does spring it they are probably civilians anyway.'

The best serial was fortunately saved to last – an SBS-style operation to rescue hostages held on board a ship by the Cornish Liberation Army. The very nature of a modern ship, masses of metal bulkheads and easily secured compartments, plus the difficulty of approaching silently and then gaining access without being spotted, makes a ship rescue the most complex operation imaginable, a Special Forces nightmare. The operation was organized by an SBS SNCO attached to OTW and employed three twin-engined RIBs (Rigid Inflatable Boats) driven by SBS coxswains, which can reach speeds of sixty knots in the open sea. The target was the *Ramehead*, a former cargo ship now moored permanently in Portland and used by the SBS for training in close-quarter combat afloat. SB do not do things by halves. All their training is done with live rounds with live hostages, and the inside of the *Ramehead* is so decorated with bullet holes it is a wonder some of the steel bulkheads are still standing.

On board the *Sir Geraint* the O group was given very competently by Russ Corn, who realized that some of his brothers were desperately hoping for a glaring error they could highlight. Matt Skuse was not among them. 'The matter is closed,' he said, though still smarting over the incident. 'I don't want to make too much of it.' The situation was complicated by a choppy sea which was to make boarding the RIBs much more difficult; there was no way the ship's captain would open the doors, letting them step into the awaiting boats. Instead they had to climb over the side on rope ladders with the ship wallowing in the swell so one moment you are banged against the side, the next swinging out over the oggin. The RIBs were pitching and rolling and a couple of YOs landed with a thump, including Neil Watkinson, who was still favouring the ankle he had cracked climbing two months earlier.

Neil, Shaggy and Dan Bailey had been rock climbing on the sea cliffs at Torquay just before summer leave. Shaggy with his experience as an E6 climber can appear to be the crazy one once he is thirty feet off the ground – and sometimes on it: he does things, takes risks and gets away with it. Unfortunately Neil, in trying to emulate some daring manoeuvre, was traversing across the cliff face without ropes, and fell off. Dan heard this great cry and looked around to see Neil fall. He dropped sixty feet, cracked his ankle and to complete his humiliation had to be rescued by the coastguard.

Five miles out to sea and the cox'ns open up the throttle on the RIBs. It is too choppy to really go for it but at thirty knots the boat is bouncing, skimming in the trough between waves and occasionally leaping from the top of the wave, getting air to accompanying whoops from the batch. A mile out to sea the speed drops, and the engine howl dies away in the wind, replaced by a muted *phut phut* that can hardly be heard. Nary a sound carries from the other RIBs a hundred metres away. The silent covert approach brings the RIBs around the back of the harbour wall, dropping off a mythical section. (In the plan this section would have installed themselves in a position overlooking the *Ramehead* where they could pick off any of the Cornish terrorists who showed themselves on deck.)

About ten minutes to midnight the RIBs enter the harbour as silently as possible. One swings into the lee of the *Ramehead* hugging underneath the stern anchor chain and Woodall leads three men up a ladder. Then the sign is given to the other RIBs to open up to full throttle ahead. Within half a minute both boatloads are up the gangplank and storming into the wardroom where the hostages are held. A flash bang grenade, a fusillade of shots and two of the terrorists are down. Then the plans start to go a little awry. Mike Tanner's section, having cleared the wardroom, should cover Andy Harker as he drops down to the next deck; instead Tanner leads his guys straight down into trouble.

'Everyone got a bit excited,' says Skuse. 'Harker was one of the section commanders and because it was an SB-style op he got over-excited and wound up Russ when they were planning it. Mike Tanner was not given strict enough guidelines so he just went charging in like a bull in a china shop. He was cuffing it, so took rather longer than he should clearing the top deck, then went straight on down instead of acting as my back-up section.'

In clearing another room and further exceeding his brief Tanner fires half a mag into the forward room and then charges through it.

Unfortunately the terrorist throws a grenade (thunder flash) which explodes beneath his feet as he charges in. It is only an exercise but even Mike admits that in real life he would be very dead or at the very least singing soprano in the Corps choir. Finding Mike had done his job Harks rushes on clearing cabins until he bumps into the other squad coming in the other direction. A few shots were exchanged and had it been for real that would have been a very messy blue on blue.

As the corridors are cleared it is apparent that the YOs still have a lot to learn about such ops. The odd cabin is not cleared properly and when two sections converge – radio comms being non-existent in the metal belly of the ship – disaster is but a trigger finger away. As ever hours waiting are dissipated in under five minutes of action. Final Nail is finished.

As they unload all the Bergens on to the jetty, Bob Baxendale managed to step backwards off the pontoon into the harbour while Rob Lunn ran down the gangway, completely avoided solid ground and joined him in the oggin. To celebrate the final meeting of the FRV Club, Ashby, eccentric as ever on a chill October night, stripped off his denims and leapt in to join them, stark naked. That's it for practical soldiering until they join their units, so why not celebrate with a dip in Portland harbour. All that is left at CTC is drill, lectures, tidying loose ends and finally the Pass Out.

Over and Pass Out

Is this the real life –
Is this just fantasy –
Caught in a landslide –
No escape from reality –
Open your eyes.

Freddie Mercury, 'Bohemian Rhapsody'

IT IS FUNNY that after fifty-one weeks of training there should still not be a chance to relax. With Final Nail hammered in, the batch had only three weeks left and there were still not enough hours in the day. The Officers' Mess was now heaving with the addition of another thirty-odd YOs from Sept. '92 and in OTW pressure on space meant that Wolsey was now camping in with the other DS, as his office was now occupied by the new batch officer.

(All the spare kit and munitions, including several thousand rounds of blank ammo, had been cleared out and used up on Final Nail. It is one of the peculiarities of service life that if you have not used up all your allotted ammo on a particular exercise you'll get even less for the same exercise next year. There is nothing a soldier fears more than running out of ammunition and a good one will always have reserves stashed away, fearing, not unjustly, that the civil servants at the MoD would dearly love any excuse to cut his supplies further.)

'The pace in the last three weeks was fast and furious. Much of the day was spent going to lectures on spotting the symptoms of drink and drugs abuse in your men which could have been completed in fifteen minutes but managed to fill forty, and we had the feeling we could have been doing other things,' recalls Matt Skuse. 'The most time-consuming of all was the batch presentation that

went through rehearsal after rehearsal, draft after draft. Russ somehow came in at the top as director and six of us wrote different
chunks of script.'

The final presentation is a minor epic. Lasting some forty-five
minutes it is a review of training, performed once only in front of
parents, relatives and friends on the day of Pass Out. Combining
audio-visual and video with live action sequences it is a celebration
of batch triumph and has been, in the past, extremely funny. Sept.
'91 decided to take a rather more serious look at what they had
accomplished and what they were about to do next – their way of
telling everyone that the truth of their training lay more in pain than
in laughter. Originally Lodgie, Tanner and Lunn wrote the script,
Skuse went through over a thousand photographs while Pete Manson
was pinged to rig and operate the lights in the Falklands Hall.

The initial scriptwriters soon degenerated into unseemly squabbling. 'Apparently,' reports Andy Mac, 'one of the three kept on
talking about "big lads" and how they helped out the smaller
chaps. Coupled with a tendency to talk only of death, yomps, pain,
grit, determination and Mark Wolsey, this led to his contribution
being totally edited out by the two pixies and the rest of the batch.
Mike will hopefully stop sulking about that some time in '94.'

Like any theatrical production much of the work lay in getting
the props together. A vaulting horse for various YOs to do a hysterical vaulting display – first as overweight uncoordinated fatties,
then as lean mean fighting machines – was easy enough. Gathering
together a dozen different uniforms, from tropical lightweight to
arctic whites and a sniper's gillie suit, requires both patience and a
useful knowledge of paperwork manipulation. As ever there were
one or two who did not want to get involved. Andy Harker continued his near masochistic training regime, pushing his body further and further, but equally absented himself from social activities.
It was as if he knew that henceforth the guys he had shared training
with would pass only as ships in the night.

'Andy upset me and a lot of other people by his almost total
refusal to do anything at the presentation,' says Lodge. 'Harks
refused to appear on stage except in his gillie suit. The joke was he
wanted to go into Special Forces and didn't want his face plastered
across the video, or didn't want to make a fool of himself. He was
always terribly worried about the impression he gave. He became
obsessive about the physical side of things.'

So at the end of training Harker was still as much of an enigma as he had been at the beginning. 'We are very different, but he was good to me on the Commando Course,' continues Lodge. 'It worried me that I wouldn't have physical presence in front of a Marine troop and I saw in Andy the opportunity to understand how a Marine looks at things. He reassured me that Marines aren't expecting a YO to be a super-fit hero. He was a good friend, though at times I found him exasperatingly self-contained. I never saw how he got on so well with Russ.'

However in between writing and rewriting the script to the satisfaction of Matt Sturman – the batch never quite plucked up the courage to insert into the dress rehearsal a picture from one of Gav's magazines, in which they insisted the naked model was the spitting image of Wolsey – there were still a final Signals exam and the Final Exam to pass. Ignoring the lecture on alcohol abuse Gav Parr went out the next evening and got completely pissed. Like the rest of the batch he was getting increasingly irritated because still none of them knew what their first appointments were to be. Gav was hoping he was going to be sent to Diego Garcia for a year but he also knew the chances were low as he was going to be finishing at the bottom of the batch and was far more likely to end up in Commando Logs for a year.

'I was hoping to get Diego,' he says, 'because there are only about twenty Marines there and in the past it has been a Corps Commission appointment. But by the time the Final Exam came we had all pretty well wrapped our tits in by then as they refused to tell anybody what their appointments were until after we'd sat it. So the night before I went and had a few beers, came back to my cabin, locked the door and passed out on the floor.'

Matt Skuse was Duty Student on the day. He banged on Gav's door but got no answer so assumed he was up and about and it was not until everyone else was assembled that he realized Gav was not there. He sent a couple of the batch off to find him, to hammer on his door and wake up the dead. He turned up five minutes late for the exam looking very dishevelled and Wolsey told him to come back later. Fortunately he passed on his retake but two weeks later went on to Plymouth and Logs, back in his now accustomed position. On warning.

The worst part for many was having to relearn all that drill for the Pass Out Parade. It had seemed so pointless during the

Commando Course, but if there was ever universal agreement among the batch in those last few days it was that they had to get it right: in fact better than right. Inside CTC a few people were also doing their best to drive home to the YOs that outside Lympstone they were going right back down to the bottom of the pile.

'Even Shagger Shaw was trying to cut us down to size,' says Mike Tanner. 'telling us not to get too arrogant, too cocky. At the end of training Susie Thomson, a Wren officer, was giving us a lecture on how to behave as troop officers when interviewing people. She just didn't like Wolsey and said, "For heaven's sake don't do it like your boss does, swanning around in such an arrogant fashion." Suddenly thirty blokes sat up to attention, glaring at her all thinking, "Don't slag off the Boss or it's out the window, lady." Imagine, she accused us of being thirty clones of Wolsey, thirty arrogant people, which as you can imagine didn't go down well.

'He was tremendously liked in the batch, there was no one without exception who didn't think he was a superb bloke. By the end of training we realized he had a hell of an ego – an ego the size of a truck. He's a bloody nice guy, it's just he knows he is good. He is one of those characters around whom folklore arises – stories of going AWOL in Norway, jumping off boats in Dartmouth. His NCOs and men think he's brilliant.'

Taffinder's initial misgivings about Wolsey's reputation had long since gelled into a much clearer picture of his character. 'He was an extremely charismatic course officer,' he says. 'He played it very well, started off distant from the batch and got closer as the months went by. He was hard but never harsh. His Commando Course was probably the most enlightened yet taxing in all my time at Lympstone. He adores the business of professional hands-on soldiering and communicated that to his batch. The difficulty for Mark is that there comes a time in any officer's career when sword wielding turns into pen pushing and Mark is a dedicated sword wielder. He needs a job where the adrenalin flows like a waterfall.'

Wolsey had jacked up one final treat for the batch – a weekend run ashore in New York over Halloween. Virgin Atlantic had given them a healthy deal on the air fares and in exchange the batch went on a sponsored run around Manhattan for the Trevor Jones Trust – one of Richard Branson's favourite charities. Otherwise they bought a lot of jeans, drank even more beer and just failed to get

Over and Pass Out

into serious trouble in Christopher Street with a bunch of militant men with moustaches who were definitely not Royal Marines.

Eventually the final day came. Friday 6 November 1992. The pass out presentation went very slickly, a mixture of pathos and humour that had more than one mum sobbing into her hanky. Andy Harker even took his sniper's hat off to reveal his bare, unmade up face for the final curtain call. When the batch marched out on to the parade ground to the strains of 'Scotland the Brave' none of the watching parents and staff knew that the words they were sub-vocalizing were deeply and eloquently obscene.

'The tune was "Scotland the Brave", but the batch all knew it as "Down in the Glen",' says Andy Goldsmith who first learnt it in agricultural college and has since taught it to the Argyll and Sutherland Highlanders. 'We would sing it in the back of four-tonners to celebrate Endex. We'd be threaders, frozen through and shattered and it would start with this universal wail, like bagpipes, then I'd stamp my foot and it would begin.'

Fortunately nobody sang the words out loud, nobody dropped either clangers or swords on the drill square and for once not a soul moaned about Russ getting the Sword. Andy Harker picked up the CGRM's Prize and the Herbert Lott Award of a pair of binoculars and a cheque for placing second. Rob Lunn picked up the Commandant's Prize of a book for 'showing the most improvement throughout training' and Pete Evans won the Commandant's Essay Prize for the best essay on an amphibious topic – a strange but honourable award for a YO who had struggled long and hard to achieve a goal that at times only he had thought possible.

That evening the batch, with girlfriends in tow, took Wolsey, his team and their partners to a pizza joint in Exeter – organized by Scran King Pete Manson, the YO with the biggest appetite in the batch, in itself an impressive achievement – where they presented the Boss with a very smart black leather briefcase – 'perfect for going to Staff College, sir.' Brian Adcock was blissfully happy for he had finally acquired a girlfriend – Sophie, a delightful blonde Scots lass he had met in Edinburgh with Bob Rob – who seemed to reciprocate his passion. The drinking was not up to its usual excess, with a cloud of bittersweet sadness cloying the air. Now they all knew their next postings, they also knew that it was possible that they might never see some of their batch mates again.

A few perhaps recalled Mike Taffinder's words just two days into the course – a year and a lifetime ago. 'Much will be uncertain but I can promise one thing and that is that in this room today you will find the best male friend you will ever make. Today the batch spirit starts.' Proving his point, at his own batch's thirtieth anniversary reunion all but one of the surviving fourteen (one had been killed in Borneo, one died of a rare disease) 'plus our drill instructor and course officer' had turned up from all corners of the globe. Batch spirit lives on but that is something once again for the future to prove.

Royal Marines are not good at showing their emotions in public. They hate goodbyes; hugs and kisses on the cheeks are absolutely *verboten*. But a handshake was not really sufficient to say farewell to men with whom you have shared everything – from your blackest depression, your darkest secrets, to your sleeping bag, your last cup of tea or in Goldsmith's case his last cigarette.

Instead they rushed outside the restaurant to the banks of the canal. There they all stripped naked, sprinted on to a pedestrian bridge that spanned the water and, as one, hurled themselves thirty feet into the dark chilly waters beneath.

It was an unusual way to say goodbye.

Past, Present and Future

We know what we are, but know not what we may be.
William Shakespeare, *Hamlet*

'WE WERE NINE in a RIB boat – five Marines, two merchant mariners, the foreign office adviser and me – miles north of Diego Garcia checking the offshore islands in the Chagos Archipelago for yachts or any Russian or Mauritian ships illegally taking the fish off the coral reefs in British territorial waters. The lagoon was thirty miles across, renowned for dangerous coral heads that rise from the bottom to two feet below water, and for ocean-going sharks looking for easy prey inside the lagoon. Dangerous waters in a small open boat.

'One moment we could see miles, the next vis suddenly closed down; we lost radio comms with the ship, the temperature dropped rapidly until everybody – we were all dressed in tropical lightweight gear – started feeling the chill; it was raining hard, visibility was down to fifty feet and falling. I had to snurgle us out, crawling along following bits of coral head. To hit it at ten knots would sink us, rip the bottom out of the boat, and we'd be shark bait. It was a little bit hairy – one of my corporals admitted later he thought we would have a nasty incident. After fifty minutes we got comms with the ship again, vis rose, an hour later we had line of sight.

'So it's not entirely boring out here,' says Matt Skuse, from the comfort of his luxury suite on Diego Garcia. 'My major complaint about training is that they never taught me anything about sharks, they're bloody dangerous animals. I've snorkelled here trying to get the anchor up from a coral head and a massive great shark swims between me and the boat. I've seen thousands of the things. The sea boils with fish, thirty-foot sharks and sea turtles, coral and shells and God knows what.'

Diego Garcia is closer by far to the Equator than to any continental land mass. A small horseshoe-shaped island with a giant lagoon, all of twelve miles long and four wide, it is no more than a speck on most atlases marooned in the middle of the Indian Ocean. However, it also possesses the second longest runway in the world, capable of taking B52s, AWACS, US3s and other huge military transports. Diego is owned by Britain but used by the USA as a rapid response base. If anything serious flared up in the Middle East Diego is capable of acting as a springboard, base camp and munitions dump. It is inhabited by 1,500 US Navy and Airforce personnel, 1,500 Ipak and Mauritian workers to do all the third-rate jobs and forty-two Brits. For twelve months from November '91 one of the Brits in Naval Party 1002, on his first command appointment after training, was Matt Skuse.

'Diego Garcia is seen as an arduous draft for Spams [US Navy personnel] – after this they get a preferential one,' he says. 'So millions of dollars have been pumped into facilities. It has a gym twice the size of CTC, a cinema that shows films twice a night, bowling alleys – everything is free. My room is awesome, it has its own kitchen, bathroom, TV, video, double bed, air conditioning, a two-piece suite. The scenery is ridiculous – if it isn't the Bounty in Paradise ads it should have been.

'I'm the training officer for twenty-two Marines, who basically act as a Customs force on the island. I'm here in front of Spams who think Marines are superhuman athletes, so there is a constant peer pressure on me from people I don't know. Where Commando training was all about being tough and showing initiative, I haven't been able to show that out here. Pretty much as soon as you have that green lid you don't have to prove it again. The hardest things here physically have been a couple of bicycle rides. You can't get the Marines here excited about a night ambush or a load carry, which is quite testing.

'There is a temptation to try and be liked when you are standing out in front of Marines, especially standing out in front of only four or five. I've never seen the entire detachment in one place at one time – the most was sixteen. I feel as if they are looking in my eyes so the best way to get that feeling of a job well done is to get them to respect your decisions, being good at your job and being cool, the man who always has a slick putdown when a necky Marine pipes up, so I can't have my kit fall out of my webbing when I pick it up, and I can't reverse the Land Rover into the wall.

'This job's about growing up. Where CTC was about understanding how I worked, making me know how I felt about various things, discovering things about myself, the job now is about discovering things about other people, different types of people and being able to ping them for what they are. You have to know when to say "go and fill up twenty sandbags" and when to say "Marine Hodge, I don't think this wall is high enough, what do you think?" "I agree, sir, there isn't enough room to get down behind it." So he goes and makes the wall higher.'

Long before he had a green lid, probably even before he wore nappies, Mike Tanner was exuding confidence the way most of us exude sweat. In June '92 standing on the edge of a clearing in the Guyanese rainforest, clutching a piece of paper masquerading as a map, Mike was sweating for real. Inside and out. He might have been a troop commander for nine months, he had survived the rigours of a Norwegian winter, but now he had to take a leap of faith … and expect his men to follow him into the jungle.

Most of Guyana, some 85 per cent, consists of thick, all but impenetrable jungle, the sort of rainforest where naturalists wet themselves because there are more undiscovered species leaping and chittering in the canopy than you find in the whole of Northern Europe. Ninety feet down, it is always gloomy because the sun cannot break through to warm the forest floor. The rain however can. And does. In Guyana it rains a lot for eight months and not at all for the rest. One hundred inches of water a year makes a rainforest live up to its name but it makes yomping very hard work.

Map reading is a basic Marine skill: if a man has a green beret he should be able to read a map. The problem with reading maps in Guyana is that once you leave the fertile plain at sea level 'accuracy' and 'map' are two mutually contradictory terms. The grid squares are neatly uniform on the piece of paper but on the forest floor one is two kilometres and the next might be either one or three kilometres and if you get a little bit lost you may never know where you are again. The only way is to take a compass bearing and follow it.

'We walked on a compass bearing for three days,' recalls Tanner, safe in the haven of the Officers' Mess at Norton Manor Camp. 'It's a bit of a confidence test marching on a bearing like that, worrying if you're where you should be and with all the blokes looking at you and thinking "Has the boss got it wrong?"; worrying constantly that you have walked for days in the wrong direction and are lost right in the middle of the thickest jungle in the world with no one having a clue where you are and the fastest pace you can travel at, hacking your way through, is a few miles a day. Training had given me confidence so when we were in Norway and it was minus thirty degrees and people were starting to go down, I knew I could still hack it but this was getting much more nerve-racking by the end.

'By the third day we should have been there but I couldn't recognize our objective. Fortunately we walked another five hundred metres and found we were only a hundred metres away from it. Achieving that was an incredible feat, I was jumping up and down, it was one of the best feelings in my life.'

Mike Tanner continues to be deeply in love with the Royal Marines, he simply adores being an officer, relishes the joys of command. 'You have to learn to be comfortable with being in charge of people. The first time I got pinged for section commander in training it was everyone stand to attention, then after a while I got more comfortable with it,' he says. 'Same with my troop. When I joined I was mega Pussers, everything was by the book – full inspections every morning, we marched everywhere round camp. Now we haven't lost standards but I have relaxed and I don't feel I have to do everything by the pan – they are happy I'm the boss, I don't feel I have to stand up and prove myself every five minutes.'

A year away from Lympstone the members of YO batch Sept. '91 had changed once more. One was dead, another had seen two of his men die and most had faced testing conditions that made training seem like a piece of cake. Only twelve members of the batch were able to enjoy the delights of being a troop officer in a Commando. Not everybody got to tackle sharks for fifteen months like Matt Skuse. For the others their first year out of training was sometimes frustrating, often tedious and not always fun.

In September 1993 after completing two years' training all the YOs were promoted to Lieutenant and then each started to work out what he wished to do in the future. Second jobs in the Corps can be pretty boring so officers are given the opportunity to specialize. (Recruits are encouraged to gain either a Specialist Qualification (SQ) or a Technical Qualification (TQ) as 60 per cent of Marines are specialist trained.) In practice options for officers are limited to specific weapons-oriented specialities – Weapons Training Officer (the equivalent of a Platoon Weapons qualification), Support

Weapons (mortars and anti-tank weapons), or Assault Engineer. In some cases they might also go for the very tough six-week Sniper's Course, which has given the Marines the reputation of being among the best snipers in the world – but few officers do. Other options open to them include becoming a PT and Sports Officer, an MLO (Mountain Leader), a Helicopter Pilot, Signals Officer (an eight-month course), Landing Craft Officer or going into Special Forces.

After Pass Out four YOs – Manson, Woodall, David and Shetler-Jones – went to command troops in Comacchio Group, based like 45 up in Arbroath. Originally formed in 1980 to protect North Sea oil rigs Comacchio is named after the battle of 2 April 1945 when 2 Commando Brigade fought their way into strong German defences on the shores of Lake Comacchio in Italy. The oil rig protection side is now handled from Poole so Comacchio's prime role is the guarding of nuclear weapons, both on bases like Coolport and Faslane and any convoys carrying nuclear weapons while in transit. It is not considered to be a great posting though at least the YO does get to command Marines.

The problem according to Jezz Woodall is motivation. Stuck inside a base on the west coast of Scotland for weeks on end where 'the accommodation's shit, the scran's worse and its usually raining' is not good for morale. 'The opportunities for getting out in the field are limited,' he says from the depths of a concrete bunker somewhere in Scotland – 'I can't tell you where otherwise I shall have to kill you,' he laughs. 'Training is nothing special, we are in a security-type role where we sit around waiting for something to happen, awaiting a terrorist attack, an armed incursion.

'Of course we understand the compliment that to defend nuclear weapons requires your best troops and God forbid anything should ever happen. It's a real challenge to keep the Marines motivated, beyond sitting in a wooden hut at the gate of the installations.'

The greatest drama for both Jezz and Tim David seemed to be writing off their respective cars, so in November '93 with a great sigh of relief Jezz headed south to join 42 Commando as the unit training officer. Pete Manson had left earlier for RAF Wittering for six weeks' flying grading with the eventual intention of flying helicopters. One-time mountain bike racer, David was appointed for a two-year stint as second in command of the Royal Marine biathlon team, in which he is basically a full-time paid athlete who spends a lot of time on skis in Norway.

The indomitable Phil Shetler-Jones, as expected, achieved instant rapport with his men, and even managed to win a Comacchio company competition as best troop commander. A man who had never owned a watch in training, who during command appointments would be constantly asking the time, celebrated his first troop by buying both a watch and a Filofax in a sometimes vain attempt to organize his life. In January '94 he joined HMS *Fearless* as Landing Deck Officer to spend a year at sea.

The bum postings were generally considered to have gone to Pete Evans and Gav Parr who passed out at the bottom of the batch and subsequently drew the Commando Logistic Regiment, based at Seaton Barracks in Plymouth. The Marines pride themselves on being able to do everything themselves so they are not dependent on anyone else's good offices for guns, petrol, trucks and ammo. The seven hundred men at Logs provide all the essential admin that enables 3 Commando Brigade to go to war.

Gavin, of course, arrived in trouble again. He seems to exist, if not thrive, on a diet of warnings but this final Commandant's Warning, caused by missing the Final Exam, was a classic even by his standards. Fortunately he was soon relieved of that, though very nearly ended back on it again over a small matter of unpaid tailor's bills. Logs he claimed was not as bad as it first appeared and Plymouth was the perfect stamping ground for his nocturnal activities.

Off duty Gav continued his two favourite pursuits, of trapping and downing pints with equal alacrity. He was at last more at ease in the company of his peers and the nod cut he once sported was now grown out so he resembles a former skinhead hoping to get into raves more easily. Sadly he still talks more and more of not surviving the cut. Part of him seems destined for ever to charge into authority: indeed that he has survived so long is close to miraculous. Gav's line is always 'Well, if Wolsey can survive then so can I', but he lacks Wolsey's ability to be simultaneously charming and mischievous. A fearsome figure because he's so bloody big, he naturally puts people in authority on the defensive and when he gets aggressive they may give way and resent that weakness and him forever more.

However, Gav's second appointment was as 42's Assault Engineer troop officer. In November '93 he went on the Royal Engineers' three-month course at Chatham to learn about the intricacies of commanding men who know a lot of extremely dangerous things –

how to both build and blow up bridges, how to set and disarm booby traps. For Gav the best part is the prospect of a Northern Ireland tour in November 1994.

While Parr is destined for a turbulent career, Pete Evans waxes lyrical about the opportunities Logs allows for a career. 'You get to understand how the Army works, see the chain of command more clearly and they're not half as dumb as we were led to believe in training by the likes of Sergeant Coyle.'

Off duty Pete remains Lieutenant Plug, jointly obsessed with pulling nurses ('That must be because they see such terrible things on duty,' commented one loyal colleague, 'that even Pete can look beautiful off duty') and a determination to forge a proper career in the Marines. He has always had that determination in spades. Dissatisfied with a normal working life, he was the oldest of the batch and intelligent enough to find some of the demands upon his time intellectually diminishing.

'Training wasn't an environment I was going to enjoy myself or flourish in,' he says. 'Initially I thought it was a bummer that the troop I got at Logs was not a real infantry troop but what I did get to see is everything at brigade level, to understand the wider picture whereas most troop commanders never see beyond company level. As a Full Career Officer I really enjoyed my time there.'

Perhaps it was that in training Pete never had any luck. In his first appointment he proffed from the off, even managing to appear in a couple of episodes of a TV documentary series on the Royal Marines, in one of which he had to give an O group to half the officers up in Norway. Less happy was having to bring back the dead body of a man he had just done Arctic training with. 'I had a drink with him the night before he died,' he says, shaking his head in sorrow. 'He was in a 27-ton vehicle, lost control and went off the road into a river. Most times you would get away with it. He didn't and I brought him home thinking all the way what a waste.'

Pete has enjoyed the antics of Logs where each troop appears to possess a couple of professional Del Boys to hustle and cajole essential supplies out of nowhere. 'When 42 went to Cyprus they took all their own gas bottles. Unfortunately the bottles in Cyprus had a different attachment and when Marines can't eat they get rather upset. Even more serious was when the fridge went tits up in the middle of a Cyprus summer – the prospect of no cold beer in the Mess is a national emergency – so we had to fix that.'

Pete's starring role on TV also landed him a plum six-month posting in January '94 – as a UN observer in Bosnia. 'I want to be a Landing Craft Officer and so I had six months to kill before the course started in September. Everyone said I was much too young to work for the UN but I applied and the guy had seen one of the TV shows in which I had been negotiating for some non-combatants to cross a border. Just the sort of thing I could be doing in Bosnia. For once it was a case of right place, right time, so I'm well chuffed. The only drag is that I won't be allowed to carry a weapon, which will make me the only unarmed man in the country!'

Gav and Pete would have regular drinks with Harker, Stovin-Bradford, Watkinson and Adcock who were all with 42 Commando, based at Bickleigh Barracks, eight miles outside Plymouth. While 42 spent most of their year in the UK, with a single six-week exercise, Tudor Lance, in the Mediterranean, 40 and 45 had, on paper, an altogether more exciting time. Tanner, Attwood, Lunn and McInerney who went to be troop commanders with 40, at Norton Manor Camp in Taunton, spent six weeks Arctic training in Norway followed in November '93 by a six-month tour to Belfast. In between Tanner went to the Caribbean and McInerney and Lunn to Kuwait. Corn, Baxendale, Ashby and Robinson went to 45, based in Arbroath, but spent the first part of 1993 in Norway, followed by five months in Belize. Because they are based so far from the other Commandos – sharing RM *Condor* with Comacchio – 45 have developed a very individual mentality, if primarily in the art of having fun.

Andy Harker was always going the Special Forces route. If the words 'SBS' were mentioned in training it was the only time he displayed signs of emotion. But most important was first to command a rifle troop. That is the most vital test for a Corps Commission officer, for inevitably you will end up commanding a man, possibly a friend, who served alongside you in a unit.

'There was one guy in my troop to begin with who eventually went back to Lympstone on a Corporals' course, whom I had served with. Even though we used to go out for a drink together he knows better than to call me Andy, he always refers to me as "sir" even if we're off duty,' says Harker knotting his blond eyebrows firmly together. To Andy physical fitness had always been everything. In training the others had always taken the piss at the 'my body is a temple' routine, but to him it was real. He never drank and tried to eat the right foods. At 42 he continued his rigid training schedule, pushing his body further and further in preparation for the SBS selection test in September '93.

To universal surprise he blew out on the first twenty-mile yomp. Simply put, he had overtrained and he realized it. To Andy Harker failure at a physical task was something that simply did not happen and because of his age (twenty-five) he was already too old to apply to be an ML and November '93 was his last chance for SBS selection.

'It was certainly a bit of a disaster,' he said candidly just before his second crack at selection. 'It taught me you can't go into anything thinking you will sail through. It was good for me, however, and I'm a better person for it and I've changed my attitude to training. I gave up running and concentrated on yomping with weights on. I have to pass because for me it's the only way ahead and I don't want to have to join SAS because of my age.' In November '93 Andy Harker took the SBS selection tests for the second time. Although perfectly fit he chose halfway through to remove himself from the course. He may in the future apply to the SAS but is currently considering his options.

Brian Adcock also had thoughts of going into Special Forces but instead got selected for flying training in May '94 and promptly – after picking good advice from the master of the scam, Wolsey – managed to get himself on an expedition cycling from Nairobi to Cape Town. Unlike many of his contemporaries Brian is still restless, single once more, unsure of what to do or where he is going. Initially he found life at Bickleigh trying. It did not help that early on he managed to have an ND (Negligent Discharge) in front of his men, who were already pretty anarchic not having had a troop officer for the past five months.

'The real world is quite a lot different from how I perceived it,' he says. 'I expected the Mess to be a much friendlier place. We weren't made to feel that welcome, just expected to get in there and get on with it. My troop gave me a hard time when I first turned up as they hadn't had an officer for ages, my sergeant found it difficult to let go of the reins. I didn't know the score, they didn't know how to come to me. A lot of men were taking time off left, right and centre of their own accord: I had to get to grips with that, which they didn't like.

'I came dashing out of Lympstone, expecting things to be carried out at the same frenetic pace. I had to drop a gear, calm myself down. I found the NCOs blocking me. We went to Sennybridge and I wanted to do lots of extra things when they weren't working, as the days were relatively free, and it was hard to force it through. I think I could have done it before, it is something you either have or you don't. The actual Marines are pretty much what I expected, some are rogues, some are hideous and so on but we're not carrying any baggage. If Marines don't respect an officer his life can be very difficult. I don't order, I ask. One question you need to ask in your initial interviews is do you have any dependent children – too many and they can become a risk. One Marine came in and said, "Yes sir, I have three children to three different women and I am paying maintenance to all three"!'

According to a senior officer at 42, Brian 'had a hard task and has coped with it pretty well'. Unlike Adcock, Neil Watkinson was very fortunate in having a 'brilliant troop sergeant' who kept his men in line while they got the measure of their eccentric officer. Neil's, shall we say, idiosyncratic approach to man management has raised a few eyebrows. 'He's had his men writing essays,' hissed Chalkie in horror. Neil was unrepentant, saying, 'It was quite interesting and revealing.' He also purloined some of Mark Wolsey's better ideas from the Commando Course and refined them. He took his men caving and even cave diving – well, some of them wanted to go diving, but as the life expectancy of a cave diver is about seven dives and none of these boys had any scuba kit, a wiser head prevailed and they all returned to Bickleigh, wet, muddy and still alive. In November '93 Neil became Assistant Adjutant at 42 but expects to leave the Corps as soon as his five-year SSC (Short Service Career) is up.

Chalkie Stovin-Bradford continues to go out with 'Fluffikins' (Katie) but has also managed to establish a reputation as a 'beast master and phys monster' – while his choral ability and natural bonhomie quickly made him friends in the Mess. He was the officer in charge of the Royal Marine troop at the Royal Tournament in 1993, abseiling from the roof, doing assault courses in full kit – in front of an audience. Given Chalkie's ability to pile on the pounds when he is not fully active it was a good thing he spent three months in Brunei doing jungle training in late '93. In January '94 he returned to Lympstone to take a recruit troop through training. The irony was not lost on him.

Up at Taunton with 40 Commando Rob Lunn settled relatively easily into the role of troop commander. His brusque manner unsettled a few people but the physical weaknesses that were sometimes apparent at CTC did not show themselves in the harsh freezing conditions in Norway. His temper, however, was tested to the full and found wanting during a brief spell in Kuwait. Training Kuwaiti soldiers, who have a somewhat different concept of timekeeping and discipline to Royal Marines, led to regular outbursts of shouting, followed by incandescent rage. When Rob returned to Taunton he was known to all and sundry as 'Genghis'.

Aided by his easy-going approach and ability to cultivate senior officers Andy McInerney managed to grab the biggest room in the Officers' Mess. His social life was improved immeasurably by the purchase of not one but two cars, the second being forced upon him after his pride and joy, a sports car, spun off the road and was all but totalled. His relationship with Andrea finally sank in the summer of '93 when he discovered she had booked herself in on a TA course and was intending to stay at Norton Manor Camp. 'It's as though she wants to keep an eye on me,' he wailed, 'I can't think why … well, actually I can' – one reason why being a dead fish sent to him by another spurned paramour, which with perfect timing arrived in the post room just as the camp split on their three-week summer leave. For some other completely unrelated reason Andy Mac still remains unable to look at, let alone eat, Pussers sausages.

After Norway Paul Attwood's next six months at home were 'a bit dull unfortunately. In Norway it was the coldest winter for some years but all four of us coped pretty well with the skiing and the conditions. A few of my lads got frostbite but compared to Bob Rob we had no real dramas. When Tanner went to the Caribbean and the other two went off to Kuwait my company got left behind. I ended up doing a three-week training course with school cadets.

'It was amusing to see everything from the other side of the fence and we had to work hard to get the boys and girls interested in the forces, rather than each other,' he chuckles. 'We spent two nights a week out in the field and I had to sleep in the middle to prevent any "fraternizing". It made me think that after the tour of Northern Ireland I'd like to take a recruit troop through training and use the time to get fit before trying out for the Special Forces or ML.'

'We had a week in Norway which was a real tight survival situation,' says Mark 'Bob' Robinson. 'The weather closed in completely, visibility was about two feet and the temperature was far below freezing. Eventually we had to make a decision whether to get out and make an RV with the snowcats or stay put in the tents. We set out in a total white-out and the only thing we could do was follow the compass bearing exactly. Fortunately we hit the vehicles spot on.'

Having survived that ordeal unscathed it was doubly distressing for Bob to lose two of his troop on the final exercise a few weeks later. The weather was fine – as fine as it gets in the Arctic Circle – but one morning when the men were stirring one of the corporals could not get any answer from a three-man tent. 'He called me over, we pulled open the flap and the tent was full of toxic fumes,' he says. 'We pulled them out and I gave one mouth to mouth for about twenty minutes. It was too late. Two died but one guy was pulled back from the brink.'

Arctic tents are designed with two flysheets, giving them two layers of insulation and two doors. Such an accident should never have happened, for in drills the Marines are taught never to use a stove inside a tent without opening the flaps for ventilation. But waking up on a freezing morning they had probably lit the stove for warmth which quickly burnt off the oxygen and they dozed back off. One realized what was up but passed out before he could open the flap into fresh air. When the signaller came to the tent he found one of the three men lying face down, having made it through the first door but not the second.

'Everyone felt responsible all the way up the ladder,' says Bob, reluctant to talk about it months after the event. 'At the time, rather than establish what happened I just had to deal with my blokes' reactions. Being Marines they usually brush it under the carpet and I've done that too, to a certain extent. I often think what would have happened if I had checked them one more time, got everyone moving a few minutes earlier, but that would have been simply a matter of luck because there was no reason to do so.'

Bob was a troop commander in Wolsey's old outfit, Zulu Company – 'so I heard some interesting stories about him. It was the place to be all right. All the things Wolsey talked about were here. Training prepared me totally but there was still a massive learning curve. I doubt myself all the time, I learn from my

mistakes, from the little things that go wrong. In truth it was a varied year but it ended well in Belize.'

Zulu Company were involved in drug enforcement work, supporting the local police force, attempting to prevent the country
becoming another staging post on the narcotics highway. 'We are
able to close down drug cartel operations easier, we can put the
frighteners on them which the police can't do because the gangs
terrorize their families. We got our information from the police on
various individuals, then we'd monitor them, set up road-blocks and
do raids. We had some big hauls of cocaine, crack, marijuana and
blokes armed with automatic weapons.

'The rest of the time we were on jungle patrols, updating maps,
bringing back medical reports on the conditions of the Indians and
outlying villages. We always work in support of the Belize Defence
Force (BDF) but they are fairly tinpot and I'm not sure how they'll
survive without us if we leave for good.'

In contrast Bob Baxendale had a superb year, discovering that
training had prepared him well and his natural exuberance 'plus the
help of some excellent corporals and sergeants' carried him through
the initial small mistakes. 'I've been very impressed with the calibre
of the Marines,' he says. 'On live firing exercises they are very cool
and go through their drills very efficiently. They also adapted well
from the extremes of freezing cold in Norway to the heat of the
Central American jungle. Although it can appear worse in the cold
in Norway you just have to be able to ski, whereas in the jungle
people can be feet away from you and you can't see them, minor
cuts and bruises get infected and swell up quickly. Dehydration is a
danger because you get soaked in sweat, the rain is so warm it
makes no difference and the water in your bottles is sterotabbed so
it tastes like tepid swimming pool water. Early on before we had
acclimatized a couple of the lads went down with heat exhaustion.'

On his return to England in November '93 Bob took up a position as the Derby area schools career liaison officer. If this sounds
like a strange appointment he chose it deliberately because the
Sheffield Eagles – a first division Rugby League club – had offered
him a contract to play either at loose forward or in the second row.
Although he played primarily Union at school and university Bob
had become one of the driving forces and captain of the Scottish
Schoolboys' League team. 'The Corps have been very good about
it,' he says. 'I'm not allowed to sign a binding contract, I have to

play as an amateur and the Eagles will just pay my expenses. I've always wanted to do it and this is my chance to see whether I can cut it at the top levels.'

In November '93 Russ Corn thought he had managed to wangle staying on in Condor but instead found himself back at Lympstone taking through a recruit troop. 'However,' he says, 'in late May '94 I'm taking over the training of the NECIC team, which is for a NATO competition to be held in September which tests the physical and infantry skills of teams from different regiments from armies all over Europe. I'll have to pick eight men and a sergeant and train them up for ten weeks before the competition. The Marines don't usually like to play at things like this unless they can win, which they did last year. I was introduced to CG in Belize who asked me what I was doing next. When I told him all he said was, "You'd better win, or don't bother coming back."

'In Belize we did a lot of border patrolling. I was chasing a cattle rustler over the river into Mexico,' he says. 'We settled down to wait for him to come back then it poured with rain, the river flooded and he never came back over the border. Another time on the Guatemalan border we picked up dozens of illegal immigrants who it transpired were being shipped over to vote for the ruling PUP party. I don't think they were terribly pleased with our activities.

'Norway was a tough winter, it was so cold and we've never lost three men in one winter before. I was with Zulu Company when the Sergeant Major died. He was asphyxiated in an over-snow vehicle and died of carbon monoxide poisoning. In training you think you've had hard exercises like the day we went over Pen-y-Fan but four days after Pass Out I was doing mountain training in Scotland which is far far harder. Norway throws up even more extreme weather conditions. We'd had about ten feet of snow and then it rained one day when we were on the move. You can just brush snow off your white nylons, but in the rains we were soaked to the skin within ten minutes and then the freezing winds whipped in. We were lucky to get out of that with only a couple of lads getting frost nip.'

Being the Sword winner, he soon discovered, was a double-edged honour. 'When I got here the company had the Sword of Honour winner from the Sept. '90 batch so it wasn't that new. You get introduced to all the visiting brass as a Sword of Honour winner and the lads in the troop are impressed – like they are with a King's Badgeman – but people would also love to see a Sword winner fucking up.'

It goes without saying that Russ didn't and has no intention of doing so in the future. Because his Sword rival Phil Ashby had already done Arctic training in his SSLC, he was not sent to Norway and so did not get a troop immediately. Instead he went to Brunei on the Jungle Warfare Instructors' course, which he loved. On his return to Condor he was given about half of the anti-tank troop (eighty-eight strong) to command. In his superficially quiet way Shaggy is as much of a crazy maverick as Wolsey was. In another era he could have been an explorer, searching for the source of the Nile, or a lost city of Gold up the Orinoco. In the nineties he veers between a charismatic leader and a charismatic nutter.

His men regard him in a strange light, a mixture of respect and awe, especially during the Belize posting where for relaxation he would take them up to the top of jungle waterfalls, and then slide back down again. It was something of a miracle that nobody got seriously injured, but even amidst all the cuts and bruises Shaggy came out unscathed. He is also now a qualified skydiver which adds further potentially lethal strings to the bow of a man who seems to know no fear.

'Shaggy always does his own thing, follows his own path,' says Russ Corn, whose career first at Cambridge and now in the Marines has closely shadowed his. 'He only takes people on at what he's good at, he won't stay up all night trying to drink you under the table because he'll end up there too. We went on a ski mountaineering holiday at CTC and I passed Shaggy doing Mach 3, fell down and dropped what seemed to be five hundred feet down the slope. He was fine, of course, but he's still a nutter.' On New Year's Day 1994 Shaggy and his girlfriend, Anna, were climbing in Scotland when they were caught in an avalanche and swept two hundred and fifty feet. Despite his trying to protect her Anna broke her back and had to spend weeks recuperating in hospital. Shaggy cut his finger.

29 Commando Regiment Royal Artillery is one of a handful of army regiments for whom the Royal Marines have great respect. (They also respect the Paras greatly, but just don't ask them to admit it.) 29 provide artillery support for the Corps and each member has

successfully completed an All Arms Commando Course and wears a green lid in his own right. They also like to play practical jokes on young Royal Marine officers attached to them.

Dan Bailey was standing in the bar at the Citadel in Plymouth in his dinner jacket preparing to attend his first regimental dinner, clutching as instructed the white envelope that had been passed to him when the Adjutant rushed up and told him that suspicious characters had been spotted. 'We were divided into pairs and each given a radio,' says Dan. 'We rushed outside and saw these suspects. My partner rushed ahead and I was suddenly stopped by these MPs [Military Policemen] who demanded to know what I was doing with a piece of military equipment dressed in a DJ. They asked to see my ID card – which had been taken off me earlier in the afternoon "to register my number". As I didn't have it they dragged me off to the guard room where they discovered this envelope full of white powder. Then they started to try and freak me out.

'I realized that it was all a set-up and so started fooling around and trying to escape. Eventually they let me out after two hours, whereupon I was late for the dinner and promptly fined for being late.'

While Dan realizes that understanding artillery tactics will prove invaluable one day he did not enjoy much of his time with 29 and was, at times, messed around. He never had a proper troop to command and, as one of the prime social movers and organizers in the batch, certainly missed his mates. 'I went on a crash course to learn about guns, how to fire them and how to work in an OP calling down fire from 105 mm or the bigger 4.5 inch naval guns. However, I'm not a gunner so they don't really trust me, so in the way of commanding men, of being Numero Uno responsible for thirty guys I have dipped out. I won't mind if I get a rifle troop for my next appointment.'

He was getting a bit depressed at the lack of command appointments, shunting from one odd job to the next until going to Belize. Dan had a great tour, capped off by two weeks' leave in Barbados, over which it would be wise to draw a bikini bottom. After jungle training he was an umpire in exercises, set up range firing ('OK, so the Range Qual Course wasn't such a waste of time as it seemed'), trained the Belize Defence Force and went on anti-drug patrols. 'On the live firing the BDF were so very inexperienced that they made Pete Joy look like a sharpshooter,' he laughs. Dan was hoping that his next posting would be to a Commando unit. He was very disappointed when his next appointment was to Comacchio Group. He is currently getting himself very fit with the intention of applying to join the SBS.

'We were doing a big night march in northern Kenya – I'd call it a yomp but the soldiers just laugh at me – or they would have done if they weren't finding it such hard work,' recalls Matt Lodge. 'It was pitch black and we ended up marching within a hundred metres of this pride of lions. Suddenly all we heard was this tremendous roaring; everyone – me included – threw themselves on the ground and there was this sound of weapons being cocked. Then we realized that we only had blank ammo, so I got everyone up on their feet and we marched off very quickly in to the night. It woke them all up.'

Owing to a lack of available troop appointments, four YOs shipped out to different army regiments accompanied by assorted howls of derision from those going to Commando units, harmonizing with green-tinged wails from those off to Comacchio. Matt Lodge joined the 2nd Battalion Princess of Wales Regiment continuing a historic link between the Marines and the Queen's Regiment – which recently became the Princess of Wales and is universally known as 'the Squidgies'.

'I am slightly unusual for a Royal Marine officer,' he says. 'I did take over from another Marine, but he was a Tanner figure – a little slimmer and a lot fitter, fitting their stereotype of a great hulk of a man. In training the physical side was not the easiest for me but I did a run within a couple of weeks of arriving in Canterbury and came seventh in battalion – in the batch I'd have come halfway at best.'

For Matt – as well as escaping the debris of his relationship with Amanda – the advantage was learning a bit about the Army and getting to command a full troop of twenty-eight men for eighteen months. In November '93 he went to Fermanagh on a six-month tour of duty, where in January '94 he was joined by Bob Rob.

'The men are much more professional than Sergeant Coyle led me to expect,' he says, 'though they aren't Marines. They are southeast London lads, sub-Essex boys and when they go out of camp they put on their earrings, their shell suits and their baggy suits – outfits a boot neck would never be seen dead in. The main difference is that they are only soldiers when they are in uniform and a Marine is a soldier whatever he is wearing.

'They are far more forthcoming with outward signs of obedience and respect. A Marine won't salute if he can get away with it. Here it's "yes sir, no sir, three bags full sir" and then they do nothing about it. If you don't provide fitness training a lot of guys won't bother. After twelve months I started to get homesick for the Corps. Things are different and there are frustrations but at least I can blame them on life with Perce.'

Pretty inseparable in training, Stan Harris and Steve Hussey joined 3 Royal Irish Regiment at Portadown for twelve months. For the first few days confusion reigned as the battalion did not seem to know what to do with them. Eventually they were shipped off on an acclimatization package and returned to be given full twenty-eight man platoons. Stan quickly ran into trouble when the regiment's 2 i/c decreed that they should both wear army uniforms with no identifying Marine insignia. Steve, always more easy-going, complied with a groan, but Stan held out, complaining to friends at 42 Commando, 'I worked too damn hard for my lid for some Pongo colonel to make me take it off.' Eventually he bowed to the inevitable but promptly grew a moustache and started smoking a pipe – perhaps a subtle form of revenge from a twenty-one year old who celebrated getting his green lid with a discreet tattoo of a dagger on his inner thigh – just below the panty line, where it has been admired by several members of the opposite sex. One advantage they did have with the RIR is that because the men all live locally they are allowed 'more leash' to fraternize and go out clubbing. Not that Steve, who remains resolutely faithful to his constant Emma, would consider such a thing.

He did however have to face a potentially dangerous incident when in command of a road-block in County Down on the main road from Belfast to Dublin. 'A white box van was stopped which contained a very flustered driver,' he recalls. 'He had been hi-jacked by a group of masked gunmen just outside Crossmaglen, blindfolded and left in a barn for two hours, then returned to his van and instructed to drive to Belfast. I decided to treat the van as suspect, cordoned off the road to seal the area and evacuated both troops and civilians to a safe distance, assuming that the vehicle had been booby-trapped. I found my training kicking in immediately, the adrenalin covered any butterflies in my stomach. When we had carried out all the instructions I crawled to within a hundred metres of the truck and looked through the scope of my SA80 to see if I could spot anything. It turned out to be a "one times false" [the term given to a hoax] which was rather disappointing.'

Six months later Stan, too, had to establish a cordon when a VBIED (Vehicle Borne Improvised Explosive Device) was discovered by the RUC in a housing estate in Portadown. 'My role,' he says, 'was to ensure that the cordon remained sècure so that the various agencies could work unimpeded inside it. The NCOs of the RIR tend to be very experienced at dealing with various incidents, which obviously makes my job far easier.'

In November '93 both were allowed to put their green lids back on. Stan became a troop commander with 42 Commando in Plymouth and may be returning to Ulster in November '94. In January '94 Steve went to the Army Air Corps Training Centre at Middle Wallop for an intensive three-week flying grading course and is hoping to make the grade as a helicopter pilot.

'I now know why Marines call all other army units Pongos,' says Andy Goldsmith, who spent a year as a platoon commander with the 1st Battalion Argyll and Sutherland Highlanders. 'They are quite capable of wearing one shirt all week, and keeping the same pair of socks on until they get holes in. With Marines it is always one shirt one day, then change. When they go into town the Jocks all have rave haircuts and shirts, jewellery and pointy boots with shiny buckles which would make most boot necks shudder.'

Andy found regimental life very formal compared to the somewhat easy-going attitude that prevails in most Royal Marine Messes. 'They are a very old-fashioned regiment, fiercely proud of their traditions and hard-won battle honours,' he says, 'but it's always suits for dinners, gin and tonics brought on a silver salver by a Jock in tartan trews and no T-shirts in the Mess. The orderly officer at Lympstone simply slings a belt with a beeper and a pistol over his denims but at the Argylls he has to don spit and polish brogues, snow-white spats, a kilt, red and white socks, a Sam Browne with a sword and a stick. I've kept all my own kit which hasn't been that hard as the Army appears to expect Marine officers to behave in a certain way. You are expected to be loud, rude, blunt and aggressive and you are not expected to be tactful. The only penalty is that everyone from the CO down calls me "Booty" which I can live with.

'I've fought very hard to stay out of a kilt,' he laughs. 'Every time I pass the QM he asks if I want to come in for a fitting. However I have worn one on social occasions. There is a tradition in the Mess that if a girl asks you what's under your kilt you have to buy her a drink. The first party in Germany I got asked within five minutes; the eventual upshot was she got pissed and I got lucky.'

Although initially Andy was relieved to get away from the batch mates with whom he had lived and breathed for fifteen months, it did not take him long to yearn for the company of other green lids, which was difficult as he spent the first nine months in Germany. As for the soldiering he immediately found himself physically far fitter than his men – the fastest man in his company and one who quickly incurred a reputation as a 'phys monster which isn't difficult among a group of men who will happily sleep for twenty-four hours at a stretch'.

The Argylls had just abandoned their 432s – armoured personnel carriers – and many found reverting to the role of foot infantry both a culture and a physical shock. 'We had a kit inspection prior to a major exercise at Vogelsang on the Belgian border,' he recalls. 'We found some extraordinary things in their Bergens, cans of shaving foam, bottles of aftershave, thick books, Walkmans, cuddly toys. They were so used to kipping in the back of the 432s they'd have brought the kitchen sink if they had to.

'We had a yomp of maybe thirty kay but only carrying webbing and weapons so I set off and found I had to stop every quarter of a mile to let them all catch up. Then after one rest stop I managed to lose the last two Jocks in the line; they fell asleep and no one woke them up. I discovered they were missing three kay later – shades of Pete Joy's Rifle – and it took four hours to find them. I gave them such a dressing down that my troop sergeant was so certain I was going to thump them that he turned all the platoon with their backs to me so they wouldn't see!'

While Andy enjoyed battling with the thick Glaswegian slang, ultimately he was very relieved to get back into the Corps. 'Marines have a reputation with the Jocks for being a bit dim,' he says, smoking furiously, 'but when I think of some of their "Ruperts" – young post-Sandhurst officers – I've met a lot of smarter nods. But they certainly dress better off duty.'

In winning his green lid Charlton Jackson became one of only a handful of JDF officers ever to do so. Displaying such physical and mental tenacity is appreciated in Kingston and Charlton is now highly regarded and expected to go far.

For Trevor Henry his much longed for return to Jamaica was to prove disastrous. Elections in the island tend to be violent, often bloody affairs where the role of the JDF can become blurred and politics can quickly become embroiled in gunfire. On 27 March 1993 (three days before the elections) soldiers burst into the JLP (Jamaican Labour Party) offices in Brownstown, St Anne. In the subsequent altercation three men including Police Constable Rupert Sinclair were shot dead and a female office worker wounded. Subsequent to an investigation Lieutenant Henry and a Lance Corporal Maxwell were charged with murder.

According to testimony at a court hearing on 6 September a witness in the next office heard PC Sinclair identify himself with his hands held above his head, then saw him beaten by the soldiers and shot at point blank range. The trial hearing for Henry and Maxwell was set for 11 October. Trevor was not in court to hear his fate, nor did he ever stand trial. In early September he was diagnosed as suffering from throat cancer. Within three weeks he was dead.

Of the thirty-three YOs who began training on 4 September 1991, nine either resigned their commissions or were 'withdrawn from training'. Andrew Parlour returned to the USA and has disappeared back into civilian life. Mark Collins was rumoured to be the manager of a pub while Martin Webster is believed to have applied to join the police force. The author was unable to contact them.

Donning the uniform of a Naval officer was the best thing Jason McQueen ever did. He might have been unsettled at Lympstone but the lessons he learnt there served him well when he went to Dartmouth. 'The hardest thing at Dartmouth is being chucked out,' he says. 'To begin with they applied tremendous pressure in musters and inspections but I'd had far worse at CTC. I was in a single cell and I found myself showing the new guys how to do hospital corners. They expect you to learn from the seniors but they don't always help the newcomers as the Navy is much more rigid and hierarchical.'

Jason passed out in the top four of his class and spent six months working in anti-smuggling operations in Hong Kong, working with a couple of SBS fast RIB drivers. He then joined HMS *Southampton* in the Gulf to complete the necessary eight months' fleet time before taking his Fleetboard in September '93. 'That was the final weeding stage,' he says. 'You get grilled for a whole day. Fail it and you're plain Mister the next day.'

He garnered a first class pass which means he got higher than 70 per cent on all subjects – more important, it gave him seniority and extra cash. After a four-month 'X' Course as seaman officer he went to his 'first real seaborne appointment which means I've become a useful asset to the Navy'. In the spring of '94 he was promoted to a complement commissioned Lieutenant. Jason's long-term ambition is to join the hydrographic branch of the Navy. 'I see a lot of officers being thrown out with no qualifications. If I get into that branch there will always be a career for me after the Navy.'

Andy Rowley teaches PT at King's School, Wimbledon, and still has the same girlfriend. 'I have never regretted my decision,' he insists.

Rory Thomson went back to bar work as assistant manager of the Frigate and Firkin pub in Olympia, west London, grew his hair long and had his ear pierced. In May '94 he was planning to travel to Australia and the Far East. 'For a while I thought about the possibility of going back to the Marines after getting a college degree,' he says, 'but the longer I spent away from Lympstone the more alien it became. Most of my friends know what I did before working here but I don't talk about it much. I do miss some of the guys.'

After returning to Exeter University in October '93 Martin Wood took his final exams for his MBA and then went on to study for his dissertation attached to the Mergers and Acquisitions Department at Swiss Bank. He harbours no resentment about being kicked out, happily confessing, 'I knew it was coming, I wasn't cut out to be a Marine officer – I realized that within a month of joining but I didn't want to quit so I coasted along until I was thrown out. When the axe came I was half hoping I might actually get a green beret but I was already prepared with a three-month holiday job in Turkey and the MBA course standing by.'

Typically enough he affects no recollection of the hard time he suffered at the hands of his former batch mates. 'I had a good time, I learnt a lot of things,' he says ingenuously. 'I genuinely enjoyed myself, it was good for my confidence and the next best thing to doing National Service. I made some good friends and had a good laugh.' However, he has not kept in touch with any of his former colleagues.

'In January 1993 I received a formal letter of discharge,' writes Pete Joy. 'I also joined the City of London Royal Marine Reserve as a recruit and once the paperwork was out of the way, spent two weeks in May pounding around the Bottom Field for old time's sake on the RMR Commando Course to finally get my "coveted green beret". Eventually I'll apply for an RMR commission though whether I'll get one after what Wolsey and Taffinder may have written about me in the files is another matter. Believe it or not at RMR London I'm considered a very good Marine.

'I went in a successful graduate and a blue, popular among my fellows, expecting and expected to do very well at CTC. Instead I stumbled from one problem to another until I was finally kicked out in ignominy. Furthermore in getting sacked I've effectively wasted two years of my life (the second in a desk job in London as something to do while I sorted my life out) and lost my good reputation. Getting my beret at least gives me *something* to show for all that precious time and physical effort. The only way I can rationalize what happened is to try to ensure that that training will not be wasted and in the RMR I can use that training.'

After spending the summer of 1993 working as a Camp Counsellor in California Pete had the choice of applying for a commission in the Royal Engineers or studying for an M.Phil. in international relations at Cambridge. The Engineers turned him down and so he returned to Cambridge. While his experience at CTC still rankles, Pete now feels less hard done by, though somehow he still cannot accept that the fault was largely of his own making, insisting that bad luck was to blame. Perversely if he had shown the same dogged determination to prove himself that he has shown since he was sacked, he would have succeeded in the first place. Perhaps it is for the best; there are some people who are not cut out for the restrictions of military life.

After he left Lympstone the anger and frustration that had been building up inside Jools Ostling came to a dramatic head. 'I did rather go off the rails when I came out. I was pretty rebellious when I thought I had my freedom back,' he says. 'I had this girlfriend who I was pen pals with, from that Easter onwards we got on really well. She was up in Huddersfield and coming back from seeing her one time I went crazy and got nicked doing 150 mph on my bike. I ran away from a police car on the M1 for thirty three-miles, bobbing and weaving on the hard shoulder.'

Condemned to travel on a bicycle Jools started to teach A level economics, GCSE maths and rowing at his old school, right opposite where Andy Rowley teaches at King's School, Wimbledon. It still makes him uncomfortable being in charge and responsible for others, and he continues to shift allegiance between teaching and working as a mechanic in the family garage, which is both 'relaxing and rewarding'. There is also the possibility of using his economics degree by coordinating a relief operation in Eritrea.

'This last year I have been wondering what I want to do,' he says. 'My mind was very restless. I feel I am still sixteen but when I was sixteen I felt twenty-five. I seem to be a dominant character but I don't like taking responsibility for other people in a formal situation. I take a pride in welding, knowing what has to be done. There are no boring jobs, there are boring people. I'm only twenty-three and I wasn't planning on starting a career until I was twenty-eight.'

He misses the camaraderie of the Royal Marines which he never had before and cannot resurrect in Civvy Street. He reminisces happily about his time in the Corps but it's as if he were talking about another person in another lifetime. With all his internal struggles Jools would not have made a good officer and in choosing to leave he has set about discovering who he really is.

'I was definitely a bit cruel,' he admits. 'Another reason I left was because I felt I was becoming a bit of a bastard especially to women. I've decided I've done all that now, especially all the shagging, it was one of things you have to try. The girlfriend I have now – if I don't have another that'll be fine, I won't feel I'll be missing anything. She knows I've done all that.

'I did learn some lessons, I know how to iron,' he laughs. 'I'm thinking of cycling to Africa so I can live in the field, whereas before I'd have taken tarpaulins and ropes all the stuff you don't need. And map reading which will come in useful.'

Captain Mark Wolsey continues simultaneously to amaze and infuriate his colleagues. His year at the Army Staff College at Camberley (although the Royal Marines are now forging closer links with the Navy, it was at one time considered a better career appointment to attend the Army Staff College at Camberley than the Navy one at Greenwich) passed uneventfully enough, better than he had hoped. Wolsey is, cliché intended, an Action Man and he found some of the restrictions of Staff College particularly galling, with tactics and strategy still geared up to NATO confrontations with the Warsaw Pact. While the latter has ceased to exist as a military alliance the discussions always seem to end up with a 'scenario of Russian tanks driving up the M4, which simply is never going to happen again'. Wolsey sees the future of the Royal Marines as a rapid deployment force, involved in police actions like Kurdistan, and so would vociferously question the point of learning such out-dated strategy.

Being Wolsey he had a couple of other profitable sidelines, selling his convertible BMW for a profit and investing in an E-type Jaguar. Much amusement was caused when a couple of male modelling assignments he had undertaken in the past suddenly surfaced in a ski magazine but far more frighteningly on a poster campaign on the London Underground. 'I thought I'd escaped from the bugger,' said one YO. He also ran his first Marathon in April 1993 coming in in the astonishing time of two hours thirty-six minutes. His second daughter, Imogen, was born on 1 November 1993. He seems resigned to fathering only girls which is fortunate for he will be a hard act for any son to follow.

Much of his time at Staff College was spent finding out what jobs were available from January '94. Not much took his fancy and he was resigned to spending two years at the Ministry of Defence in London, in charge of buying Marine widgets for Navy ships. Instead he found himself promoted to (acting) Major and drafted to an extremely challenging operational appointment in an Army HQ, where he may well bump into some of his former protégés. Maybe fortune does favour the brave for Wolsey's career is flying ahead and provided he does not do something foolhardy (always a strong possibility) he seems destined to reach the upper echelons of the Corps. Naturally enough he talks constantly of retiring in about five years as a Major.

Colonel Mike Taffinder retired from the Royal Marines in July 1993. He now works from home as an Area Organizer for King George's Fund for Sailors and spends his spare time in his Gloucestershire garden. 'I was towed out of Lympstone in a 35-cwt. truck bedecked with flowers – the chief gardener has left CTC,' he says. 'I had always been quite clear about two things when I retired. I would never work in London and I would never commute anywhere by train. I adored my thirty-two years in the Corps and running Lympstone was the best job I ever had. But getting up in the morning and putting on a pair of jeans – after a lifetime in uniform – that's a real treat.' He was also rumoured to be growing his hair long.

Alongside the charismatic Wolsey, Major Matt Sturman often appeared to be the grey man, the pen-pusher not the sword-wielder. This would be unfair for – aside from the fact that he is by nature a courteous man whose innate concern for his charges might, at times, have made him over-protective – in his two years at CTC Matt made a large number of innovative and important changes to the way in which YO training was conducted. For a start the dreaded Range Qualifying Course was cut to a more palatable three weeks. In addition he was unhappy with the way the Thirty Miler was conducted, and subsequently the YOs were forced to rely on their own efforts without the pushing and cajoling of the DS which had become a feature of the test. He also introduced more joint training with the Royal Navy and had a number of the petty restrictions under which YOs laboured in their early days removed. 'I regard Matt Sturman as having been one of the best OCs of OTW for some time,' says Mike Taffinder. 'He was professionally excellent and both a wise and gentlemanly Wing Commander. I suspect he and Mark Wolsey did not always see eye to eye but that is not to say that they differed in any way about their mutual aim – to produce YOs who could lead the Marines in both peace and war. To a very large extent they were very successful.' He left OTW in September 1993 to study for an M.Phil. in military studies at Cambridge University.

Billy Baxter had just started his ML1 course in August '92 when he had to withdraw for family reasons. He went to 40 Commando at Taunton, where he almost became Tanner's troop sergeant, was promoted to Colour Sergeant and in September '93 applied to become a Special Duties officer. Although he passed his AIB he did not score highly enough to be accepted on the SD course. He returned to 40 Commando for the tour of Northern Ireland and may at some point apply once more for the SD position. It would be highly appropriate if one day he ended up sharing a Mess with Shetler-Jones for Billy learnt as much from teaching the course as many of the YOs – and certainly more than Martin Wood. Tom Coyle is back in operations working in a sensitive area. Toby Broomes tried to grow a moustache and is still at CTC, as is Dai 'I shouldn't tell you this, lads, but ...' Phillips. Graeme Foster has left the Corps.

Does YO training work? What walked out of Lympstone were thirty extremely fit, hard, self-confident individuals with every sharp corner knocked off, ready for anything the Corps could throw at them. Sir Henry Beverley believed that there are four essential characteristics required by a Royal Marine Officer – professional excellence, modesty, wit and a pleasant social demeanour. Without doubt the first and third of those aims were achieved. Modesty, one can safely say, is not an attribute that springs readily to mind when describing YO batch Sept. '91 – but much of their arrogance rubbed off within months of reaching a Commando unit and learning that they were very junior cogs in a grown-up wheel. Mike Taffinder worries that YOs do not leave CTC as gentlemen, for the training is geared to muscle over manners. But then how many twenty-three year olds are socially assured, at ease wherever they find themselves? These young men have looked deep inside their souls; they alone know what they found there but a great part of being a gentleman is being confident in oneself. That they have in abundance.

So what does it all mean to the individuals? Was it worth all the sweat, all the blood, the private tears? Most of the YOs do not know yet. All they know is that training was a high point in their lives, not always a pleasant one, but a time lived with a heightened awareness. Since then a couple have come face to face with death, and one has found it; others have had to cope with mind–numbing tedium. The intense camaraderie that bound them together has begun to dissipate before the encroaching tide of reality. Ironically it is Matt Skuse, not the most sensitive of chaps, who put his finger on the one thing that will always set them apart from other men.

'Most of the other lads have been serving in Commando units surrounded by people with green lids so perhaps this won't have hit them yet,' he says. 'Pretty well worldwide that green beret and the Royal Marines officer is respected. It is a peculiar feeling for me in my first job at twenty-two to find this instant respect from a major in the USMC or a captain in the US Navy. It is very odd to have a 48-year-old captain of a 300-metre-long merchant ship asking you your opinion on some matters nautical when you have been out of training for months and he has had thirty years before the mast.

'The Americans do not just pay lip-service to it, they really defer to the green beret, the whole Commando ethos. It opens a hell of a lot of doors out here, which shocked me after coming straight out of Lympstone. There it took more than a green beret to get respect.'

ACKNOWLEDGEMENTS

The author and publishers would like to thank the following for permission to reproduce material:

Louis Kronenberger, 'The Cart and the Horse' in *Our Unhappy Happy Endings*, first published by Alfred A. Knopf, reproduced by kind permission of the author's estate;

Eric Hoffer, *The Passionate State of Mind*, copyright © 1954 Eric Hoffer, reprinted by kind permission of Curtis Brown Ltd.;

Robert Frost, *The Poetry of Robert Frost*, edited by Edward Conway Latham, published by Jonathan Cape, reproduced by kind permission of the Estate of Robert Frost; and

Bohemian Rhapsody © 1975, reproduced by kind permission of B. Feldman and Co. Ltd. trading as Trident Music, London WC2H 0EA.